The Rule of Freedom

V

The Rule of Freedom
Liberalism and the Modern City

◆

PATRICK JOYCE

VERSO

London • New York

First published by Verso 2003
© Patrick Joyce 2003
All rights reserved

1 3 5 7 9 10 8 6 4 2

Verso
UK: 6 Meard Street, London W1F 0EG
USA: 180 Varick Street, New York, NY 10014–4606
www.versobooks.com

Verso is the imprint of New Left Books

ISBN 1–85984–520–7

British Library Cataloguing in Publication Data
A catalogue record for this book is available from the British Library

Library of Congress Cataloging-in-Publication Data
A catalog record for this book is available from the Library of Congress

Typeset in 10/12pt Baskerville by
SetSystems Ltd, Saffron Walden, Essex
Printed by R. R. Donnelley & Son, USA

To Rosaleen, in faith and love

Contents

List of Illustrations

Figure 1 is reproduced courtesy of Mr Chris Makepeace. Figures 1.1 to
1.3 are reproduced courtesy of Manchester University Geography Department. Figures 2.1 to 2.4 and 5.1 are reproduced by permission of the
Guildhall Library, London. Figures 3.1, 3.2 and 3.4, 4.2, 4.4, 4.5. 4.7, 5.3,
5.4 are reproduced by permission of the Local Studies and Archives
Department, Manchester Central Library. Figure 4.1 is reproduced by
permission of the Museen der Stadt Wien. Figure 4.3 is reproduced by
permission of the Mitchell Library, Glasgow. Figure 4.6 is reproduced by
permission of Halifax Central Library, and Figure 5.2 by permission of
the British Library.

Acknowledgements

This book developed over a fairly long period, and therefore I have a number of people to thank for help along the way. I received advice and encouragement from various people on particular aspects of the book, many of which I am an autodidact amateur in. Chris Perkins, Chandra Mukerji and Miles Ogborn told me about maps, and Gyan Prakash and Partha Chatterjee helped me with the Indian section. Leif Jerram was extremely generous in giving me the advantage of his knowledge on the history of architecture. More in my own neck of the woods, Miles Taylor and Bertrand Taithe directed me through aspects of nineteenth-century political and cultural history. During a recent period of teaching in the University of California, San Diego, I benefited greatly from the friendship, encouragement and insight of Richard Biernacki, Stefan Tanaka, Steven Shapin, also Chandra Mukerji. I also wish to thank other members of that remarkable institution, John R. Hall and Patrick Carroll-Burke at the Davis campus. I received encouragement at crucial times from Keith M. Baker and Mary Poovey. The role of those fertile labourers in the field of governmentality studies, Nikolas Rose and Tom Osborne, has been crucial from the start. Similarly, a number of people have been rocks of support in the entire history of the book, namely David Vincent, Simon Gunn, Patrick Curry and James Vernon, another Californian. My thanks also, and my apologies, to those I have forgotten to name.

Among those would be many who at seminars where I presented aspects of this book, in Britain, the USA, Brazil, India, Spain, Germany and Ireland, gave me sound advice and information. I wish to thank another remarkable institution, the University of Manchester, especially its History Department, for creating the congenial conditions in which this book was created. In particular I have benefited greatly from working with graduate students who have put the concept of governmentality into critical and creative historical use, especially Chris Otter, Francis Dodsworth, Tom Crook, Mindy Silverboard and Gavin Rand. Thanks to Harry Cocks too. At Verso I received the benefits of an anonymous reader, and those of an engaged editor, Robin Blackburn. The editorial advice of James Ingram was extremely helpful. I also acknowledge the thought of Michel Foucault, for the enticement to creative thought about the past as a critical inquiry shaped by the present. As always, I could not have done it without the constant support of my wife Rosaleen, and it is to her that I dedicate this book.

Patrick Joyce
Broadbottom and Manchester
September 2002

Introduction

When, at the opening of a new century, the reign of freedom seems so markedly in the ascendant, it may be timely to consider the inception of this reign in the nineteenth century, for it was then that freedom began to be used systematically as a way of governing the emerging liberal democracies of the time. To write of the rule of freedom, as I do in my title, is to employ the idea of freedom in an unusual way. When the word is used in relation to liberalism it usually denotes the freedom to be left alone in order to do what one wants to do, or it has a more positive sense as the practice of something that is good in itself. To think about freedom as a mode of ruling people is to consider the absence of restraint as a form of restraint, which is something of a paradox. It is this paradox I seek to explore in this book, the active and inventive deployment of freedom as a way of governing or ruling people. What I mean by a paradox here extends beyond the familiar recognition that to make people free it may be necessary to compel them, for this still conceives of freedom as a good in itself, whether a positive or a negative one. Freedom in this understanding is still in some sense a real entity in the world, something that government is organised *for*. Rather, I want to consider freedom as something that is ruled *through*, freedom as a formula for exercising power, and freedom, as has been said, as a technique of rule, as *technological*. I shall explain this at greater length in a moment.

I apply the term 'liberalism' to this governmental understanding of freedom throughout the book, but I also use terms like 'liberal govern-mentality' and 'governmental freedom'. It will be apparent that by 'liber-alism' I do not mean liberal politics, ideas or institutions as commonly understood, though it is obvious enough that 'liberalism' as I present it in what follows inevitably has a close relation to these. Perhaps 'liberalism' is the wrong word to employ; I hope my readers will not be confused by my use of the term. I have been at pains to indicate the senses in which it and the term 'freedom' are used. My reason for courting misunderstand-ing like this is that there has in recent years grown up a considerable body of writing on liberalism in this sense of 'governmentality', which employs these terms. It is part of existing scholarship. What I like about this scholarship is its practical, empirical character, the way in which it makes theoretical approaches work their passage. What I also like is its illumina-tion of our present political condition, as what has been called 'a history of the present'.

It informs us about how contemporary government *works*, about things like the welfare state, communication systems, schools and cities, the subject of this book.[1] It also tells us about statistics, insurance and risk, accounting, criminology and work,[2] and about the management of econ-omic life, state expertise and the development of political economy.[3] It shows us how the sciences and practices of the mind help govern the self within, and how freedom governs the self without in the world of modern mass consumption.[4] Extending beyond political sociology, governmental-ity approaches, already attentive to the history of the past anyway in writing the history of the present, have in recent times taken a decidedly more historical turn – for example, on Britain in terms of the history of moral regulation, on Russia and the Soviet Union in terms of state strategies of surveillance, on the United States in considering the govern-mental information machine, and in postcolonial history, especially that of India, on colonial governmentality.[5] In the concluding chapter I discuss some comparative possibilities thrown up by this work. Particularly import-ant for the present study of liberal governmentality and the city has been the work of the English studies scholar Mary Poovey on the epistemologi-cal categories that in nineteenth-century Britain underwrote some of the central organising categories of governmental freedom, above all the notion of 'the social' itself. Especially in the shape of the social body, this formed a central element in contemporary imaginaries of power.[6] This category of the social has been the object of sustained critical attention recently, in part through a governmentality optic.[7]

What, then, is governmentality? I will give only a brief account, as the approach now has several useful guides to which readers may turn if they wish.[8] In the words of Nikolas Rose, governmentality concerns 'the ways in which those who would exercise rule have posed to themselves the question of the reasons, justifications, means and ends of rule, and the problems, goals or ambitions that should animate it'. Here the notion of government is synonymous with political reason, the different forms of the mentality that animate govern*mentality* comprising different political rationalities. As a political rationality, governmentality is understood 'as a kind of intellectual machinery or apparatus for rendering reality thinkable in such a way that it is amenable to political programming'. Following from this, *technologies* of government are to be analysed in terms of the 'strategies, techniques and procedures through which different authorities seek to enact programmes of government'. As Rose says,

> This is not a matter of the implementation of idealized schemata in the real by an act of will, but of the complex assemblage of diverse forces (legal, architectural, professional, administrative, financial, judgemental), techniques (notation, computation, calculation, examination, evaluation), devices (surveys and charts, systems of training, building forms) that promise to regulate decisions and actions of individuals, groups, organisations in relation to authoritative criteria.[9]

So defined, how does governmentality historically emerge? It is Michel Foucault's elaboration of the term which has defined this area of study.[10] I present this narrative here, briefly, as it helps frame my own. I recognise that it is sweeping, contestable and hence provisional. None the less, it gets me started. As Mitchell Dean paraphrases Foucault's argument, the separation of governmentality from sovereignty in the sixteenth century involved the development of a notion of government as an activity, or an 'art', that is immanent to the state. The government of the state became autonomous and distinct from different versions of sovereignty, for instance 'divine right' theories of rule, as well as from the personage of the sovereign. From being conceived of as based upon a transcendent form of authority exercised over subjects within a definite territory, government from that time had to take into account the nature of the things to be governed and their 'disposition', the latter term denoting 'the spatial and strategic arrangements of things and humans and the ordered possibilities of their movement within a particular territory'.[11] This involved fostering these resources of things and humans so as to increase the means of subsistence, and to augment the wealth, strength and greatness of the state by increasing the happiness and prosperity of its inhabitants, and by multiplying their numbers. In this way 'population' became a principle of rule, and bio-power its expression. A governable 'economy' and 'society' began to emerge, but these were not yet fully autonomous, as they were to be in 'liberalism'. The so-called 'police' form of governmentality that can be said to have preceded the 'liberalism' that emerged, at least politically, in the early nineteenth century sought to operate on a territory and its inhabitants which were transparent to knowledge. The conduct of persons in all domains of life was to be specified and scrutinised.

By contrast, 'liberalism' ceded governance to an unknowable, and now opaque, object of rule, that of the liberal subject. Liberalism was shy of too much governing, and it confronted itself with realities – markets, civil society, families and, in my case, cities – in which these subjects could be identified. These realities had their own internal logics and mechanisms of self-regulation which had to be respected. Liberalism therefore depended on cultivating a certain sort of self, one that was reflexive and self-watching.[12] Yet this self, as it were, also watched liberalism, in the sense that liberal governmentality depended, and depends, upon cultivating persons who could, and can, practise freedom by constantly questioning its limits. In liberalism rule is ceded to a self that must constantly monitor the very civil society and political power that are at once the guarantee of freedom and its threat. A certain instability, but also a certain suppleness evident in the capacity to thrive upon this instability, seem evident in liberalism, and perhaps explain something of its durability. In chapter 3 I approach some of these aspects more directly, in terms of the development of an ethics of liberal governance.

However, it should not be thought that sovereignty is simply superseded by liberalism in the modern world, for as Dean, among others, makes clear, sovereignty has its own subsequent history, particularly in the state's concern for its own preservation as an end of sovereignty.[13] My book, however, is not a history of modern sovereignty, nor do I examine other sorts of modern political rationality beyond liberalism, which Foucault did briefly consider,[14] though I do in the conclusion make reference to 'non-western' forms of governmentality, and I consider colonial ones at some length. Consistently with his position, Foucault also recognised that 'liberalism' did not simply supersede 'police' forms of governmentality, so that both forms can be said to continue into the era of liberalism, in much of continental Europe in the nineteenth century, and later, needing to be distinguished from the rather different pattern I think evident in a more 'liberal' Britain and the United States. None the less, the continuation of 'police' within the belly of liberal rule in Britain in the nineteenth century will later be apparent, and its presence in British rule in nine-teenth-century Ireland, but also within metropolitan governmentality itself, has recently been argued strongly by Patrick Carroll-Burke.[15]

As well as abjuring a study of modern governmentality in general, neither do I make any pretence of writing a history of the category of freedom, related as this is to the question of different political ration-alities, though I do in the final chapter make some reference to this history. Rather, my aim is to use the approach I have outlined as a means to my own end of writing an historical narrative of the relationship between freedom and the city, one that attempts to be sensitive to the contingencies of time and place in the traditional spirit, if not always the traditional manner, of historians. This aim departs to some degree from the more static and atemporal qualities evident in at least some social science sensibilities, including those apparent in many of the existing studies on governmentality (and not completely absent in Nikolas Rose's formulations above, for instance the idea that those who govern *actively* pose to themselves the question of the means and ends of rule, and that 'authorities' seek to make reality amenable to 'political programming', which seems to be in some tension with his advocacy of the idea that strategies of governance are not idealised schemes realised by an act of will).

These more atemporal qualities were not absent in Foucault's work either, and they have in fact been noted from within the social science literature on actor network theory by John Law, who has drawn attention to the ways in which an interest in the broad sweep of 'strategies', as Foucault termed these, as opposed to immediate and messy 'tactics',[16] has a tendency to give the historian, or the sociologist, too much licence in banishing a knowing subject from the exercise.[17] By 'strategies' I mean in my context the same thing as the political rationalities of which I speak here, with their attendant technologies, especially the political rationality of liberalism. Alongside this static quality, and arising from it, there is a marked repetitive quality to the way in which strategies seem continuously to repeat themselves, as if these strategies of power were already in place before their tactical and historical instantiation. As an historian I am interested in tactics as well as strategies, though I fear I may have too much strategy for some historians, and too many tactics for some sociolo-gists. I hope not. None the less, one must insist, in the end, that even if realised through tactics, strategies, or rationalities, do exist at a more 'structural' level than tactics, so that some historians' complaints that these approaches avoid the messiness of history are pretty much beside the point. Strategies cannot be derived by simply adding up tactics, and the aim of this book is to isolate and delineate strategies of governance, strategies which undoubtedly had an overarching coherence beyond their discursive articulation and were something more than the sum of the intentions of those involved.

I therefore wish to write what might be called a socio-cultural history of governmentality. In order to do this, certain of the preconceptions of an established social history need to be questioned, and developed. This questioning can be understood as part of the shift in contemporary social thought from conceiving of society as a thing, to thinking about the social as a process. This in turn involves a move away from the idea of a static and monolithic social *order* to the idea of social *ordering* as a fluid, open and many-stranded activity. Following on from this interest in *ordering*, in my account questions of *agency* gain prominence beside, if not over, ones of *representation*, and a concern with what things *mean* (representation) cedes some precedence to how they *work*. At various times I am concerned with the sorts of agency that need to be brought into play in order for things to work in the way they do. Parallel to this I am interested in seeing the social world in terms of action or doing, in terms of practice, of what I later call the *performance* of people, but also of things. I am aware that I may so far run the risk of trying the patience of my non-specialist readers, as these and other terms may be unfamiliar or unclear, or both. I would ask these readers' indulgence for a little while longer, after which I will, quite literally, bring these terms down to earth, and indeed below the earth, by my example of an exceedingly ordinary Victorian street scene. My book is indeed made up of these (extra-)ordinary things.

One particular conjunction of theoretical influences that I have found especially helpful is the combination of science studies, actor network theory and what might be called the historical sociology of material culture. In John Law's account, for example, the social is also performed by material things, so that labelling one thing a person and one a machine, one thing material and one thing not, is not given in the order of things but is itself a product of the complex processes of the ordering of people and things of which I speak, which themselves in total make up 'social ordering' itself.[18] So too is the underlying distinction between nature and culture or 'society', also the human and the non-human. Law here draws on the work of his colleague Bruno Latour, who locates this arbitrary division of the world historically in terms of modernity itself.[19] The process of ordering that Law describes is what he calls a technosocial one, and in this book I employ that term as well as the term technopolitical, the latter as I am explicitly concerned with power and governance. In the book I explore the technopolitical in terms of the technosocial solutions to political questions that were to be found in the material things and processes apparent in markets, sewers, roads, material objects like maps, and so on. Part of the 'political' nature of these solutions lay precisely in the way they were realised as 'technical' and so *outside* the political.

Pursuing a somewhat different, if related, intellectual track to these ones, the work of scholars in the field of material culture is particularly suggestive. Among others, that of Richard Biernacki and Chandra Mukerji is I think exemplary, the latter on how the power of the French state was engineered into the French landscape in the seventeenth century, in terms of the 'territorialisation' of the state, for example in the fortifications at the periphery and the gardens at the centre of the new French state. Biernacki is concerned with how valuations of labour power were carried over time by German and British workers at the level of practice, in the material objects and processes bound up in factory architecture, payment systems and forms of mill discipline. These reproduced in material terms implicit assumptions known at the level of practice. In terms of labour history itself this represents a shift away from thinking of 'culture' as separable from production and 'technology'. Instead of viewing culture as *for* or *around* practice, culture is now located *in* practice, and in material forms. At something of a tangent to this approach, but complementary also, James Scott's study of how material forms are involved in the knowledge-producing practices of the modern state is also of relevance here.[20]

Readers may find a certain lack of 'conflict' in the book, but it here depends on what one means by this term. In attempting to separate myself somewhat from certain social history and allied approaches, by emphasising social ordering rather than social order, I try to avoid understandings that present power as a sort of zero-sum game, in which those with power impose order on those without it. This is not to say that this understanding is not important, and, assuredly, as is plain in what follows, power was often concentrated in the hands of the few. However, I look at power and 'resistance' in a different way. In fact, there is a great deal of conflict in the book, which in the first section of chapter 5, under the heading of 'Resisting freedom', I bring together in terms of the concept of resistance, which I consider in the material as well as the human world. Foucault considered power and resistance to be inseparable, and as will be evident in the many instances of 'resistance' that come up in the first four chapters of the book, so do I.

In the long final chapter, I also take a more extended and considered look at 'conflict' in terms of the rather different outcomes to be expected when my own reading of 'resistance' is employed, namely outcomes that are heterogeneous and ambiguous in character. In fact, what I am after here is some sense of how liberalism has been so powerful and pervasive because of this very ambiguity, something at bottom owed to the way it is knitted into everyday life, as by the same token is resistance. Arising from, and contributing to, this sense of the complexity of freedom's operation, throughout the book I attempt to explore intermediate or liminal places, persons and conditions, which comprise a sort of social indeterminacy in which power and the very nature of the social order are put in question. I am also concerned, especially in chapter 5, to give some account of the various 'others' of freedom, through which it was both constituted and negotiated. In sum, I am interested in 'everyday' power and resistance, in fact in the processes making up the 'everyday' itself as a site of power. My interest is in what has been called 'normalisation',[21] something which I often term the 'naturalisation' of the world that makes up this everyday universe of common sense. Therefore, the 'great moments' of war, revolution and protest tend to be less prominent in my book than in some others. This is not to say that I wish to minimise the significance of these moments – indeed I discuss some of them in chapter 5 – but it is simply that I am coming at the problem of order and its experience from a different angle.

In particular I come at it from the angle of the city. For in the nineteenth century the city moved to the centre of the concerns of the governors about how the new society then emerging might be governed. This was especially so in Britain, which at the same time as it became the world's first industrial state became its most heavily urbanised one. It would have been possible to write the history of liberal governance in different ways, at a more macro level in terms of the categories of 'society' and 'economy', say, or at a more micro level, one of the school or the family, for example. In considering the city, I have chosen to operate between these two levels, the better to relate them. In particular this is an account of two cities, Manchester and London, though it adverts to many more. I wished to get some sense of provincial, urban Britain, and Manchester was as good a choice as any. In fact, it was a better choice than the others, for especially in the early and mid-Victorian years it was the source of prodigious political as well as economic invention (though, contrary to many accounts, as the epicentre of Britain's industrial revolution, Manchester itself was more of a mercantile than an industrial city). Despite its earlier history, it was in a sense a city created *de novo*. Altogether, it had a quite crucial role in creating the modernity that emerged in the nineteenth century, as Marx, Engels, de Tocqueville and so many others saw.

At the same time, it is impossible to write about the nineteenth-century city without writing about London, an old city, which by the mid-Victorian years had already been the greatest city in the world for some considerable time. Because of this it too was the source of prodigious novelty and invention. Therefore, there was a sense of comparison that motivated my choice, but at the same time my basic concern was to look at processes that were evident in almost all cities in Britain, but also I think in most cities of the developing liberal democracies of the west. I recognise that 'city' is a problematic term, and that in using it I am pointing to urban life more generally, although the examples I use are almost all drawn from large concentrations of population, or 'cities' for want of a better word. Therefore I include many cities in this account in a way that may seem rather promiscuous to some of my readers, as these cities were decidedly different from one another. While recognising these differences, as I say, I am looking at processes that crossed diverse political and socio-economic situations, one advantage of approaching liberalism governmentally being its capacity to suggest new typologies, correspondences and differences. In the final chapter I attempt, if not a systematic comparison, then some discussion of the possibilities of a comparative understanding of 'liberalism'. And I look at how the city functioned in colonial governmentality, seeing in the relationship of metropolitan and colonial governmentality some of the key sources of modern governmentality. There is another reason for considering Manchester and London as well, namely that these are the cities I have known best in my life, and in attempting to convey some sense of the lived experience of cities it is perhaps no bad thing to have lived in them. In this way their present forms become more effectively the archive of their past forms.

Figure 1 is a photograph of one of the principal thoroughfares in Manchester, Deansgate, taken in the 1880s. In 1869 the old Deansgate was widened and modern lighting, sewerage and water supplies were put in. There is therefore a double street, as it were, the street above ground as well as the street below, with its pipes, sewers, cables and wires.

What can this quotidian scene of Victorian life tell us about the conceptual terms I have so far used? First, *performance*, for the photograph

Figure 1   View of Deansgate, Manchester, 1880s

itself already creates a scene of a sort. Within this scene dress, deportment, manners, action, all can be seen to perform urban life and social relations at the level of practice. There is often a very direct sense of public performance by people here. For example, the rather dandyish figure with his back to us, standing in the street in the foreground of the picture, seems to strike a decidedly theatrical pose, to say nothing of the spectacle of the perilously mounted cyclist. There is therefore the performance of human beings, and in my third chapter I dwell at length on the sense of the active public performance of those who would govern. I do this in terms of what I call an ethics of governance, one that was closely related to the public display of the objectivity and neutrality of those who governed the new techno-scientific state then emerging. However, I also want to enlist my pipes and sewers here, for these things are made by humans in order to encourage matter to behave in the way humans want it to, in short to make matter perform. So, too, can one describe the buildings in view. Of course, matter did not always obey its human masters. This sense of what I call action and doing is important in the book, therefore, and relates to the allied use I make of the term 'ordering', as opposed to 'order'.

For these different levels of performance also made up the very complex process of the ordering of social life, so that many different and often competing ordering activities are present – the ordering of the massive urban development initiative of 1869, for example the ordering of the material street (kerbs, surfaces, lamps, street signs), but also other orderings, for example the ordering of men who drive vehicles, the different ordering men and women bring to their sense of how they should present themselves in the street, and so on. This is to say nothing of temporal ordering, of how old and new – wide new street and narrow old lane – continued to exist close to one another. It is by means of recognising the interaction, the patterning, of these processes of ordering that resistance *and* the coherence of what I called governmental rationalities, or strategies of governmental power, can be realised, entities that have a force and unity of their own (the concerted initiative of 1869 evinces just such a unity). However, 1869, and all the great number of initiatives in urban governance that preceded it, were themselves divided houses: for instance, the Health of Towns Association of the 1840s, which figures from time to time in this book, held different ideas about what the city should look like, and different ideas about how medicine and the body should be understood. And different associations, interests and initiatives often competed one with the other. I wish to attend to the 'tactics' that reflected these differences, but not to lose sight of the fact that, these tactics and differences notwithstanding, enduring strategies did emerge.

They emerged around what is evident in the photograph: a city of wide streets, straight lines, improved visibility, a city where people and things could circulate freely. This city was cleaner and better lit than ever before. In short, a certain freedom was realised. And this freedom was realised around the city and the person as both now themselves sites of free movement, free association, with the person now freely choosing, responsible and therefore self-monitoring. Indeed, the city and its streets were constituted in such a way as to remove all impediments to this person, this liberal subject, being able to exercise freedom (the impediments of danger, darkness, traffic, the very mundane impediments of unpaved roads, mud and horse droppings). The city below the street contributed equally to that above, and there was evident a sort of political economy of the sewer and pipe, a political economy of infrastructure which set up the conditions of possibility in which freedom might be exercised. This freedom is where I take 'liberalism' to reside. And the action of these pipes, sewers, roads and lights comprised what I have called the *agency* of material things. 'Conditions of possibility' is a relevant term here, for these things did not determine outcomes (for matter, no less than men, constantly failed to perform in the ways that were wanted – the clear, unobstructed road had constantly to be dug up for maintenance, for example), so that these things carried a certain capacity for action, and built into them were certain kinds of agency.

An example that comes later in the book is the changed, and new, possibilities for action, for example with privacy, that followed from the arrival of running water in the home, not least the capacity to defecate in private. One should not underestimate this landmark in what has been called the history of shit. Maps come in here also, for the 'improvements' of 1869 were the outcome of a particular imaginary of the city, and maps, the subject of my first chapter, as both cause and effect exerted their own agency by framing the thoughts and actions of city improvers, shaping their particular urban imaginaries. I make reference from time to time in what follows to social imaginaries of the city, and by this term I mean the model or diagram (imaginary is a better word) of the city contemporaries worked with, the chief of which was the city in its many different formulations as a site of freedom, alongside 'society' and the 'economy' as themselves sites of freedom. Let us not, however, forget our dandy in the photograph, for he signifies something of the freedom liberal freedom sought to colonise and use, the freedom that exceeds liberal freedom, and which provokes it into action just as it eludes it. *Resistance* is again apparent.

In general I combine two ways of proceeding in the book. The first can be called interpretive, in that my attention is given to the interpretation, or, better, reinterpretation, of existing historical and other accounts in the light of my interest in liberal governmentality. I wish to establish how a historical narrative based upon the analytic of 'liberalism' can do justice to the sweep of historical change, so that I can make the governmentality arguments stick historically. For instance, in chapters 1 and 2 I dwell upon the considerable literature on maps and on public health in order to reinterpret these in the light of my own concerns. However, I then go on to a more empirical, 'case study' method, picking up the themes of my interpretive sections by concentrating on particular instances, for example the Ordnance Survey in chapter 1 and markets and abattoirs in chapter 2. My method here is metaphoric as well as empirical, in that the logic of my procedure is led by the association of one metaphoric dimension of my theme with another. In chapter 2, for example, where my interpretive section draws on how the life processes of the city were utilised by governance, what I call the vitalisation of the city, I follow the theme of life through to blood and to death, the death of animals and thence human death. In chapter 3 the general theme of the creation of openness or publicity in liberalism leads me into an empirical exemplification of publicity in the form of the public library, itself a kind of metaphor for the light of knowledge. The other chapters take a similar form, and are composed in the following manner.

In chapter 1 the significance of knowledge for governance is considered: before populations can be governed they must be known or identified. I open by considering a range of such means of knowing, for instance the new Penny Post of the time, but the chapter concentrates on statistics and cartography. In the new liberal state, governmentality depended upon reaching a balance which involved not only knowing the governed but *not* knowing them as well. An enduring theme of contemporary governmentality emerges in the chapter, in terms of the importance of the 'social' in the political imaginaries of those who would govern. Perhaps more than anything else at the time, the city was the focus of this new interest in the social. While I talk of the state, the chapter proceeds to question notions of an all-seeing state. It in part does this in the discussion of statistics, but especially that of maps, for the state is to be seen not simply as the author of the knowledge it helped create, but also as the *outcome* of this knowledge. This means that the state and governmentality were reproduced in material forms, and therefore in 'liberalism' itself. What was reproduced was often highly indeterminate and dispersed. This is considered in terms of the map and its putative 'liberalism'. The abiding interest in *performance* in the book also emerges here, in terms of the human performance of the objectivity and ethical neutrality held to have been contained in statistical knowledge itself. The Ordnance Survey is the chief historical object of interest in the chapter, not least in the manifestations of British rule in Ireland.

In considering maps and statistics, this chapter is concerned with the creation of the epistemological foundations of the new political subjectivities emerging at the time, both collective and individual. This creation was partly by the state, but also went on outside it (processes of urbanisation, the mechanisation of labour, the development of commodity capitalism). It amounted to what has often been called modernity, in the sense of the consolidation of the objectification, abstraction and standardisation of time and space that have come to mark modern life. Politically, only when the world was rendered into abstraction could it be made objective, and only when it was made objective could it become available for modern sorts of governance. At the time these developments were apparent, for example, in the emergence of a standard 'railway time' across Europe, rather late in fact, in the 1880s and 1890s. It was only in 1894 that an international agreement on standard time and time zones was signed.[22] Outside the state, and indeed outside governmentality itself, technological change was important: in particular, the steam engine determined the rhythm of time independent of nature, helping to consolidate 'homogenous and empty time'.[23] The state was itself important at particular times, for instance in the standardisation of mensuration evident in the Napoleonic regime in post-Revolutionary France.[24]

Once the governed was identified, through these processes of abstraction and objectification, it could then be operated upon so as to secure governance. This is the next stage in governmentality taken up in chapter 2, called 'The Water and the Blood of the City'. Securing governance involved realising the world in terms of various self-regulating entities, in effect a process of what I call 'naturalisation', so that at the time the social and society became seen as quasi-natural in operation. So too did the city, and in the first section of the chapter, on the 'civic toilette', I consider this process of naturalisation in terms of the realisation of the city as a place of free circulation. The social imaginary of the city that was involved was that of what is called the 'sanitary city'. The aspect of what I have termed 'technosocial' solutions to political problems is developed here. In the second section, a more anthropological understanding of the social is employed to probe contemporary notions of the distinction between the social and the natural. This is considered in terms of the reform of markets, especially meat markets, where some of the most profound contemporary anxieties about governance seem to have been located. I locate these anxieties in the transition from animal to edible, from flesh to meat, including the market among the many liminal spaces and conditions that I consider throughout this book. The chapter ends with a consideration of the human dead, and the place of the new cemeteries of the time in the governance of the city.

In chapter 3 I attend directly to more explicit and articulated formulations of governance, the first section, called 'Performing liberalism', being concerned with how the governors sought to work upon themselves, as well as upon others, in the elaboration of an ethics of governance. Such an ethics was articulated in the emergence of the early civil service. Again the concept of performance is evident in terms of the behaviour and actions of those who would govern, in how they presented themselves to the world. Before this, in the opening of the chapter, I attempt to distinguish politics and the political, in the sense of organised conflict, especially party conflict, from governance, a distinction that I think is not usually made in the governmentality literature. Therefore, alongside 'society' and 'economy' I would see politics as itself emerging as an autonomous, and to some extent self-regulating, entity at this time, as distinct from administration and sovereignty. The emergence of a 'non-political' administration is itself in turn seen to be an aspect of this change.

Therefore, I identify liberalism as something that was worked out *as* moral struggle, in which its *agonistic* qualities explain something of its subtlety and continuity, but also as something worked out *in* struggle with the ambiguous morality of politics. It is here especially that 'strategies' are seen to be embedded in 'tactics'. If the state is sometimes hard to find, I think it can be identified fairly clearly in the second quarter of the nineteenth century in terms of the gradual but increasingly emphatic and positive embrace of freedom as the central principle of state rule. This was especially evident in contrast to the eighteenth-century state. I further take up the matter of securing liberal governance, opened in the previous chapter, in respect of the urban as now a *direct* and a political realisation of liberal community, one that depended above all on openness, and on exposure to what I call 'the light of publicity'. The Municipal Corporations Act of 1835 was a central element in this. Policing is one of the subjects considered in terms of this creation of urban liberal communities. In the final section of the chapter I consider the library as a sort of technology of liberal publicity, something dedicated to the transmission and the absolute transparency of knowledge, just as notions of liberal community were concerned to develop transparency in institutions and practices of the city at large. In directing the light of publicity in a particular way, the library also exemplified the central place of education in creating liberal community and in performing the liberal self.

Chapter 4 represents a move from the governance of space to the governance of time, again something not usually considered in the governmentality literature. The argument moves forward historically in regard to certain failings of the 'sanitary city' or at least the contemporary necessity to complement reform underground, as it were, by reform overground, by the attempt to moralise the city of free circulation, correcting the failings and extending the possibilities of unfettered circulation. Once the city had been, at least to some extent, secured as a neutral public space of free circulation, it was necessary to moralise this space, a process in fact largely taking place through the action of time. What I call the moral city and the social city in this chapter are what I refer to earlier as social imaginaries of the city, but a better way of putting it would be that they were certain kinds of problem spaces upon which governance could operate. Conceived as such, liberal community was then realised in terms of the built forms of the moral and social cities, and it is these forms that I examine in some detail in the chapter, bringing aesthetic considerations into play alongside moral and political ones. In this chapter I also consider the increasingly demotic nature of the governance of time and space, employing, not over-rigorously, the idea of a transition from the panopticon, the one viewing the many, to the omniopticon, the many viewing the many. Part of this is what I call the institution of the ordinary in the ideas and practices of governance, something which was accelerated greatly in the social city. Developments here take the account into the early twentieth century.

The long chapter 5, as I have said, opens with an account of 'resistance' and how this has figured in the book so far. The opening also presages a more systematic account of the negotiation of liberal governmentality in the two sections of this chapter, on knowing the city, and moving in the city. This account explores some of the 'others' of freedom, in a sense already encountered in the book, namely the 'others' freedom generated in order to constitute itself, for example the city of darkness to which it opposed its own light of publicity. However, I also consider freedom's 'others' in terms of other contemporary valuations of freedom, which might themselves be the repressed others of liberal freedom. In particular I consider the public free and easy in the first section of the chapter. Again, the notion of liminal spaces and conditions comes into play. As suggested by the title of the chapter, 'The Republic of the Streets', the street was the most troubled and volatile arena of governance, and if it was a sort of omniopticon, it was very unstable and undependable. In dividing the chapter as I do, I also want to get at dimensions of knowledge and conduct which extended beyond political governance as understood in the previous parts of the book, but which had a complex relation to this governance.

This complexity I proceed to explore in terms of maps, directories, guides and a range of literary writings on the city, recognising in these the governmentality of conduct in the world of consumption and in the aesthetic sphere, something that seems to have preceded the operations of the liberal state and liberal governmentality themselves. These operations can be located in the civil society emerging often much earlier than explicit, political articulations of governance, but this emergence can none the less be seen as a consequence of governmental liberalism in so far as this depended upon governing through a free civil society but also a free economy in which the burgeoning world of consumption operated. In contrast to the more state-directed and political governmentality emerging in the early nineteenth century, these 'extra-political' dimensions of conduct might be called quasi-governmental, in recognition of the manifold connections but also differences between the everyday conduct of conduct and governmentality itself. In the chapter I therefore wish to explore both 'resistance' and this indeterminate terrain between everyday conduct and governmentality. This account therefore throws back into the eighteenth century and earlier other possibilities for writing the history of governing through freedom, just as Mary Poovey's work on the eighteenth-century 'sciences' of wealth and society suggests how intellectual developments presaged nineteenth-century political ones.

Perhaps above all in the chapter I want to get at some sense of the experience of city life, so that I have emphasised bodily and habitual modes of *using* the city in terms of moving in it. Most of this account of moving in the city is in fact of walking in it. I counterpoint what I call 'liberal' walking with other ways of walking, official ways of passing through the city with other ways of passing, ones which complemented but also undermined dominant forms. I end with a disquisition on the omnibus. This is developed in terms of modes of transport in the city in the concluding chapter by means of a rather different example, that not of the late nineteenth-century city and its omnibus but of the late twentieth-century Los Angeles freeway. This is part of an attempt to develop some comparative aspects in the study of liberal governmentality, an attempt taken further in the study of colonial governmentality in India, and of the place of the city in this. Perhaps I might add here that while this book has been based on a large amount of reading in primary and secondary sources, much of it takes the form of an exploration of certain key texts and instances, so that I have felt it appropriate to limit reference to these, rather than to the whole range of material I have consulted, much of which has indeed not served the purpose of this extended worrying away at the historical utility of the concept of governmental freedom.

Notes

Throughout the book place of publication is given as London though the work cited may in some cases be published elsewhere also. Information on publishers is not given for books published before 1950.

1. Thomas Osborne, Andrew Barry and Nikolas Rose (eds), *Foucault and Political Reason: Liberalism, Neo-Liberalism and Rationalities of Government* (London: UCL Press, 1996).
2. Colin Gordon, Peter Miller and Graham Burchell (eds), *The Foucault Effect: Studies in Governmentality* (Hemel Hempstead: Harvester Wheatsheaf, 1991).
3. Mike Gane and Terry Johnson (eds), *Foucault's New Domains* (London: Routledge, 1993).
4. Nikolas Rose, *Governing the Soul: The Shaping of the Private Self* (2nd edition, London: Free Association Books, 1999), and *Powers of Freedom: Reframing Political Thought* (Cambridge: Cambridge University Press, 1999).
5. Alan Hunt, *Governing Morals: A Social History of Moral Regulation* (Cambridge: Cambridge University Press, 1999); Matthew G. Hannah, *Governmentality and the Mastery of Territory in Nineteenth-Century America* (Cambridge: Cambridge University Press, 2000); Oleg Kharkhordin, *The Collective and the Individual in Russia: A Study of Practices* (London: California University Press, 1999); Gyan Prakash, *Another Reason: Science and the Imagination of Modern India* (London: Princeton University Press, 1999); Nicholas Dirks, *Castes of Mind: Colonialism and the Making of Modern India* (London: Princeton University Press, 2001).
6. Mary Poovey, *Making a Social Body: British Cultural Formation 1830–1864* (Chicago: University of Chicago Press, 1995), and *A History of the Modern Fact: Problems of Knowledge in the Sciences of Wealth and Society* (Chicago: University of Chicago Press, 1998); also see Steven Shapin, *A Social History of Truth: Civility and Science in Seventeenth-Century England* (Chicago: University of Chicago Press, 1994).
7. Patrick Joyce (ed.), *The Social in Question: New Bearings in History and the Social Sciences* (London: Routledge, 2002).
8. As well as the works already cited, see Mitchell Dean, *Governmentality* (London: Sage, 1999).
9. Nikolas Rose, 'Governing "advanced" liberal societies', in Thomas Osborne et al. (eds), *Foucault and Political Reason*, pp. 41–2.
10. Michel Foucault, 'Governmentality', in Colin Gordon et al. (eds), *The Foucault Effect*.
11. Mitchell Dean, *Governmentality*, pp. 103–6, and chapter 5.
12. For an account of liberalism, see Nikolas Rose, 'Governing "advanced" liberal societies', pp. 43–7 and *passim*, also on 'advanced liberalism', *Powers of Freedom*, chapter 4; and see Colin Gordon, 'Governmental Rationality: An Introduction', in Colin Gordon et al. (eds), *The Foucault Effect*.
13. Mitchell Dean, *Governmentality*, p. 106. On modern sovereignty taking the form of popular versions of the democratic will, see Keith Baker, 'A Foucauldian French

Revolution?', in Jan Goldstein (ed.), *Foucault and the Writing of History* (Chicago: University of Chicago Press, 1995), pp. 195, 205.

14. None the less, not only did Foucault think of discipline, governmentality and sovereignty as making up a triangle which defined modern governance in the west, but he also considered modern governmentality as taking different forms. As well as liberalism, which locates rule in the rational conduct of the governed, there is *raison d'état*, which locates it in the state as itself a sovereign individual, and there is what Foucault called the 'cosmo-theological', in which the location of rule is in transcendent Truth, human or divine (in his example of Communism). See Graham Burchell, citing Michel Foucault, 'Naissance de la biopolitique', course at the Collège de France, Paris, 1979, in Burchell's lecture, 'Historical Subjects: Races, Nations, Classes. The Limits of Liberal Rationalities of Government', a copy of which the author has kindly presented me with.

15. Patrick Carroll-Burke, 'Medical Police and the History of Public Health', *Medical History*, No. 26:4, 2002.

16. John Law, *Organising Modernity* (Oxford: Blackwell, 1994), esp. 'Introduction'.

17. Michel Foucault, *History of Sexuality*, volume 1 (London: Penguin, 1990), pp. 94–5.

18. John Law, 'Introduction', *Organising Modernity*.

19. Bruno Latour, *We Have Never Been Modern* (Hemel Hempstead: Harvester Wheatsheaf, 1993). See also his 'Gabriel Tarde and the End of the Social', in Patrick Joyce (ed.), *The Social in Question*.

20. Richard Biernacki, *The Fabrication of Labour: Germany and Britain, 1640–1914* (London: University of California Press, 1995); 'Work and Culture in the Reception of Class Ideologies', in John R. Hall (ed.), *Re-Working-Class* (London: Cornell University Press, 1997) and his *Time, Place, and Action: Ventures Beyond the Cultural Turn* (forthcoming); Chandra Mukerji, *Territorial Ambitions and The Gardens of Versailles* (Cambridge: Cambridge University Press, 1997); James Scott, *Seeing Like a State: How Certain Schemes to Improve the Human Condition Have Failed* (London: Yale University Press, 1998); see also Ken Alder, *Engineering the Revolution: Arms and Enlightenment in France, 1763–1815* (London: Princeton University Press, 1997).

21. In thinking about 'normalisation', one might invoke less heterodox sources than Foucault, namely Pocock and Skinner, who, from a somewhat different angle, none the less see that what it is possible to achieve in politics depends upon what can be legitimised, and what it is possible to legitimise depends on certain normative principles which function as limiting factors regardless of motivation. See Quentin Skinner, *Liberty before Liberalism* (Cambridge: Cambridge University Press, 1998), p. 105, and G.J.A. Pocock, 'Introduction', *Virtue, Commerce, and History: Essays on Political Thought and History, Chiefly in the Eighteenth Century* (Cambridge: Cambridge University Press, 1985).

22. Wolfgang Schivelbusch, *The Railway Journey: The Industrialisation of Time and Space in the Nineteenth Century* (Leamington Spa: Berg, 1986), esp. chapter 3.

23. Christoph Asendorf, *Batteries of Life: On the Story of Things and Their Perception in Modernity* (London: University of California Press, 1993), esp. chapter 10.

24. Witold Kula, *Measures and Men* (London: Princeton University Press, 1996), esp. chapter 21.

1

Maps, Numbers and the City

Knowing the Governed

In order for the liberal state to operate it was first necessary for it to identify those it sought to govern. Shortly after the first Reform Act of 1832 this state set about naming its subjects. The extension of democracy in the Act, however minimal, was parallel to the extension of knowledge concerning the subjects of the state. The Act itself, but also the Municipal Corporations Act of 1835, represented an extension of knowledge in the political sphere. This was evident in the compilation, under increasingly centralised authority, of electoral registers and ratebooks. Outside the political sphere as such, the Registration of Births, Deaths and Marriages Act of 1836 was a major step in the attempt to identify the nature of the 'society' liberalism increasingly sought to govern in accordance with. With the institution of the national census in 1800, aggregate knowledge of the population became available on an unprecedented scale. After the institution of civil registration, from 1841 the census became increasingly elaborate, as it was now possible to collate many different items of information about the population. Before this time, the Home Office was collecting criminal statistics as early as 1810, and state educational surveys were made after 1818. The eighteenth-century state had certainly known those over whom it sought to govern, a knowledge driven by the expansion of the state, but this need for knowledge was shaped by the exigencies of the 'military-fiscal' state rather than a desire for governance through the vital characteristics of populations, and the rapidly evolving notion of 'the social'.[1] What was new, also, in early and mid-nineteenth-century Britain was that power began to pass to the administrators who compiled this increasingly intensive state knowledge.[2]

However, what is equally striking is the limited nature of this knowledge, at least in retrospective view. Information on individuals was for a long time limited. For example, under the 1836 Act registration by street and parish was sufficient, and house numbers were not given.[3] The principle of legal compulsion in the collection of information was also limited. Direct surveillance by the state was itself quite restricted: it was not until 1911 that the Official Secrets Act was passed.[4] In crucial respects the liberal state depended on knowing enough not to have to know more.[5] What it knew, or sought to know, was vital to it, but of equal importance was securing the trust of citizens by not attempting to know too much.[6] This balance, of knowing what to know and what not to know, was being worked out for the first time in the early and mid-nineteenth century, and if state knowing deepened in time, then this balance was at the heart of liberal political reason and central to its subsequent development.

From around the beginning of the twentieth century, when knowledge of individuals fed more powerfully into knowledge of aggregates, governance through collective and 'social' subjects deepened. The National Insurance legislation of 1911 was one example of the institution of these new regimes of the social. The legislation depended on a level of information not available earlier. For the first time long-term records on individuals were kept, beyond the previously available census, and the life events recorded in the 1836 Act. This in fact depended upon the deliberate destruction of local bodies of knowledge, those of the friendly societies which ran what welfare system there previously was. Yet at the same time, in line with a liberal state knowing what not to know, there was also the deliberate decision, against much contemporary feeling, not to know about the private life of the citizen, only about such things as made a 'social' administration possible and efficient. Despite the limitations to the state's knowledge in the nineteenth century there was none the less a steady, if uneven, diminution of the importance of local information before the 1911 legislation. The principle that civil registration took precedence over parochial registration was itself a sign of this, though the resistance of the power that in this case enshrined the local, namely the Church of England, was marked, just as the dislike of those who were to be calculated was often volubly expressed at the time, and not only by the poor.[7]

The history of the letter helps trace something of this retreat of the local. Letter delivery before the Penny Post of 1840 depended on local knowledge and face-to-face contact, in part because delivery was dependent on the payment of costs by the addressee. The system of cheap state postal delivery served to link names to addresses and residences in a way which depended on formal and impersonal systems of information (for instance, the commercial postal directories that developed so rapidly at this time, and which, while specific to each city, were published in uniform editions by national concerns). The Penny Post served to accelerate the numbering of house doors and the fixing of street signs and of letter-boxes. However, there were once again limits to change, because the less well-off tended to use the post less, and when they did so, later in the century, they favoured the more public postcard rather than the letter.[8]

Despite these limits, the Penny Post can, on the one hand, be understood as conducive to the growth of privacy and the individuation of the subject. House and person were attached, increasing individual identity, just as the folded, and literally 'enveloped', letter enhanced and protected individual identity and liberty. Letter writing itself encouraged self-reflection and a consideration of viewpoints other than one's own in such a way that one became a 'subject' in letter writing, someone made singular by 'personal' and direct contact with another.[9] However, on the other hand, the logic of the Penny Post was conducive to the creation of the collective as well. Names were taken out of the context of the locality, circulating in a new sort of 'public' arena. By the same token, the limited information collected in the Act of 1836 was none the less of 'public' access, unlike the information collected in the census. In the process of securing this access, one knew oneself as a person who was an individual, but in choosing to exercise one's right to this access, one constituted oneself as part of a collective, as a new sort of public and a new sort of collective political subject.

At the epistemological level I am concerned with here, one concerned with the cognitive possibilities available at the time, people became available to be identified as individual and collective objects and subjects for governance.[10] In the example of the cheap post I think that this availability for identification was translated into a governmental intervention that can be regarded as a relatively early example of a liberal political technology in action. It explicitly emphasised privacy, represented and consolidated a sphere of freely circulating information, but yet, for all the emphasis on privacy, was openly dependent on transparent procedures, not linked to local, and hidden, forms of knowledge. The cultivation of the self was intimately related to new forms of collective subjectivity, and these became implicated in governance. Somewhat later, the electric telegraph can be understood as composing what has been called a 'perfect material base' for liberal government.[11] The very materiality of the telegraph is important here: the telegraph system was pervasive and yet it did not possess a centre. It appeared to increase the diversity of contact in society without any unnecessary intervention of the state. Territorial space was reconfigured in a way that was compatible with liberal rule, and if not quite a political technology in the developed way of the Post, this further example drawn from communications systems indicates something of the dynamics of the constitution of political subjectivity. In the following chapter I will consider something more of these technologies of governance, in terms of how subjects once known and identified were then operated upon to secure their subjectivity.

Here, in what follows, my emphasis on the epistemological underpinnings of governance in the liberal state is upon information rather than communications systems, and upon more direct ways of identifying political subjects, something which at the time owed a great deal to cartography and statistics, and it is these which will be my concern for the rest of this chapter. In both areas a similar process to that evident in the case of the Penny Post is apparent, namely the mutual constitution of the individual and the collective at an epistemological level, in terms of the availability of certain subject positions for the purposes of governance. Maps and statistics were especially significant in the case of the city, which was so much the arena in which the problems and possibilities of liberal governance were located. However, whether and how available epistemological possibilities translated into the operations of rule, let alone 'liberal' rule, is nothing if not an open question: so far the account might indicate that a pre-ordained (liberal) state functioned simply as the source of the knowledge which it operated through, as if the state was both prescient and systematic in its operations. On the contrary, an exploration of these two areas, especially cartography, suggests that, if not quite blind, the state – itself a problematic concept – felt its way into the future, and that seeing like a state, to adopt James Scott's term, was a haphazard affair.[12] Rather than being a source of the knowledge it operated through, it might be nearer the mark to say that the state was in important measure the outcome of this knowledge.

Counting the state and the city

Particularly in Britain and France, the early nineteenth century saw the eclipse of an older 'political arithmetic' by what was increasingly to become modern statistics.[13] Political arithmetic was associated with the centralised bureaucracies of the absolutist state, and the information it conveyed was often the privileged secret of the state. By contrast, the new statistical thinking was frequently pioneered outside the state, by makers of opinion about the condition of 'society', such as doctors and clergymen.[14] Statistics in Britain and elsewhere in fact helped constitute the very 'civil society' in whose name it sought to speak. It maintained that 'society' was more important than the state or government. Statistics uncovered those 'laws' of the social, knowledge of which would enable correct governance to take place, a governance which respected the 'natural' self-regulation of society, and allowed governance to be 'at a distance' from it.[15] 'Social science' itself grew up in intimate relation to this new way of thinking by means of number and 'social facts'. Emerging in civil society, statistics did not, however, abrogate the power of the state, but rather augmented it in a new way.[16]

In the emerging democratic sphere of politics this 'governing by numbers' involved a power that was both calculated and calculating.[17] It depended on those who governed calculating the operations of democracy and using such calculations as a justification for, and a means of, power. It also depended on inculcating calculation among those who were to be governed, shaping them as, quite literally, democratically accountable, and hence responsible, citizens. In this light, 'democracy' was itself nothing more than a gigantic political technology based on number. In democratic republican regimes, for instance the nineteenth-century United States, the pedagogy of numbers took on very pointedly political forms, involved as this was in the creation of democratic citizens.[18] Elsewhere, as in nineteenth-century Britain, more qualified forms of liberal democratic regime clung to numerical forms of mensuration which, unlike the decimal system, did not lend themselves so readily to inculcating the greatest rationality in the greatest possible number of people (though the USA did reject parts of the metric system). However, Britain was at one with other modern states at the time in stabilising mensuration: the imperial system of weights and measures was enacted in Britain in 1824.[19]

Whatever the form of liberalism, there appears to have been in general a thrust that was everywhere 'democratic', or at least concerned with what objects and subjects had in common. Statistics only made sense if the common personhood of all those who were counted was somehow more important than their differences. Autonomous persons were counted in statistics, not members of estates. Autonomised, equalised subjects were therefore brought into being by this new form of knowledge. This equalisation was thus itself part of that general process of objectification and standardisation considered above, something widely characteristic of this time. The 'quantification' statistics made possible meant a standardisation in which judgements of quality were taken away from those who did the measuring, as well as extracted from the instruments of measure themselves, and what was measured. The calculating apparatus evolved at this time was as a consequence closely tied to the idea of objectivity. In fact it has been argued that 'objectivity' replaced the social trust that was lost in complex societies such as urban, industrial Britain was then becoming.[20] However, it may be nearer the mark to say that statistics did not replace trust, but remade trust on a new basis, so that it became one expression of the liberal balancing act of knowing and not knowing, its deliberately limited and targeted sort of knowledge reflecting the sense of the limitations of what needed to be known.

This elaboration of objectivity was involved with what has been called the 'technicization of politics'.[21] What was involved was the accumulation of increasingly specialised knowledge about governing. In order to govern people and processes occurring at a *distance* from power (as in the new forms of civil society then emerging), it was necessary to turn these into traces that could be mobilised and accumulated, much in the manner of the natural sciences and their technical operations. These operations are made possible by what Bruno Latour has called the 'immutable mobile', the trace that can be made both visible and stable, and hence knowable and therefore manageable for the ends of power.[22] The map, quite simply, could be folded and put into the pocket, or otherwise easily stored, an ease of use increasing as the century went on. Both the statistic and the map can be understood in this way therefore, as traces that enabled the coordination of incredibly complex systems like states, particularly governmentally liberal ones. In respect of liberal governmentality, a political rationality that sought explicitly to 'rule at a distance', statistics was therefore of particular importance as part of what was both the material practice and the rhetoric of liberal objectivity. It identified the objectively given and hence 'natural' operation of the social world, a world of what were called at the time 'social facts', the facts of a domain that, like the natural one, was newly objectivised precisely by such means as these 'facts'.

Statistics can be said to have lent themselves to liberalism in at least two major ways therefore, the first through the operation of the discursive practices of objectivity and neutrality, which took matters of power out of the political sphere, making them often matters of 'science', and thereby preventing political intervention in the realms they operated upon. (In the next chapter I will consider how technology, in the form of civil engineering, complemented science in this way.) A putatively de-politicised sphere, in fact alive with power and politics, thus opened up the second major way in which liberalism was to advance, namely the deployment of statistics to define and understand the supposedly freely operating and 'natural' domains of the social, from society itself to the individual self. The earliest forerunners of statistical science were in fact closely involved with ideas of nature and with the operations of natural science, as in the post-Restoration *Natural and Political Observations* (1662) of John Graunt.[23]

When ideas of social 'law', 'science' and 'facts' emerged they drew on this established understanding of objectivity. Statistics thus gave rise to a public rhetoric of disinterestedness, and to the idea of fairness and rule following: of course, as has been noted, standardised forms of mensuration might curb power as well as instituting it, so constraining the governers as well as the governed. Statistics against statistics, as it were, objectivity against objectivity. This was evident from early on: before the elite London, later Royal, Statistical Society was in fact founded, there existed a shadowy 'London Statistical Society', which in 1825, authored by a 'Committee of Artisans', probably of Owenite leanings, published a radical and critical compilation of statistics entitled *Statistics Illustrative of the Territorial Extent and Population, Commerce, Taxation, Consumption, Insolvency, and Crime of the British Empire*. This sported the motto 'Every line a moral, every page a history'.[24] The politics of knowledge was not all one-way, not all top-down.

Objectivity carried with it the notion of rationality: a premium was put not only on the superior rationality of what could be quantified and known statistically, but also on the person who employed statistics to think and consider. The idea that the decimal system was a more rational system than older ones was a reflection of this. The particular form of reason that became prominent was an historical and empirical one. It was in explicit defence of this form of reason, as against the abstract, deductive style of Ricardian economics, that Richard Jones set about creating the statistical section of the British Association for the Advancement of Science in 1833.[25] It was indeed as the empirical arm of political economy that statistics gained much of its prominence in Britain and France at this time, creating what rapidly became known as 'social economy', with its 'social facts'.[26] The British Association was symptomatic of the development of 'expert' opinion outside the state, an opinion which thereafter continued in close connection with it.

Many political intellectuals of the time, Charles Babbage and Thomas Malthus among them, were very active in the Association's statistical section and in the Statistical Society of London which came out of it. The effects of this expert opinion were felt directly in the state: in 1837 the General Registrar's Office was set up to supervise the extended census of 1841. After 1841 an increasing amount of information on the populace was gathered in the decennial census of Britain. From the 1830s the civil service used and generated statistics at an ever-increasing rate, and in close association with the reforming currents of the time, whether in the Board of Trade (whose statistical department was founded in 1832), the War Office and Admiralty, the Poor Law Commission, the Home Office or, from 1839, the Privy Council on Education.[27] The civil servants who directed these statistical efforts were closely associated with the London and provincial statistical societies, and with 'reform' groups such as the Central Society of Education and the Health of Towns Association. Somewhat later, William Farr, who as Registrar General of the General Register Office was the central figure organising the three censuses of 1851 to 1871, was not only regarded as the greatest medical statistician of the century but was also directly involved in the public health and sanitation movements.[28]

The pioneers of 'social medicine', such as Thomas Percival of Manchester, who set up a Board of Health in the town as early as 1796, were early exponents of statistics. The Manchester Statistical Society, founded in 1833, was the first such society in the world, pre-dating the London one. It continued to be the most important society outside London.[29] It was a Manchester MP who was responsible for setting up the Board of Trade's statistical department. James Kay, later Kay-Shuttleworth, treasurer of the Manchester Society, and secretary to the Manchester Board of Health in the 1830s, continued the tradition begun by men like Percival. The deployment of statistics in this case involved the elaboration of the link between physical health and moral or social health, particularly as these were represented in the city.[30] Local societies and national institutions collected 'vital statistics', concerned in their intrinsic nature with the events of the body's history. They were the object of what Foucault called 'bio-power', that power over, and through, the events of the body's life and death that was a defining mark of political modernity.

Kay-Shuttleworth was indeed a figure of major national significance: he was a prime mover in forming the Committee of Council on Education in 1839, and was the first secretary to the Board of Education. This career pattern in itself serves to indicate the linked concerns of men such as him: almost all the statistical societies' activists were also deeply involved in a range of other philanthropic and reforming activities. Typical of these was the Manchester and Salford District Provident Society, a so-called 'visiting society', concerned to make personal contact with the poor complement the knowledge of the poor that statistics brought, something in fact necessitated by one of the major contradictions thrown up by statistics themselves, namely that in the statistical aggregate the 'individual' was inevitably lost to view.[31] This contradiction was in fact played out in social reform movements themselves, such as the Charity Organisation Society, where arguments for direct contact were mounted *against* social statistics, so that the victory of social statistics was not achieved overnight.

A number of the key members of the Manchester Society were educated in the Enlightenment traditions of the Scottish universities, with their strong emphasis on the sciences of the social, including 'social medicine'. Kay-Shuttleworth and Manchester are good examples of the significance of these circles of the provincial intelligentsia. Such circles, as in Manchester, were often made up of co-religionists.[32] The individuals concerned were also frequently inter-married, such marriage links extending their influence to the centre from the provinces. The first two vice-presidents of the Manchester Society were Lieutenant-Colonel Shaw Kennedy and John Kennedy, the latter a major cotton industrialist in the city (the two were not related). John Kennedy's daughter married Edwin Chadwick, a Manchester man himself, and the greatest of all exponents of sanitary reform and its attendant statistical knowledge. Shaw Kennedy became Inspector General of the Irish Constabulary in Dublin, and thus one link between social policy and the new meanings of 'police'.[33] The daughter of W.R. Greg of Styal, a leading paternalist cotton employer and a prominent figure in the Manchester Society, was married to the daughter of the editor of *The Economist*, a major organ of liberal reform and of the science of statistics.[34] In Manchester it was the Unitarian connection that served as the religious element binding the Society, though the influence of the denomination in fact extended into most of the reforming initiatives in the city.

These reforming elements comprised something like a liberal project at the time, so cohesive were their social and intellectual connections, and so concentrated their sense of purpose. This project, and these projectors, will be a presence in the account that follows in this book. They should not be thought of as a class, for instance a bourgeoisie. They did not think of themselves as such, but as the 'opulent classes', or the 'wealthy and influential inhabitants' of the city.[35] They might be thought of as the makers of a class perhaps, those who helped create the epistemological foundations upon which forms of social identity could be based (forms that were of course not only of a 'middle-class' kind, but that formed the staple, for instance, of popular radical and later socialist accounts of the social and its class entities). The concern of these men of influence was to establish a society which would involve the 'total exclusion of party politics'.[36] Only by the truth of statistics could a sure and certain knowledge be formed which would deny the (very real) divisions of religion and politics amongst men of property, and so establish a sense of what a 'middle class' could be.[37]

The Manchester Statistical Society was made up of the leading industrialists and bankers of the city, complemented by its most prominent medical practitioners. No mere statisticians, they described themselves as 'industrious gentlemen'. In its first report of 1834 the Society referred to its members as 'gentlemen for the most part accustomed to meet in private society, and whose habits and opinions are not uncongenial. At its first institution it was considered desirable to unite the members as closely as possible by the attractions of agreeable social intercourse, and it was determined that the meetings should occur every month'.[38] Its members were young (under 40), of 'philanthropic and literary taste', and in its early days meetings were regularly held in the (extremely opulent) homes of these opulent gentlemen. The ambience was very much that of the club in fact, an environment that was distinctively masculine in character. The Society was indeed organised rather like a club – its membership was restricted, subscriptions were substantial and new members had to be vouched for by old ones and could be easily blackballed.[39]

The development of governmental statistical 'expertise' elsewhere highlights the gendering of the process apparent in this case.[40] In the United States, for example, the early, amateur phase of expertise, marked in a similar way to Manchester's by the gentlemen's club and the political magazine, eventually gave way, as it had beforehand in Britain and Europe, to the development of professional expertise and social science. However, professionalisation in the United States was as masculine an affair as in the earlier phase: the overtones of neutrality attaching to science were themselves associated with masculinity. Women were indeed involved in the development of governmental statistical expertise, but more at the level of 'social work', as opposed to 'social science'. Their contribution was associated with understandings of their 'natural' condition as essentially passive and immobile, located in a domestic space which was personal and local, as opposed to scientific, neutral and objective, and, also in the case of the United States, national (men were associated with the production of governmental knowledge both at and of the national level in a very striking way). 'Social work', such as the visiting society referred to in the Manchester case, involved the anything but neutral dimensions of the personal, the local, the moral and the practical. Indeed it has been argued that the 'spatial gaze' involved in the operations of governmental power was itself gendered, 'abstract space' tending to a mobile, active and synoptic masculinised gaze, as opposed to the passivity and immobility of a feminised gaze.[41]

In the case of the Manchester Statistical Society the kind of social intercourse evident in this club was reflected in the character of the social knowledge the Society produced. It was said of the members by one of their early contemporaries that our founders 'were men, highly individual but of similar mould, religious but unsentimental, social but serious minded, eager for reform but saved from extremes by fundamental common sense and the capacity for compromise'.[42] Gentlemanly social intercourse therefore gave rise to a kind of gentlemanly knowledge which, through the agency of plain number and 'facts', was serious and unsentimental, akin to common sense, in fact the sort of knowledge that led away from 'extremes'. As with the progenitors of modern science itself, the men of the Royal Society in the seventeenth century, the virtues of the gentleman informed the intrinsic nature of knowledge, in this case those of a reworked gentlemanly code, that of the 'industrious gentleman'. The form of social knowledge, as once the form of natural knowledge, can be seen therefore as in important measure an extension of the daily 'social' of these men, that of their practice of the everyday. In both cases, empirical knowledge took on the virtues of the English gentleman.[43]

In fact, the social history of the truth of statistical knowledge as a whole hinged on just this sort of reproduction of truth in everyday life. In this sense truth can be said to be 'performed'. In the seventeenth century the cultural resources of gentlemanly status were mobilised to produce notions of scientific truth, which involved the living out of notions of knowledge and truth in terms designed to establish the standing of an empirical notion of detached witnessing as the mark of veracity. This notion of truth was established in the scientist Robert Boyle's performance of his own scientific persona, and in turn the Society's public performance of this persona.[44] In early nineteenth-century Manchester the truth of statistics was performed in the persona of the Society's members, performed upon themselves as a means of constituting the identity of their immediate circle, and performed in the city at large, and beyond, in terms of the public representation of their activities (for instance, in the public presentation of their work in the city as disinterested and scientific).[45]

The gentlemen of the London Statistical Society were of a somewhat different kind. As in Manchester, the aim was to transcend political and religious passions and bias, and, as one of the early founders of the Society put it, drive out 'the daemon of Discord', so as to establish the 'Eden of Philosophy'. In order to demonstrate freedom from bias of any sort, a body of Fellows was established which reflected all sections of the governing classes, including contingents from the law, 'Political Society', the arts, the medical profession and especially 'the Nobility and Gentry of England', who, as *echt* gentlemen, would add the necessary sheen to this public performance of inclusiveness and neutrality. The Fellows, and the Council, in fact comprised some of the most influential political, administrative and intellectual figures in Britain (including Gladstone, Chadwick, Nassau Senior and Malthus), and if political rationalities can be said to have any clearly defined locations, then institutions like these have a good claim as, if not the birthplaces, then at least the academies of such forms of reason.[46] Later on, the National Association for the Promotion of Social Science was another such academy.

This London academy had its own professors, most notably those of the new science of political economy (including Malthus and Richard Jones), but there was a firm distinction in the deliberations of the Society between 'political economy and political philosophy', together with the 'facts', on the one hand, as opposed to 'mere abstraction', on the other. These 'facts' would serve as the 'secure ground' and 'foundations of these sciences'. Secure ground was by no means to be found solely in number in these early days, for it was only in the later part of the century that 'statistics' came to be understood as primarily mathematical, in distinction to the body of 'social facts'. Up to then, the performance of neutrality by number was sought where possible, but it was the larger battle of historical and empirical over abstract and inductive forms of reason that witnessed the greatest victory of the 'social fact'.[47] As has been seen, the London Society was itself a weapon in this war, so that the construction of a particular kind of Society, as outlined above, was an engagement not only in the public performance of neutrality but also in the reason wars themselves.

This understanding of the performance of truth, and the mobilisations of the cultural resources involved, has consequences for understanding the nature of the state, especially the liberal state, which more than other versions of the state can be understood as ramified in the circuits of the performances and cultural mobilisations which established the sorts of truth it increasingly came to rely upon as it became dispersed in civil society. These circuits were realised in terms of just such social and cultural contexts of class and power as those apparent in the case of the 'industrious gentlemen' of Manchester and in the London situation. Rather than simply a centralised, directive power, the development of statistics indicates this dispersed and circuitous nature of the state and its expertise, which was particularly marked in the first half of the century, before the (still limited) move towards a more professional and central-ised bureaucracy with the Northcote–Trevelyan reforms of 1853–4.

None the less, the directive power of the modern state in the gener-ation of statistics should not be minimised. Beyond Britain, the most systematic account of governmentality and statistics is that of Matthew G. Hannah on the USA.[48] While not underestimating state power, he dem-onstrates a similar understanding of the state as the outcome as well as the author of statistical knowledge, and a similar recognition of the performance of power in terms of an ethics of governance within those who would seek to govern, especially in this case the director of the US census, Francis A. Walker. Hannah's account concerns the census in particular. Later than in Europe, particularly in the 1870s and 1880s in the aftermath of the Civil War, there developed very similar epistemologi-cal operations on state territory as in Europe. Extending beyond the census, but especially apparent there, were the twin processes of what Hannah calls 'abstraction' and 'assortment'. These processes were gener-alised across nation-states, and were apparent in Britain also, so that it is useful to dwell on the US example in a little more detail.

The former term, 'abstraction', involves creating an 'observational field' across which 'agents of the governmental gaze can travel without significant impediment, and throughout which they can expect to be provided with complete and accurate information'.[49] Typically, this is provided by the map, so that the map and census statistics are closely related, though one might also think of the creation of observational fields in terms of 'grids of specifications', or systems according to which 'different kinds of governmental objects are divided, contrasted and related'.[50] Such grids of specification are, for example, gender, race, age, nationality, occupation and class, but also spatial specifications. 'Governmental objects' themselves, in terms of the operations of 'assortment', are understood in terms whereby 'the units being observed (whether resources, people or activities) are unambiguously identified and distinguished one from another' in terms of their location in particular grids of specifications and the observational fields to which the latter are related. Drawing systematically on Foucault's work, this detailed account of the development of the US census indicates how populations were now both unified and differentiated as new objects and subjects of governance.

The cultural authority of the census itself in part rested on the wider cultural authority of the male gaze and male power, which were implied in the careful constitution of objectivity in the operations of the US census. For example, the US census authorities' management not only of census categories, as above, but also of the actual collection and compilation of statistical information so as to appear natural and neutral thus allowed society and the individual to operate freely in their own 'natural' domains framed by this careful creation of knowledge as neutral and automatic.[51] Elements of the 'liberalism' of the census can therefore be seen to lie here no less in Britain and Europe than in the United States. Indeed, intellectual cooperation between the new professionals in state knowledge was increasingly marked after the first international statistical congress, held in Brussels, in 1853.[52]

In terms of the pioneering days of statistics, the Manchester Statistical Society members' interests in the 1830s were centred upon social categories which pre-existed their statistical investigations, namely 'the working classes' and the 'Manufacturing Districts'. These they explored in a determinedly empirical manner, employing a form of the direct witnessing of knowledge through the means of paid agents who would be the point of contact with the 'working classes' in collecting information. In turn, other agents were sent around to check against these agents, whose information was double-checked against a whole battery of other sources. At the same time, the Society was at pains to point out that its information was not trustworthy, and no conclusions could be drawn without a great deal of further study.[53] These agents of the Society might also include the 'stipendiary visitors of the poor' of the Manchester and Salford District Provident Society, so that the Provident Society, based on the reconstitution of direct human contact with the poor, was in effect indistinguishable from the Statistical Society, direct empirical witnessing and number complementing human conduct.[54] As is apparent from the Society's papers, which also show how it was in contact with similar societies throughout Britain and Europe, the activities of these societies were rapidly spreading into all areas of public policy, for example in the presentation of criminal statistics to visiting justices at their Sessions,[55] though the city was the chief focus of interest. And, as chapter 5 will show, statistics spread far beyond social investigation and public policy into a myriad of other ways of knowing the city.

These pre-existing categories of the contemporary 'social problem' – class and the 'Manufacturing District' – through the activities of the Manchester Statistical Society itself, came to be redefined in *urban* terms: as a problem, and a solution, specific to the city itself, and knowable in statistical terms. Among the first exercises of the Society was the anatomisation of the social-cum-occupational groups that made up the city's population, not just the 'working classes' but, for example, the handloom weavers (who were considered a key element in the 'social problem' of the time, the Society having a special sub-committee on them), so that the city was thereby constructed as a mosaic of elements of a 'social' and statistical character.[56] This mosaic, in turn, involved the segmentation of the city and the towns into 'districts' and other subdivisions, which, while to some extent reflecting existing perceptions of the social composition of urban life, reconfigured these perceptions in terms of a new sort of certitude based on statistically verifiable entities,[57] just as it reconfigured contemporary perceptions of class and manufacturing Britain. The aim of the Society was to promote what they called 'local' knowledge of 'political and social economy', so that the city became itself the active and reforming subject of statistical knowledge through the cultivation of its own self-knowledge. In a quite literal sense too, Society members were also central to making Manchester a 'city', in terms of the incorporation of the city in 1838. Three major figures in the Society had a central role in the city's incorporation: Richard Cobden led the agitation, William Nield was the chairman of the committee for promoting incorporation, and Thomas Potter became the first mayor of the city. Many Society members were municipal aldermen in the early days.[58] This production of a new kind of city closely involved its mapping, many of the individuals, societies and groups involved in statistics also being involved in mapping the state and the city.

Mapping the state and the city

In producing a version of the city that was amenable to governance, the map shared in the epistemic characteristics of statistics. The cognitive nature of both turned on a particular version of space, 'abstract space', which had first been elaborated at least as early as the seventeenth century. This now lent itself to the social sciences as once it had been integral to the foundation of the natural ones. As 'the elusive heart of the epistemology associated with modernity',[59] space was rendered abstract. The spatial dimension of 'modern abstraction' was both isotropic and absolute. Geometric models assumed that space was continuous and uniform in all directions (isotropic), and therefore uniformly subject to mathematical laws. In addition to this mathematical regularity, absolute space was independent of all time, matter and motion.[60] Fundamental to the transportation of the idea of space into the social sciences was the idea of functional equivalence, the notion that space was reducible to formal schemata or grids, in which the elements of the schemata could be reproduced as equivalents one of another. As a consequence of this, abstract space was 'symbolically and materially associated with homologies: seriality; repetitious actions; reproducible products; interchangeable places, behaviours and activities'.[61] Associated with the idea of functional equivalence was also the equation of value with quantity. The epistemic foundations of statistics will be clear. Homology and seriality made classification, comparison and counting possible.

The epistemic foundations of maps will be similarly apparent. 'Abstract space' was the foundation of the modern map. In the 'realisation' of space literal and imaginative ways of seeing predominated very strongly. Visuality was central to how abstract space was conceived. And, as the visualised, finished product of this operation of realisation was the centre of attention, the process of realisation tended to obscure the social labour which had created this product. The abstract, and gendered, gaze of the map was literally superior: the view from above was detached, part of a visual rhetoric of modernity which privileged the observer with a vantage point separate from the observed. Thus, vision's claims to truth conflated the observed with its self-effacing and 'naturalistic' representation. The cartographic surveyor, one whose gaze is detached and looking always *upon* its object, is a particularly important exemplification of this visual rhetoric. The processes of map production were obscured by a rhetoric that objectified the map.

Of course, maps had preceded the idea of abstract space, and maps continued to reflect the uneven development of abstract space itself. However, the consolidation of abstraction is amply apparent in the history of the map. Michel de Certeau described how the map has disengaged itself from the itineraries that were once its condition of possibility. (Older maps were at first more like itineraries, in which the network of the points making up the itinerary was measured in terms, for instance, of the time taken to traverse these points or stops.)[62] Between the fifteenth and the seventeenth centuries, maps became more autonomous, or disengaged. The proliferation of narrative figures (for example, ships or animals) still had the function of indicating the operations that made possible the plan or map. These marked the historical operations that resulted in the map, and, unlike later maps, were not a decorative gloss on the text. Map historians have described the triumph of the 'empirical map', particularly marked in Cook's mapping of the Pacific.[63] Unlike the 'rationalist map', which deduced from rational principles what could not be mapped and what could (drawing in capes and bays, for instance, in inductive fashion), the empirical map left empty what could not be surveyed.

The modern map in turn reinforced the idea of abstraction upon which it was based. It standardised what it represented. Measured against an abstract grid of space, what was represented – towns, streets, coastlines – became essentially one. The standardisation of scale served to homogenise space, substituting space for what has been called 'place', namely lived, particularised positionality. This standardisation of space was further accentuated by the increasingly sophisticated printing of maps, especially in the nineteenth century. Standardisation involved in turn classification and ordering, one thing being read in terms of another. This inevitably meant the inclusion of some things and the exclusion of others. For example, maps were never explicitly gendered. Maps are therefore of interest for what they leave out as well as what they put in. In turn, because reality became knowable in standardised form, it became amenable to ordering. In short, the modern map is essential to power and to the practices of governance.[64] The practices it encouraged, in the makers but also the users of maps, can be said to partake of the abstract rationality of the map. It was like statistics in this respect, as it was in its encouragement of the view that what it described was objective and natural.

These aspects are particularly apparent in the case of the survey method of triangulation. For it was triangulation, developed first in early modern Europe, especially France, and then in the British mapping of

India in the early nineteenth century, which most faithfully represented this characteristically Enlightenment view of the world. Triangulation offered the potential perfection of the map's relationship with the territory. Triangulation 'defines an exact equivalence between the geographical archive and the world'.[65] It made it possible to conceive of a map constructed on a scale of 1:1. What the map historian of India Matthew Edney calls the 'technological fix' offered by triangulation served to intensify the Enlightenment's 'cartographic illusion' of the mimetic map. The absurdity of this aspiration is apparent. The map would be the same size as the territory it represented. In fact it would *be* the territory. The intrinsic meaning of the map would thereby be negated, namely that it is a conventional representation of the world.

In this aspiration to perfection, it was forgotten that the view of the surveyor and map maker were already informed by a history of spatial practices. In particular, the omniscient eye of the cartographer had been trained by the practice of the surveyor. As Edney argues, the mathematical promise of perfection was always at variance with the practice of surveying.[66] Like all instruments of state power, the survey upon which the mapping of India was based was an exercise in negotiation and mediation, and was marked by contestation. The knowledge the survey generated was 'the map more of the power relations between the conqueror and the conquered than of some topographical reality'.[67] It is in this sense that I want to approach the mapping of Ireland later in this chapter. However, in considering the epistemological foundations of governance and the identification of the objects and subjects who were to be ruled, it was the promise of perfection that perhaps mattered as much as the practice of mapping.

For it was the conquerors' belief that they were creating the perfect map that enabled them to rule India. The map therefore constructed British India as an object of rule. In this regard, it can be said that the practice and reception of instruments of governance may sometimes be of secondary importance: what seems to have mattered here as much as these was the creation of the illusion of a rational, and therefore governable, space, that of a mapped 'India'. Rule in India was dependent on the creation of a space within which a systematic archive of knowledge of this space might be created. This was 'a rational and ordered space that could be governed in a rational and ordered manner', a space that was white, but also male. The rationality of this space, in line with the belief in mathematical perfection, was in fact viewed in terms of an ideology of transcendent law and sovereignty. This space and its contents, including

its subjects, were configured as scientific and rational in line with this
geometrisation of space. They were also understood as liberal and Christian, in opposition to Asian rule, which was mystical, irrational and
despotic.[68] This distinguished the East India Company state from other
'oriental' states and marked it most clearly as an *imperial* one. The
meaning of British rule was incorporated into the very acts of surveying
and mapping, the latter in turn reproducing this meaning.[69]

However, it will be apparent that the same sort of processes were at
work in the metropolitan state, and it is evident that metropolitan and
colonial governmentality were closely related, though the liberalism of
the latter was never anything but highly qualified and ambiguous. The
mapping of India preceded the intensive mapping of the metropolitan
state. The Great Trigonometrical Survey's origins were in the last decade
of the eighteenth century, and 1817 saw its actual birth, under the
responsibility of the Calcutta government. The mapping of Ireland, like
the mapping of India, had a major influence on metropolitan developments. In turn, the Ordnance Survey mapping of Ireland between 1824
and 1846 had a considerable influence on the Indian work. The British
were in fact ahead of other states: with the exceptions of India and
Ireland, and the results of Napoleon's expedition to Egypt, there was no
systematic, trigonometrical survey of any European colony until 1870. At
home things were very different. There, unlike India, for example, the
exigencies of a rapidly developing liberal governance meant that the map
developed alongside the general creation of a political subject which in
its rationality would be self-governing.

In order to explore these dimensions of maps and power it is first
necessary to say something more about the single most important influence in the history of the contemporary map in Britain, namely the
Ordnance Survey. The Survey owed a great deal to the example of the
eighteenth-century French state, especially that of Louis XV. The European states' mapping of their own territories developed systematically
after 1600, the French case being the most highly developed.[70] The
mapping of the modern state as a single, uniform, territorial entity, unlike
the mapping of the multiple territories and jurisdictions of the dynastic
state, was a major outcome of the objectifications 'abstract space' made
possible at this time.[71] The (literal) delineation of boundaries and fron-
tiers in this regime of the unequivocal, geometrical line, and the setting
apart of the state from the ruler and the character of rulership, also the
naturalisation of the state as (again literally) grounded in the putatively
physical reality of a territory, were all aspects of a wider process involving

the 'territorialisation' of the state, and the consolidation of what can be referred to as the 'state country'.[72] What is striking about contemporary cartography is the relatively late date of some of these developments. Only in the 1790s, when in fact the initiative in state cartography began to slowly shift from France to Britain,[73] did Europe itself come to be consistently mapped as the uniformly presented sum of the different territorial entities making up the individual states.[74] State map-making exercises in Britain were then still very limited: the official mapping of Britain was said to be very deficient in comparison with other European states. In 1790 Britain had no accurate national maps nor any survey upon which these could be placed.

I write here of the 'modern' state, and it is apparent that states that were not liberal in the usual sense of the term, such as that of *ancien régime* France, shared a similar cartographic history to those more recognisably liberal, such as Britain. Liberal governmentality, not the same thing as liberalism commonly understood, therefore developed contrary to the distinctions of conventional political analysis. At the same time the modern state, whether governmentally liberal or not, shared many knowledge-producing discourses and practices. However, if the distinction between liberal governmentality and 'police' is useful, the emergence of liberalism out of but also alongside a 'police' form of governmentality is none the less apparent in the case of state mapping. Here the map as a *public* document seems to be a significant departure. The state maps of eighteenth-century France were in fact for public consumption as well as state use, just as at different times their development depended on *private* patronage beyond the sphere of the state in a nascent public, and 'social', sphere. These can be contrasted with the Habsburg (quasi-dynastic and 'police') maps of 1774, only three jealously guarded and hand-drawn copies of which were kept by the state.

This projection of civil society into both the production and consumption of maps can therefore be said to mark their 'liberalism', and this was especially evident in the case of the Ordnance Survey (OS). The 'state space' of the OS was in fact an amalgam of civilian and military cartographic influences.[75] Always spurred on by rebellion and war – the Jacobite Rebellion of 1745, the Napoleonic Wars – state mapping in Britain was none the less profoundly shaped not only by civilian mapping and surveying (county and estate mapping especially), but also by the demands and active interventions of scientific and 'improving' bodies, for instance the Agricultural Societies in the countryside and the Literary and Philosophical Societies in the towns, as in the case of Manchester. These

urban organisations were directly responsible for the institution of the
6 inch to the mile OS mapping of the north of England in the 1840s. The
'military-fiscal' state of the eighteenth century was transformed in these
ways, but the military influence on state knowledge remained important
throughout the nineteenth century. The Board of Ordnance and the
Ordnance Corps were themselves rather strange hybrids of civilian and
military personnel and jurisdictions.[76] It was Thomas Colby, Major-General
(Superintendent) of the OS from 1820 to 1846, who represented the
decisive shift to the accommodation of social needs and demands over
military ones. Colby, a Fellow of the Royal Society, founded the survey
techniques and organisations that were subsequently to be used for more
than a century. He also represented the decisive shift to the use of
scientific expertise in the Survey.

As was the case with statistics, the liberal state can be understood in its
epistemological dimensions as a composite of all these influences, which
were in fact frequently in conflict. The cultural production of political
truth involved the same ramifications in cultural performance, the same
mobilisations of cultural resources, as in the example of statistics. It also
involved the material instantiation of the state, for instance in the form of
the map itself. However, contrary to the idea of a prescient state, it was by
no means clear to many contemporaries closely involved that the state was
the proper agent of a national survey and national mapping, and indeed
that these were even needed at all. Many felt that it could all be left to
commercial interests, and where it was felt that it could not, then there
were often bitter conflicts within the OS itself between military and civilian
surveying and cartographic traditions. As a material instantiation or
ramification of the state, the OS map can be understood as an 'immutable
mobile', carrying state spaces of different and often volatile kinds. The
state can be understood as 'realised' through various techniques (cartography and surveying) and objects (maps) which contained these different
techniques, competencies and indeed agencies, as so many 'layers' of state
knowledge, acting as what might be called small object-machines of power
(one could easily carry a map on one's person).

The surveyor's theodolite can be understood in a similar fashion, a
similarity shared with the navigator's astrolabe, which was 'a memory for
the structure of the heavens', encoding knowledge that could not be
represented internally within human subjects. The astrolabe therefore
functioned as 'a physical residuum of generations of astronomical practice', and as 'a sedimentation of representations of cosmic regularities'.[77]
Understood in this way, the map can be understood as an epistemology *in*

practice. In viewing a map, one was, however unconsciously, learning about how perception worked: as in the use of the stereoscope at the time, say, one was not only entertaining oneself but learning ways of seeing and perceiving. Knowledge of the 'outside' world was learned, but knowledge of the body was also learned, and the body itself trained, by the use of the object. The body acted in concert with the object to form a hybrid, provisional site of knowledge formation, any rigid object–subject distinction again not being evident.

Understanding the state and governmentality in relation to maps in this way means that different sorts of knowledge, competency and agency are, as it were, 'engineered' into material objects and the material world. Things shape and delimit the way actions can be done, and doing affects knowing. Precisely because they are material, things carry meanings at the level of the habitus, the level of implicit and habitual practices, which are often outside discourse *per se,* and so because of this may be relatively immune to what is arguably the more changeful realm of discourse. Older forms of knowledge and agency in things may be unusually persistent over time. These older forms, in varying stages of decay, can in a sense be said to haunt objects and the material world. As well as this, however, there is a parallel volatility to this stability, one evident in how the sociologist of science Andrew Pickering sees the operations of scientists and engineers as setting up the conditions in which matter 'performs' and the material is in control. Devices, experiments and, in this case, maps can be seen therefore as stabilisations of the material in which agency is captured efficiently to perform its duty, but never captured totally in the sense that the material forever eludes these temporary captures.[78] In objects, in this case Ordnance Survey maps, the 'layering' of different sorts of knowledge and competency would appear to be both stable and volatile, therefore something unusually complex and multiform. Bearing in mind this stability and volatility, it is difficult to assign any one particular form of political rationality to these material objects, in this case maps. None the less, it may be useful to think of the 'liberal' rationality and attendant subjectivities of the OS map as inhering in a particular kind of state space that was especially open, plural, deeply layered and indeed itself volatile. This space might be understood as a material and representational distillation of civil society itself.

The maps and town plans of the 1830s and 1840s can be looked at in this light, achieving as they did an unprecedented degree of inclusiveness. The sheer plenitude of the information is striking, most clearly in the city plans (see for example Figure 1.1 and Figures 1.2 and 1.3 (pages 54–5))

Figure 1.1   Six inch to the mile OS Manchester city centre map, 1849

on sanitary detail, a vital ingredient in contemporary imaginings of the
social; on historical detail, so that there is a temporal layering as well; on
political and administrative detail; and on economic detail, as well as the
wealth of information on living spaces and conditions. This plenitude
involved what was almost a positive invitation to interpretation: with so
much information available it became possible to combine the different
elements of this information in hitherto undreamt-of ways. This was
especially the case for those who governed, but also for those who were
governed, in that Ordnance Survey material was becoming increasingly
publicly available, and commercial mapping unashamedly plagiarised the
OS. In chapter 5, drawing in part upon understandings of modernity as
witnessing at once the objectification and the re-enchantment of the
world, I want to consider how the very objectivity of the map was
inseparable from fantasy, the fantasy of the governors but also the
governed. Not only was the abstract and objective map peopled by all
kinds of texts and images, but its very abstraction and objectivity invited
fantasy (for example, the geometric space of city atlases excited new kinds
of imaginings of the city, as well as in practice bringing people into new

and unexpected encounters in using these works of the later nineteenth century).

The *unprecedented* nature of the variety of information published on the OS maps and plans should be emphasised. Reflecting the extraordinary multiplicity of state and civil society inputs into this mapping, this plurality can be understood as inviting and exciting a freedom of choice in interpreting maps, and therefore in this political sense the exercise of 'liberal' freedom, on the part of the subjectivity of the governed as well as the operations of those who would govern. This freedom would in its volatility in turn have involved exceeding liberal freedom, exciting the potential to read these maps against the grain of dominant meanings, though it is precisely the capacity of 'liberalism' to embrace this excess in the form of an agonistic liberal tolerance and plurality that is interesting. (Something of this is taken up in more detail in chapter 3.) This agonism, I think, represented something of the sheer plurality, riskiness and contradiction of liberal governmentality, a certain restlessness which defies our attempts to capture liberalism in easy formulations. In terms of what in fact only with reservation can be called dominant meanings, bearing in mind the complex composition and material forms of carto-graphic knowledge, the most elaborate city plans were in practice the preserve of those who governed. The really big-scale, 1:528 inch plans of the 1840s and 1850s were often paid for and commissioned by town authorities, and most were not published. Comparison between the many different elements present in the maps and especially the plans was, however, possible only because of the underlying abstract rationality of the spatial medium, so that the seeming 'objectivity' and 'reality' of the map was a decided provocation to action and to governmental interven-tion – if the world was solid like this, it could be shaped in different fashions. The OS maps and plans not only reflected prior governing projects, but through the direct agency of their representational forms also served to actively shape such projects.

Reflecting this plenitude of information was an unprecedented degree of openness in the representation of urban spaces. In particular, the interiors of military barracks and prisons were shown, as were interiors of a host of other 'public' buildings. It is as if the early nineteenth-century liberal state in its age of first innocence was willing to reveal itself. This was not so much the case later. After the 1870s prisons were not shown in this way, and details on Army building structures were limited. The interiors of lunatic asylums were not shown after 1916. The interior of other sorts of building were not shown after 1893. The detailed 'sanitary' information shown up to and around the mid-nineteenth century was not shown later either. There was also marked fluidity to the OS maps, as these changes indicate: there was a considerable degree of change in what was represented between map issues, increasing the possibility of choice by reading one map against another. In general, the later the map the less it shows.[79] Again, these temporary, and temporal, dimensions of the map indicate the epistemological volatility spoken of earlier, how maps were *temporary* captures of knowledge and material agency (though haunted still by older presences).

In terms of 'historical epistemology', the political subjectivities that seem to have been involved in these maps and plans were similar to those evident in the Penny Post. The rationality of the modern map depended upon its universality. It dealt in the outcomes of 'functional equivalence', and with a standardised space which created a realm different from the hierarchic and the God-given. Like statistics in this respect, it had a certain 'democratic' potentiality. If not inherently 'liberal', it certainly opened up a sphere in which the universal, human subject of liberalism could begin to be identified and operated upon. On the one hand, the increasingly universalistic language of the map was conducive to the imagining of collectivities on the part of those who sought to rule but also of those who were ruled. On the other hand, the possibility of imagining the collective went hand in hand with imagining the individual. This was because the abstraction of the map meant that it was opened to all. One person could read its generalised discourse as well as another. One reading was therefore as good as another. This oscillation between individuation and totalisation, if not perhaps intrinsic to liberalism or to the nineteenth century itself, was greatly consolidated then, and liberalism without it becomes, literally, unthinkable.

This relationship between the collective and the individual became increasingly important as the use of the map and plan for the negotiation of the city was popularly disseminated in the second half of the nineteenth century, something which happened in the form particularly of city guides and street atlases. The map represented the city as a place of standardised entities through which common identities could be realised. For example, the built environment was increasingly uniformly represented, and because population was represented only through this representation of uniformity, the city dweller was in the process collectivised or massified. City populations were, quite literally, oriented with reference to common symbols. The Ordnance Survey further 'democratised' city space in that, unlike many previous city maps, it did not depend on subscribers. It therefore did not need to include aspects called for by the subscriber, such as the house of the aristocrat or city merchant. Though necessarily marked by exclusions and omissions, the Ordnance Survey was less exclusive than almost all previous maps. More things were represented than ever before to more people, in ways that were increasingly standardised. Yet, at the same time, the map increasingly made everyone his or her own guide to the city, sometimes with the map in hand, guiding the steps of the walker.

If this gave the Survey, and maps more widely, a certain 'liberal' character, then the disciplinary, and 'police', dimensions of the state were never far away. This was particularly the case in semi-colonial Ireland.[80] In the course of the first half of the nineteenth century the Ordnance Survey became in effect an important cultural arbiter of the territory of the British. The 1841 Survey Act gave the OS legal authority to collect the names of places in Britain and Ireland. One was legally obliged to tell the the names of places. These names thereafter became a sort of property of the Survey, in that, once represented on the map, they took 'official' status, and tended to be fixed in this form. This was nowhere more evident than in Ireland. Power over the name, in Britain as a whole as well as in Ireland, was paralleled by power over the space the name demarcated, for the 1841 Act also gave the OS the legal authority to ascertain boundary divisions (a right given in Ireland in 1825). However, it never recorded private property boundaries, these remaining in a private, indeed 'liberal', realm. It also 'officially' mapped fields and parishes for the first time. What had earlier been relatively unfixed and subject to extra-governmental jurisdiction now became fixed by the state.[81]

What these names and boundaries represented itself took increasingly abstract form. This is evident in the history of the contour. In the eighteenth century and the early nineteenth century elaborate hatching techniques were developed for representing relief, especially for military purposes. The OS rapidly brought the hill sketching upon which these techniques were based under the sovereignty of the contour. The older techniques were said to be based on 'taste, imagination, and fancy'. Hatching was still to some extent used, but came to be based solely on the contour and not on the eye and the imagination. By the late 1840s the contour had made its introduction in the Survey. By the late nineteenth century it dominated OS maps.[82] The sheer size of these Ordnance Survey undertakings should be emphasised. The outdoor staff of the OS in Britain between 1800 and 1820 numbered usually around twenty people. After 1820 the growth was immense: by 1837 the Irish OS employed over 2,000 workers and its final costs were over £800,000.[83]

The Irish Ordnance Survey itself helps explicate the complex 'layering' of knowledge and competence evident in the map as an object, and something also of the openness and plenitude of information that marked the operation of liberal governmentality in this area. This is particularly the case in terms of historical and ethnographic elements in the map. Even though the Irish case was not the same as mainland Britain, it points to many of the processes going on in the metropolitan state as well. I therefore dwell on the Irish case partly for its own sake, as a semi-colonial encounter, and partly because of its wider relevance. If the mapping of British India, as has been seen, told more of the power relations of conquerors and conquered than of some topographical reality, so too does the Irish case indicate the mapping of the power relations evident within both Ireland and Britain, and between the two. Whether in India, Ireland or Britain, the role of intermediaries, or translators, of local knowledge into objectivised, cartographic knowledge was crucial, especially so but not solely in the colonial sphere.

In Ireland, in terms of historical and ethnographic material, John O'Donovan was probably the most crucial figure of all.[84] He was employed by the Irish Ordnance Survey to research the most 'authentic' and accurate versions of the historical material that would go on the OS maps, above all the most precise re-presentation of Irish-language place-names in English. This research he conducted in the most assiduous way, one that not only made this largely autodidact man into one of the greatest contemporary scholars of Irish language and culture, but also took him far beyond book learning into seeking out in his seemingly endless journeying across the country a particularly direct encounter with this culture and language in their everyday use. Born and raised in a small farming setting, one in which his family were immensely proud of their Irishness, he and others in the Topographical Department of the Irish Survey in fact established a body of scholarship on Irish culture which would serve as the lodestar of a great deal of Irish nationalism later in the century.[85] Indeed, those involved in the Department itself, Catholics as they were, often had distinct nationalist leanings themselves. Therefore, it is apparent that the transmission of this sort of cultural knowledge onto the map, as a means of confirming an 'authentic' Irish culture, negotiated and indeed resisted forms of state power evident in the map. In the same way, it is quite apparent that in other contexts, including Britain itself, maps could be read in ways that undermined the power evident in the map's intentions. For example, ethnographic material on maps of Britain was in part the result of a similar movement in folklore and language studies to that in Ireland, in Britain especially evident in dialect studies, and that material could be, and was, taken up as part of a refashioned notion of an authentic 'popular' culture and popular identity, not only by scholars but also by the poor themselves, in a radical and oppositional way.[86]

However, at the same time these negotiations of meaning can be seen to have taken place within the terms of reference set by the Survey and the maps themselves, and therefore within the new power relations the maps instituted. This does not mean that governmental forms were inevitable winners in this process, but simply that they had a powerful role, though not the only one, in serving to reconfigure the field within which power, and its negotiation and resistance, could operate. O'Donovan was introduced to the Survey through his association with T.A. Larcom, Thomas Colby's deputy in Ireland.[87] Larcom employed O'Donovan to teach him Irish, which he felt was essential to his task as the head of the Irish Survey. In the drive for 'authenticity' the state was as involved as its intermediaries. Indeed, like Larcom, O'Donovan himself was a very typical example of the contemporary absorption in folklore and language studies, a fascination with cultural authenticity that developed from the late eighteenth century and was deeply influential across Europe and beyond. State knowledge, in the form of the Survey map, can be seen to have inserted this kind of ethnographic knowledge into 'state space', as one element in the plurality that in the British case I have understood as representing its governmental liberalism.

In earlier forms of the state, pre-dating liberalism, one can see this incorporation of 'local' knowledge into state knowledge. As Chandra Mukerji argues, in the case of the seventeenth-century French state, and the 'early modern fieldwork' that represented local knowledge in this case, it was the cartographic 'nearsightedness' of this knowledge, as opposed to James Scott's emphasis on the objectivised, abstract gaze of power, that perhaps mattered most.[88] In the form of the knowledge attendant upon forestry reform, central government in France came to know the human landscape, which in turn helped to convince those who were themselves part of this landscape that the state knew them intimately, in terms of how they related to the geographical terrain in which they lived. In turn, the actual *use* of maps, for example in the adjudication of property rights, itself served to reproduce the state, and thereby reinforce state knowledge (of course, use had other effects too). These aspects can also be understood as elements in the development of nineteenth-century maps as a mode of governance, namely the reproduction and validation of power through *use* (in which consciousness might not come into play at all), and the capacity of the state to convince its subjects that in the more intimate parts of their being they were known: for example, that they were known in the knowledge of the townlands of the Irish peasant, or in that of the streets of the British worker, though in both cases known in terms that might be foreign to the object of knowledge. Both aspects applied even more in the nineteenth century, when many different kinds of knowledge reached an unprecedented level of cartographic expression, and a more open and plural, also volatile, 'liberal' spatial regime seems to have been evident. One was known governmentally by a form of knowledge that appeared to allow one latitude to interpret, a latitude that was at the same time not simply an illusion.

However, it is perhaps also the mode in which cultural 'authenticity' was achieved that reveals something of what was arguably the liberalism of the map. Authenticity was understood as the product of a form of scholarship that was, not unlike statistics, neutral and disinterested. The scholarly methods of O'Donovan and his like depended upon an empirical and scientific encounter with the text, as opposed to the flights of fancy of an earlier, pre-anthropological rationalism.[89] And it is clear that he was not unlike his master Larcom in this respect, a man who learned Irish in order to bring the authentic to his job: both men seem to have agreed that authenticity in the reproduction of Irish place-names was dependent upon choosing the form of spelling then prevailing which was most consistent with ancient orthography. O'Donovan tried to relate contemporary spelling to contemporary spoken pronunciation, but there is no doubting in his work the dominance of the written, in a still largely oral culture, or the pre-eminence of empirical, textual scholarship. In the definitive form of the place-name itself it was Larcom's version that ultimately counted, however, not least his version of Victorian moral correctness, so that, for example, he forbade the use of the suffix 'gob' as vulgar.

In thinking about the place of the Ordnance Survey map in the reconfiguration of the field within which power and its negotiations operated, this instance of the anglicisation of Irish place-names has rightly been seen as a major step in the cultural anglicisation of Ireland, so that the map was now primarily for non-Irish speakers' use, with the result that the English language had hegemony. This is how the matter has been presented in some quarters,[90] though in others a defence of the British for respecting Irish traditions is apparent.[91] I would suggest that in many respects both parties are correct, but neither of the two formulations does justice to the subtle operations of governmentality.[92] The reconfiguration of the field of power of which I speak, involving, for example, the style of orthographic and folklore scholarship that I describe, needs in turn itself to be seen as part of a larger discursive and institutional framework, so that one can think about the ways in which historical and ethnographic knowledge were inserted into what I call 'state space' in terms of this framework.

One aspect of this framework is the location of scholarship within the form of the 'fieldwork'-based, ethnographic 'Memoir', which was part of the activity of the Irish Ordnance Survey. Though only one such Memoir was completed, that of the Londonderry area in 1837, its character is revealing. The document is structured in terms of understanding the locality in terms of its 'natural state', including its natural history, and then its so-called 'artificial state', including accounts of towns and of history and antiquities.[93] Finally the territory was understood in terms of what was called its 'general state', including knowledge about manufactures and 'social economy', and in this general state statistics were to be freely employed. One can see how in this compendium of the territory historical and cultural information was itself framed within an overall view in which it was one constituent in conceiving of the true 'state' of the locality. The aspiration to an encyclopaedic knowledge of the territory is striking. The processes of which I speak are evident too in the dispersal of historical and cultural material within a field of knowledge embracing not only the statistical, but also a Victorian view of knowledge as crucially instrumental in shaping the self-culture of the person. O'Donovan was a frequent contributor to the *Dublin Penny Magazine,* itself modelled on the example of Charles Knight and Henry Brougham's *Penny Magazine* in Britain, a great emblem of the contemporary drive of opinion makers towards the 'Improvement' of the self and society. The Dublin magazine published articles not only on Irish language and culture, but also on 'useful knowledge' more generally, including information on arts, sciences and manufactures.

In the person of O'Donovan himself it is possible to discern some of the processes of translation going on between cultures, in Britain as well as Ireland. O'Donovan was part of the oral culture that he chronicled, and of the culture that did the chronicling. I will take the instance of one of his fieldwork Survey letters in which he describes coming across an 'old-style country school' in the ruins of Ballintober Abbey, County

Mayo.[94] He encouraged the old master to talk to him about the ancient legends of the place. O'Donovan affected a joking style with the man, in which he actively debunks the sublime and romantic associations of the Abbey. But elsewhere in his letters it is clear that, deeply familiar as he was with the realities of rural Ireland, he none the less conceived of its landscape as both romantic and sublime. He appears to inhabit both worlds. He asks the teacher, a Mr Hennelly, whether his account is true. He clearly feels that it is not. In the account of Mr Hennelly it is obvious that another idea of truth is apparent, one that the actions of the Ordnance Survey in Ireland and elsewhere subordinated to a new notion of what truth was.

The old schoolmaster goes on, describing his account: 'As true, sir, as if it had been penned down by a philosophic historian who saw the occurrence with his own clear eye.' This schoolmaster evidently himself knew this wider world of scholarship, but is aware of another tradition of truth telling.

> You see, sir, it is purely preserved by tradition, which is as true the vehicle of historical knowledge as writing. Besides, sir, you must remark that writers of history generally paint and colour, and it is well known that almost every historian from Livy down to Hume have so coloured their narratives and favoured one party more than another, that it is impossible for us of the present-day to see the naked truth among their colourings. But traditions generally transmit to posterity a pure and naked account of things as they are, without any artificial colouring.[95]

O'Donovan elsewhere in his letters gives expression to a version of truth that, for all his complexity as a translator of the indigenous culture, seems to have informed his practice most, one in another mental world from an understanding of the naked truth of tradition:

> Why have most men believed in illusions for 5000 years? Why did not reason dawn upon them sooner? Was it necessary that they should so long remain ignorant of the real laws of nature? Why were the early monks such liars? . . . Why did not the Christian religion establish peace in Christendom? Why did Christian writers tell more lies than Plutarch, Livy, Herodotus and Tacitus?[96]

The state space of the British in Ireland, also in Britain, was, as I have said, always contested and volatile. While historical information and temporal layering always continued to be a feature of Ordnance mapping, the fate of the 'Memoir' indicates something of this volatility. The idea of producing Memoirs for the rest of Ireland was shelved because of conflicts

within the Ordnance Survey, and between the Survey and the Topographical Department. Familiar arguments continued as to whether mapping
should be a military and not a civil exercise. It was felt that activities like
those of the Department should properly be the concern of commerce,
not government. It was also felt that the Department was too political,
and would stir up political passions in Ireland. There was also much
discussion about the location of political authority in this matter, as to
whether it should lie in Dublin or London. In the end, there was no
doubt about the final location of authority, namely the Prime Minister in
London, Robert Peel. Although there was sufficient opinion in favour of
continuing the Memoirs, and Peel instituted a government Committee of
Inquiry which recommended that a scaled-down version be allowed, he
would have none of this.[97] The interests of 'economy' were uppermost,
economic government in this case confounding the government of information, though, as will be apparent in chapter 3, 'economical government' was an intrinsic part of liberal governmentality as well.

Returning to the side of the water in which the heart of governmentality beat most powerfully, perhaps the clearest example of the map in the
service of a liberal form of governmentality was what can be called the
social mapping developing at this time. The period between 1835 and
1855 marked a revolution in the history of non-topographical cartography.[98] Social mapping, especially the mapping of populations, was at the
heart of this revolution. Before this time, no map of population distribu-
tions or density was known of in Britain. 'Flow maps' of population
movement originated in 1844, and the use of graduated circles to represent population concentrations a little later. Every technique of the new
cartography originated in this period in fact. The Irish Railway Committee
Report of 1837 pioneered much of this, under the influence of H.D.
Harness, an engineer of the Royal Military Academy. The influence of
developments in Ireland was again apparent in the 1841 Irish census. The
maps produced for this had a great influence on social mapping in Britain
as a whole.

T.A. Larcom of the Irish Ordnance Survey followed Harness in using
maps to represent statistics on literacy rates, population density and living
standards. The link of statistics and mapping was therefore very close. In
fact, Larcom's work for the Irish census was every bit as important as his
work for the OS. In both, heavily influenced by the publications of the
Moral and Statistical Society of France, Larcom pioneered the use of the
survey as an adjunct to the statistic, as has been seen. There was a mania
around this time for 'social' but also 'political' mapping. The final report

to Parliament on the Second Reform Act of 1867 had 530,352 hand-coloured plans. Statistical Societies, such as the Manchester society, rapidly took up mapping in the late 1830s. It was in fact the city that played the central role during this seminal period of social mapping. For it was the city upon which the most marked anxieties about the nature of the social were centred. The Health of Towns Association was behind most of the mapping activity of the 1840s, especially the large-scale OS town plans, such as the 1:528 inch Board of Health Town Plans of Warwickshire, made between 1848 and 1854.[99] Boards of Health themselves sometimes privately commissioned plans and maps. Medical practitioners also created a medical cartography at this time. There was, again, the characteristic fusion of state and extra-state expertise in these activities. However, the translation of the map into an instrument of the state was clear enough: Chadwick's seminal 1842 Report on the sanitary condition of the towns led directly to the OS maps and plans. This social mapping was also a moral mapping. The health of the city was both medical and moral, as will be apparent.[100] It is the OS plans themselves that perhaps most reveal the power inherent in maps.

The OS was in 1841 authorised by the Treasury to produce town plans of 5 feet to the mile (when it was already mapping the northern counties at the 6 inch to the mile scale).[101] Ten feet to the mile plans were published in the early 1850s for eighteen more towns in England and Wales. These were based on surveys stimulated by the evidence of witnesses to the *First Report of the Commissioners for Inquiry into the State of Large Towns and Populous Districts* (1844), and by the Public Health Act of 1848. In 1855 a third series followed, covering all towns with a population of more than 4,000. By 1892 and the end of the programme urban Britain was mapped on a scale sufficient to show detail down to the size of the doorstep, as the OS Annual Report of 1891 noted. These plans provided an unprecedented view of the city and its inhabitants. Perhaps a better term would be an unprecedented view *into* the city, for the model of vision here was the medical one of the microscope, as well as the omniscient view of the surveyor.[102]

Figures 1.2 and 1.3 are parts of the 5-feet plan for the city centre of Manchester in 1849. The plan literally opens the city to view. It 'looked into' buildings as through a microscope, discerning the inner nature of what had hitherto been hidden, as in the case of churches in both maps, or the Shambles (the old city slaughterhouse) in Figure 1.2. Previous maps had not shown the contents of buildings like this. These did, down to the level of not only the doorstep, but also the stairwell and the water

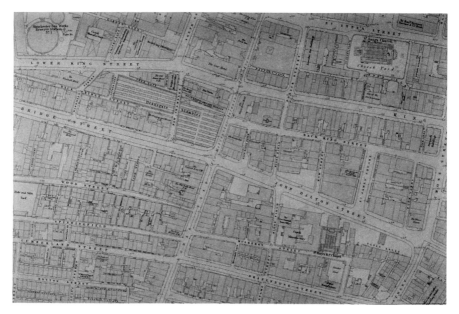

Figure 1.2   Ordnance Survey plan of Manchester city centre, 1849 (Deansgate north, and John Dalton Street area)

tap. They looked into places of social interaction, registering and emphasising the notion of what was 'public' – the place of worship, the theatre, the town hall (shown in great detail on this plan), the workhouse, banks and markets were 'public', but not places of industrial employment, for instance, and not hotels – and above all not the home. In not penetrating the home, the gaze of the map sanctioned it as a sphere of privacy, and of intimacy – it was off-limits to this form of the public gaze. As such, the domestic, feminised character of the home was also sanctioned. From this point of view, it is interesting that this masculinised gaze found in the hotel a public analogue of the home, nearer to the latter than the other more masculinised, and therefore public, city spaces and places. The freedom of this cartographic gaze did not penetrate the workplace either, the sanctity of private property being registered and reinforced in places that were in fact, especially in this part of Britain, scenes of the most intense social interaction, particularly gender interaction in cotton factories.

Of course previous maps had geometrised space like this (and shown the alleys of the city, as well as separate units of habitation), but never

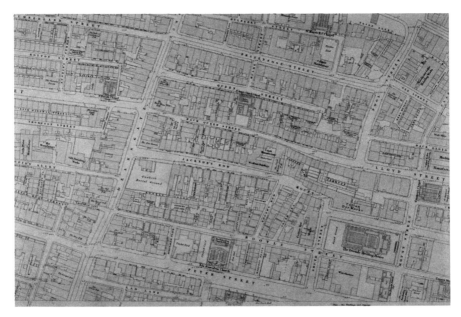

Figure 1.3 Ordnance Survey plan of Manchester city centre, 1849 (Deansgate south, and Jackson's Row area)

quite in this way, the way that an increasingly 'scientific', and vastly expensive, triangulation made possible.[103] In the plan, space is delineated, reduced to the clarity of the line. This sharpened line demarcates spaces, so that buildings, streets and so on are differentiated, but this is with reference to a common rhetoric concerning legibility. Individuation can be seen to occur therefore in tandem with the construction of epistemological potentials for the collective. All the elements are different (one dwelling is sharply different from another, to a degree that is striking and new) but all are composed of the same medium, that of an extreme form of geometrised space. In this form a 'functional equivalence' is taken to new heights, in terms of the interchangeability of standardised units. One thing is read in terms of another in ways that become ever more emphatic as the standard of measure becomes ever more standard. The spaces of the poor became in this form of representation equal to the spaces of the rich. All were composed of the same visual rhetoric. Theoretically, all were equal therefore. The poor city dweller was invited to look upon the map in the same way as the rich city dweller. They looked upon a similar condition. The standardised map made possible the imagining of the city as a collective entity in new kinds of ways, ways that were woven into the social imaginaries of the time. They were, for example, woven into Booth's famous cartographic colour codings of London's inequalities in the late nineteenth century, a radical simplification of reality upon which so much contemporary discussion and action on social welfare was based.

What this cartographic gaze looked into, and down upon, with the most dramatic effect were the city centre dwellings of the poor (see Figure 1.3, the Deansgate south map, especially, on either side of Deansgate). This was the aspect of contemporary reality standing most in need of radical simplification. In the actual built environment of the time this housing was in fact a labyrinthine jumble of courts and alleys, representing the greatest source of contemporary anxiety about the city. It was these areas that were understood to breed both immorality and ill-health. It was these streets, the courts of Manchester and the 'wynds' of Glasgow, prototypes of the late nineteenth-century 'slum', which provided the motivation for the Health of Towns Association. The streets around Deansgate, for instance Jackson's Row, Queen Street and Bootle Street to the east, and Cupid's Alley to the west, were typical of the areas where in the first half of the nineteenth century the 'courts', 'alleys', 'buildings', 'yards' and 'passages' of the old city (complete with their 'cellar dwellings') preceded the rows of uniform housing and streets, sometimes called by-law housing, that became the dominant form of 'working-class' domestic built space in the second half of the century. As will be seen in the next chapter, these new areas were the antidote to the old ones. As is evident from the plan, these old city spaces existed within easy, and threatening, walking distance of the business centre and respectable shopping streets of the town, the latter in King Street and St Ann's Square, across Deansgate from the Shambles and the labyrinths of Wood Street, itself south of Bridge Street. (St Ann's Square is just to the north of St Ann's Church, top of Figure 1.2.)

Before the rational housing of the mid- and late nineteenth century could be built, the existing irrational housing of the city had to be made rational, this paper rationality both quelling fear and providing a blueprint for action. Making these spaces legible and hence governable involved untwisting the winding alleys, and smoothing out the irregularity of the spaces of the courts and the wynds. The widening and straightening of Deansgate, seen in Figure 1 of the Introduction, was one practical exemplification of the 'paper rationality' of which I speak, a rationality made manifest and material in the built form of this street, and of the new streets of rational bylaw housing that would replace the old courts and alleys, especially in the city centre. It is to this new sort of city that attention will now be given, for once the objects and subjects of governmentality had been identified it was then necessary to secure governance over them by means of the city of free circulation.

Notes

1. John Brewer, *The Sinews of Power: War, Money and the English State 1688–1783* (London: Unwin Hyman, 1989), chapter 8.
2. David Eastwood, ' "Amplifying the Province of the Legislature": The Flow of Information and the English State in the Early Nineteenth Century', *Historical Research*, 62, 1989. See also his *Government and Community in the English Provinces, 1700–1870* (Basingstoke: Macmillan, 1997).
3. David Vincent, *The Culture of Secrecy: Britain 1832–1998* (Oxford: Oxford University Press, 1998); M.J. Cullen, *The Statistical Movement in Early Victorian Britain: The Foundations of Empirical Social Research* (Hassocks: Harvester, 1975), 'Conclusion'.
4. John Tagg, *The Burden of Representation: Essays on Photographies and Histories* (Basingstoke: Macmillan, 1988), pp. 60–5.
5. David Vincent, *The Culture of Secrecy*, chapters 1–3.
6. Thomas Osborne, 'Bureaucracy as a Vocation: Governmentality and Administration in Nineteenth-Century Britain', *Journal of Historical Sociology*, 7:3, 1994.
7. M.J. Cullen, *The Statistical Movement*, chapter 2.
8. David Vincent, 'Communications, Community and the State', in Clive Emsley and James Walvin (eds), *Artisans, Peasants and Proletarians 1760–1860* (London: Croom Helm 1985), and *The Culture of Secrecy*, pp. 68–9.
9. On letter writing and the postal service in nineteenth-century England see David Vincent, *Literacy and Popular Culture: England 1750–1914* (Cambridge: Cambridge University Press, 1989), *passim*; on letter writing and individuation, see Alain Corbin, 'Backstage', in Michelle Perrot (ed.), *A History of Private Life*, volume IV (London: Harvard University Press, 1990).
10. For a reading of the object/subject distinction see Paul Rabinow, 'Introduction' to his (ed.), *The Foucault Reader* (London: Penguin, 1986), pp. 10–11. See also Michel Foucault, 'The Subject and Power', in Hubert Dreyfus and Paul Rabinow (eds), *Michel Foucault: Beyond Structuralism and Hermeneutics* (London: University of California Press, 1982), p. 208.
11. Andrew Barry, 'Lines of Communication and Spaces of Rule', in Thomas Osborne, Andrew Barry and Nikolas Rose (eds), *Foucault and Political Reason: Liberalism, Neo-Liberalism and Rationalities of Government* (London: UCL Press, 1996).
12. James C. Scott, *Seeing Like a State: How Certain Schemes to Improve the Human Condition Have Failed* (London: Yale University Press, 1998).
13. Theodore M. Porter, *The Rise of Statistical Thinking, 1820–1900* (London: Princeton University Press, 1986).

14. Mary Poovey, *Making a Social Body: British Cultural Formation 1830–1864* (Chicago: University of Chicago Press, 1995).
15. Stefan Collini, 'Political Theory and the Science of Society in Victorian Britain', *Historical Journal*, 23:1, 1980.
16. For an extensive treatment of the history of the social, see the 'Introduction' and contributions to Patrick Joyce (ed.), *The Social in Question: New Bearings in History and the Social Sciences* (London: Routledge, 2002).
17. Nikolas Rose, 'Governing by Numbers: Figuring out Democracy', *Accounting, Organisations and Society*, 16:7, 1991. See also Nikolas Rose, *Powers of Freedom: Reframing Political Thought* (Cambridge: Cambridge University Press, 1999), chapter 6.
18. Patricia Cline Cohen, *A Calculating People: The Spread of Numeracy in Early America* (Chicago: University of Chicago Press, 1982); Paul Starr and W. Alonso (eds), *The Politics of Numbers* (New York: Russell Sage Foundation, 1987).
19. Daniel R. Headwick, *When Information Came of Age: Technologies of Knowledge in the Age of Reason and Revolution, 1700–1850* (Oxford: Oxford University Press, 2000), pp. 45–7.
20. Nikolas Rose, 'Governing by Numbers', pp. 678–9.
21. Ibid., p. 678.
22. Bruno Latour, *Science in Action* (Milton Keynes: Open University Press, 1987), and 'Visualisation and Cognition: Thinking with Eyes and Hands', *Knowledge and Society*, 6, 1986.
23. M.J. Cullen, *The Statistical Movement*, pp. 1, 2, 3, 7, 152.
24. Royal Statistical Society, *Annals of the Royal Statistical Society 1834–1934* (London, 1934), pp. 2–3.
25. Stefan Collini, 'Political Theory', *passim*.
26. Colin Gordon, 'Governmental Rationality: An Introduction', pp. 37–8, and Giovanni Procacci, 'Social Economy and the Government of Poverty', in Colin Gordon, Peter Miller and Graham Burchell (eds), *The Foucault Effect: Studies in Governmentality* (Hemel Hempstead: Harvester Wheatsheaf, 1991).
27. M.J. Cullen, *The Statistical Movement*, chapters 1–3.
28. Lawrence Goldman, 'The Origins of British Social Science: Political Economy, Natural Science and Statistics, 1830–1835', *Historical Journal*, 26:3, 1983, and 'A Peculiarity of the English? The Social Science Association and the Absence of Sociology in Nineteenth-Century Britain', *Past and Present*, 114, 1987; see also Philip Abrams, *The Origins of British Sociology: An Essay* (Chicago: University of Chicago Press, 1968). On Farr, see Edward Higgs, *A Clearer Sense of the Census: The Victorian Censuses and Historical Research* (London: HMSO, 1996), chapter 1.
29. T.S. Ashton, *Social and Economic Investigations in Manchester 1833–1933* (Manchester: Manchester University Press, 1977 edn, first published 1934); David Elesh, 'The Manchester Statistical Society: A Case Study of a Discontinuity in the History of Empirical Social Research', *Journal of the History of Behavioural Sciences*, VIII, 1972.
30. Mary Poovey, *Making a Social Body*, chapters 3, 4, and see below, pp. 65–6, 72–6.
31. On the visiting societies, see A.J. Kidd (ed.), *City, Class and Culture: Studies of Social*

Policy and Cultural Production in Nineteenth-Century Manchester (Manchester: Manchester University Press, 1985), and 'Philanthropy and the "Social History Paradigm"', *Social History*, 21:2, 1996.

32. John Seed, 'Unitarianism, Political Economy and the Antinomies of Liberal Culture in Manchester 1830–1850', *Social History*, 7:1, 1982.

33. For information on John Kennedy, Shaw Kennedy and their connections, see Simon Gunn, 'The Manchester Middle Class 1850–1880' (Manchester University PhD, 1992).

34. For W.R. Greg and the Greg family see ibid., and Simon Gunn, *The Public Culture of the Victorian Middle Class: Ritual and Authority in the English Industrial City 1840–1914* (Manchester: Manchester University Press, 2000).

35. Patrick Joyce, *Democratic Subjects: The Self and the Social in Nineteenth-Century England* (Cambridge: Cambridge University Press, 1994), p. 164.

36. *First Report of the Statistical Society*, Manchester, July 1834.

37. R.J. Morris, *Class, Sect and Party: The Making of the British Middle Class, Leeds 1820–1850* (Manchester: Manchester University Press, 1990).

38. *Rules of the Manchester Statistical Society*, 19 Nov. 1834.

39. T.R. Williamson, 'On the Origin and History of the Manchester Statistical Society', *Transactions of the Manchester Statistical Society*, 1875–6.

40. Matthew G. Hannah, *Governmentality and the Mastery of Territory in Nineteenth Century America* (Cambridge: Cambridge University Press, 2000), esp. chapters 4, 7.

41. Ibid., p. 129, also Gillian Rose, *Feminism and Geography: The Limits of Geographical Knowledge* (Cambridge: Polity, 1993).

42. T.S. Ashton, *Social and Economic Investigations*, p. 10.

43. Bruno Latour, *We Have Never Been Modern* (Hemel Hempstead: Harvester Wheatsheaf, 1993); Steven Shapin and Simon Schaffer, *Leviathan and the Air Pump: Hobbes, Boyle and the Experimental Life* (London: Princeton University Press, 1985).

44. On Boyle and the Royal Society, see Steven Shapin, *A Social History of Truth: Civility and Science in Seventeenth-Century England* (Chicago: University of Chicago Press, 1994), chapters 3 and 4.

45. Patrick Joyce, *Democratic Subjects*, pp. 161–76, for an account of the Manchester 'projectors'.

46. On the London Society, see Royal Statistical Society, *Annals of the Royal Statistical Society*, esp. pp. 5–6.

47. On different versions of the 'modern fact', see Mary Poovey, *A History of the Modern Fact: Problems of Knowledge in the Sciences of Wealth and Society* (Chicago: University of Chicago Press, 1998).

48. Matthew G. Hannah, *Governmentality and the Mastery of Territory*, chapters 2 and 5.

49. Ibid., p. 124.

50. Ibid., p. 56.

51. Ibid., pp. 135–41.

52. Harald Westergaard, *Contributions to the History of Statistics* (London, 1932); also Royal Statistical Society, *Annals of the Royal Statistical Society*, and on the development of statistics as a science, and its increasing professionalisation, see Donald A.

McKenzie, *Statistics in Britain 1865–1913: The Social Construction of Scientific Knowledge* (Edinburgh: Edinburgh University Press, 1981).

53. Manchester Statistical Society, *Report on the Condition of the Working Classes 1834–36, in an Extensive Manufacturing District in 1834, 1835, 1836* (Manchester, 1836).

54. See the 1834–6 Report, also the papers of the Manchester Statistical Society, 'Appendix to the Minutes of the Manchester Statistical Society, . . . 1833–43', at M.S. 310.6 M. 5/56, Manchester Central Reference Library, esp. *First Report of the Statistical Society*, 1833.

55. *Chaplain's Report to the Preston House of Corrections* (Preston, 1838) and see papers in M.S. 310.6.

56. Manchester Statistical Society Papers, William Langton, *The Handloom Weavers in Miles Platting*, Session 1838–9.

57. See, for example, Manchester Statistical Society Reports, *On the Educational and Other Conditions of a District in Deansgate* (Manchester, 1864).

58. T.S. Ashton, *Social and Economic Investigations*, p. 48.

59. Mary Poovey, *Making a Social Body*, p. 25.

60. Ibid., pp. 28–9.

61. Ibid., p. 29.

62. Michel de Certeau, *The Practice of Everyday Life* (London: University of California Press, 1988), pp. 120–1.

63. Barbara Belgea, 'Images of Power: Derrida, Foucault, Harley', *Cartographia*, 29:2, 1992.

64. The works of J.B. Harley have been seminal in these respects. See, for example, 'Deconstructing the Map', *Cartographia*, 26:2, 1989; 'Cartography, Ethics and Social Theory', *Cartographia*, 27:2, 1990; 'Maps, Knowledge and Power', in D. Cosgrave and S. Daniels (eds), *The Iconography of Landscape: Essays on the Symbolic Representation, Design and Use of Past Environments* (Cambridge: Cambridge University Press, 1988); see also 'Introduction to Social and Cultural Cartography', in *Cartographia: Monograph 44*, ed. R.A. Rundstrom (Toronto, 1993), also Dennis Woods, *The Power of Maps* (London: Routledge, 1993), and Geoffrey King, *Mapping Reality: An Exploration of Cultural Geographies* (Basingstoke: Macmillan, 1996).

65. Matthew Edney, *Mapping an Empire: The Geographical Construction of British India, 1765–1843* (Chicago: University of Chicago Press, 1997), p. 21.

66. Ibid., pp. 16–25.

67. Ibid., p. 25.

68. Ibid., p. 319.

69. Ibid., p. 34.

70. Michael Biggs, 'Putting the State on the Map: Cartography, Territory, and European State Formation', *Comparative Studies in Society and History*, 41:2, 1999.

71. Ibid., pp. 397–8.

72. Chandra Mukerji, *Territorial Ambitions and the Gardens of Versailles* (Cambridge: Cambridge University Press, 1997); and Patrick Carroll-Burke, 'Engineering Ireland: the Material Constitution of the Techno-Scientific State' (University of California, San Diego, PhD, 1999), also for the use of the term 'state country'.

73. Josef W. Konitz, *Cartography in France 1660–1848: Science, Engineering and Statecraft*

(Chicago: University of Chicago Press, 1987); David Buissert, *Monarchs, Ministers and Maps: The Emergence of Cartography as a Tool of Government in Early Modern Europe* (Chicago: University of Chicago Press, 1992); R.J.P. Kain, *The Cadastral Map in the Service of the State: A History of Property Mapping* (Chicago: University of Chicago Press, 1992).

74. Michael Biggs, 'Putting the State on the Map', pp. 388–9; see also Tim Owen and Elaine Philbeam, *The Ordnance Survey: Mapmakers to Britain since 1791* (Southampton: Ordnance Survey, 1992).

75. W.A. Seymour (ed.), *A History of the Ordnance Survey* (Folkestone: Dawson, 1980), chapters 1–9 for the inception and early history of the Survey; see also Sir Charles Close, *The Early Years of the Ordnance Survey* (Newton Abbot: David and Charles, 1969); J.B. Harley, *Ordnance Survey Maps: A Descriptive Manual* (Southampton: Ordnance Survey, 1993).

76. W.A. Seymour (ed.), *A History of the Ordnance Survey*, pp. 1–21.

77. Edwin Hutchins, *Cognition in the Wild* (London: MIT Press, 1995), pp. 96–7.

78. Andrew Pickering, *The Mangle of Practice: Time, Agency and Science* (London: University of Chicago Press, 1995), pp. 50–4. On the stability over time of meanings in the material world see Richard Biernacki, *The Fabrication of Labour: Germany and Britain, 1640–1914* (London: University of California Press, 1995); also his forthcoming *Time, Place, and Action: Ventures Beyond the Cultural Turn*.

79. Richard Oliver, *Ordnance Survey Maps: A Concise Guide for Historians* (London: Sir Charles Close Society, 1993), and his history of the OS, 'The Ordnance Survey in Great Britain 1835–1870' (University of Sussex PhD, 1985).

80. For a valuable discussion of the 'colonial' status of Ireland, see Derek Attridge and Marjorie Howes, 'Introduction' to their *Semicolonial Joyce* (Cambridge: Cambridge University Press, 2000).

81. David Smith, *Victorian Maps of the British Isles* (London: Batsford, 1985), chapter 3.

82. Ibid., chapter 3, 'Relief'. See also Sir H. James, *Account of the Field Survey and the Preparation of the Manuscript Plans of the Ordnance Survey* (London, 1873).

83. J.H. Andrews, *A Paper Landscape: The Ordnance Survey of Nineteenth-Century Ireland* (Oxford: Oxford University Press, 1975), p. 2.

84. Patricia Boyne, *John O'Donovan (1806–61): A Biography* (Kilkenny: Boethius, 1987).

85. Ibid., chapter 1.

86. Patrick Joyce, *Visions of the People: Industrial England and the Question of Class, 1840–1914* (Cambridge: Cambridge University Press, 1991), chapters 7–8, 10–12.

87. On Larcom, see J.H. Andrews, *A Paper Landscape, passim.*

88. Chandra Mukerji, 'Cartographic Nearsightedness and Powers of Place: The Early Modern Fieldwork of Louis de Fridour', paper presented to the Society for the Social Study of Science Meeting, San Diego, October 1999.

89. John T. Gilbert, *On the Life and Labours of John O'Donovan, LLD* (London, 1862).

90. Mary Hamer, 'Putting Ireland on the Map', *Textual Practice*, 3:2, 1989, and Brian Friel's play, *Translations* (1981).

91. See J.H. Andrews' critique of Friel in 'Commentary: Irish Placenames and the Ordnance Survey', *Cartographia*, 31:3, 1994.

92. On the Irish Survey, as well as Patricia Boyne, *John O'Donovan*, and J.H. Andrews,

A Paper Landscape (cited above), see also W.A. Seymour, *A History of the Ordnance Survey*, chapter 1, section 3, and pp. 105–6 and J.H. Andrews, *Irish Maps* (Dublin: Eason and Son, 1978), and *History in the Irish Ordnance Survey Maps: An Introduction for Irish Readers* (Kerry, Montgomeryshire: D. Archer, 1993).

93. On the 'Memoir', see Patricia Boyne, *John O'Donovan*, chapter 2, and J.H. Andrews, *A Paper Landscape*, chapter IV.

94. Patricia Boyne, *John O'Donovan*, pp. 46–9.

95. Ibid., pp. 46–7.

96. Ibid., pp. 48–9.

97. Ibid., chapter 2 for an account.

98. Arthur H. Robinson, 'The Maps of Henry Drury Harness', *Geographical Journal*, CXXI, 1955.

99. J.B. Harley, 'The Ordnance Survey Board of Health Town Plans of Warwickshire, 1848–1854', in T.R. Slater and P.J. Jarvis (eds), *Field and Forest: An Historical Geography of Warwickshire and Worcestershire* (Norwich: Geo Books, 1982); see also Richard Oliver, *Ordnance Survey Maps: A Concise Guide for Historians*.

100. H. Paterman's *Moral and Educational Statistics of England and Wales* (London, 1849) is seen as a landmark in 'social mapping'. See also Felix Driver, 'Moral Geographies: Social Science and the Urban Environment in Mid-Nineteenth Century England', *Transactions of the Institute of British Geographers*, 13 (N.S.), 1988, and *Power and Pauperism: The Workhouse System 1834–1884* (Cambridge: Cambridge University Press, 1993).

101. James Elliot, *The City in Maps: Urban Mapping to 1900* (London: British Library, 1987), chapter 5.

102. Mary Hamer, 'Putting Ireland on the Map'. See also Jonathan Crary, *Techniques of the Observer: On Visuality and Modernity* (London: Harvard University Press, 1990).

103. Comparison of runs of eighteenth- and nineteenth-century city maps and plans bears this out, for example in the case of Liverpool. George Perry's large-scale 1769 *Plan of Liverpool* has great detail but undifferentiated blocks of housing. Horwood's 1803 *Plan of the Town and Township of Liverpool, Shewing Every House*, does indeed differentiate houses but this has little of the detail seen later, and often is unclear and ambiguous as to distinctions between different built spaces. Later city guides, for example *The Stranger's Complete Guide through Liverpool* (Liverpool, 1850), often have considerable detail but many courts and alleys are not named or do not appear.

2

The Water and the Blood of the City

Naturalising the Governed

The nineteenth-century liberal governance of 'society' seems to have involved less of an emphasis upon securing power over a territory, as had earlier been the case when 'police' was the mode of rule, and more of an emphasis upon seeing, knowing and securing this 'society' as the free play of things, information and persons. Communication had to be secured in such a way as to permit free exchange and free circulation. As Foucault himself argued, in the nineteenth century architecture was superseded by communications as a mode of governmentality, and correspondingly the engineer rather than the architect became central to governance.[1] However, as I shall argue in chapter 4, once 'secured' as a place of free circulation the city was then powerfully and consistently acted upon by architects and urban planners. Under liberalism, models of free play were held to be self-evident and self-regulating, and hence subject to the 'laws' which governed this regulation. Rule, as far as possible, was to be in accordance with these laws. In short, whether it related to the self, the family, civil society, the economy or the city, the model upon which liberal rule was based was 'naturalised' in this sense of being both a self-governed and self-evident entity (though one in which intervention might be required to secure this self-governance).[2] The city itself was seen in these terms, and acted upon in these ways. It is in this sense of naturalised, self-governing entities that liberal 'freedom' is explored in this chapter, the emphasis moving from identifying liberal subjects to securing governance over them.

There were many models of the 'natural' system to which the city approximated. The body was one such model. The natural world itself, tautologically enough, was another, in the sense that social systems like the city came to be thought of in terms of the physical world of nature. In general, the relationship between the human and the natural worlds was one of constant interplay, so that the social imaginaries of the time were formed by the intense relationship of these ostensibly different worlds. This modelling of the social in terms of nature as a system was amply evident, not least in Manchester, which for many contemporaries in Britain and Europe was in the first half of the nineteenth century the 'shock city' of the age, seeming in its industrial and urban form to be the shape of things to come. Contemporary theology itself was a major conduit connecting the natural and the social worlds. The so-called 'natural' theology of William Paley, which drew evidence for the divine from the world of nature, was a profound influence on the political thought of the early nineteenth century, and also on emerging social thought, for example that of Richard Whately, Professor of Political Economy in Oxford in the early 1830s, and Archbishop of Dublin, who explicitly extended Paley's views from the natural to the social world. This sort of extension of natural theology to the social world rapidly became a commonplace of the time.

Paley was also a great influence on the Unitarians, especially in Manchester, and in this city that meant a great influence on social reform itself, so significant were Unitarians in this, as noted in the previous chapter. In turn, W.C. Taylor was a protégé of Whately. Taylor's *Natural History of Society in the Barbarous and Civilised State* (1840) argued that society had a natural history which was itself evidence of providential design.[3] Taylor was a significant figure in Manchester liberalism, serving as one of its most important intellectual spokesmen. His *Notes of a Tour in the Manufacturing Districts of Lancashire* (1842), undertaken on behalf of the Anti-Corn Law League, is an example of the new literature of 'social investigation', if one now with a decided propagandist aspect to it.[4] Taylor's *Natural History* argued that civilisation was natural to the whole of the human race. 'Barbarism' was therefore not a state of nature, the whole thrust of the argument being to emphasise that progress was integral to the human condition. This dizzying optimism was fuelled by the utterly circular belief that the state most natural to man was the state that nature had fitted him for, the state which fulfilled most completely the end for which he was made. Ultimately this end was evidenced in the workings of Providence. In this form it was the nation which embodied the 'social' expression of natural change. Just as often, it was the city. Whether the nation or the city, this belief in progress was characteristically accompanied by a horror of stasis, and of every instance of backwardness, dullness and stupidity which impeded the movement intrinsic to progress.[5]

Robert Vaughan's *The Age of Great Cities* (1843) has been called 'the most sweeping and impassioned statement of the urban ethos to appear anytime in England or anywhere in the century'.[6] Vaughan was greatly influenced by Taylor's work. Again the Manchester connection was strong: Vaughan lived in the city when he wrote the book, during which time he was also principal of Lancashire Independent College, one of the foremost Congregationalist colleges in the country. The city was seen here as blending each intelligence into a composite whole. The emphasis was upon collision, contact, flux and the benefits these would bring; in fact upon everything that was the opposite of stasis and tradition. Out of this flux of the city was generated the harmony represented by 'popular intelligence'. This city was the cradle of the voluntary association, and hence the cradle of citizenship. In fact, democracy was in this reading a direct expression of the city, for 'the people' would form the same sort of dynamic equilibrium that was evident in the city.

This city was 'the natural centre of association', in contrast to the backwardness and stupidity of the rural world. This time and this place, the Manchester of the 1840s, also gave rise to the strikingly similar understanding of the city evident in the work of Friedrich Engels. Manchester does seem to have impressed itself on several of the foundational texts of nineteenth-century social thought. In Engels' as well as in Vaughan's case, though obviously in a different key, there is the same belief in the city as the arena of modernity, in contrast to what so widely at the time was termed 'feudalism'.[7] Taylor's book was also an apologia for the manufacturing system, which was another instance (and of course another 'system') with a natural propensity towards progress. The manufacturing system itself was based upon the model of the factory as a self-regulating system, and at the time, in the 1830s and 1840s, the most potent symbol of the auto-regulative aspects of the new system of manufacture was the self-acting mule, the cotton-spinning machine, which then was the centre of so much industrial conflict and so many expressions of hope and fear about the future.[8]

The water of the city

Vaughan's work may have been an expression of an optimism about city life that was not always evident, and which lessened as time went on, but none the less the emphasis on the city as the prime arena in which the free movement central to liberal governance was to be secured was to remain dominant. This was particularly evident in the analogy of the city and the body. In viewing the city as a body, the natural systems that were invoked at the time were marked most emphatically by the medical gaze. The 'sanitary economy' of the town was like that of the body. Both were characterised by a dynamic equilibrium between living organisms and their physical environment (so that the religious vision of demotic and social equilibrium in Robert Vaughan's city was merged with this medical vision in many contemporary perceptions). The constant circulation of fluids and the continuous replenishment of vital functions were to be secured in the case of both the body and the city by the introduction of fresh particles and by the elimination of waste ones. Thomas Southwood Smith was the central intellectual figure in sanitary reform. His physiology was rooted in the idea that living organisms are inextricably bound up with their physical environments, in this case the city, so that sanitation was always a 'social' question. His theory of 'vital process' involved viewing individual human bodies as composed of constituent 'particles'; the social body in turn was made up of the entirety of the particles entering and leaving all living creatures.

This physiology has been seen as closely related to the form of medical knowledge known as 'anatomical realism', which was concerned with opening the body to view, much as in the social statistics and the cartography of the time the body of the city was opened to view. 'Anatomical realism', particularly in early nineteenth-century Manchester, was intimately involved with the rise of 'social investigation'.[9] In terms of the city and the body, therefore, 'vital process' had to be secured. The care of the city and care of the body became as one, just as the health of the city and health of the body were one. The public and private were created in parallel, and by a process of constant interaction between the two spheres. Human and non-human agency were constantly at work together. The Health of Towns Association was in fact a central element in this conjoint hygienisation of the body and the city. Securing what may be called the 'vitalisation' of the city involved its cleansing, clearing, paving, draining and ventilating, in fact what in a happy phrase Alain Corbin has called the 'civic toilette'.[10]

The social imaginary of the city upon which this view of disease and health depended conceived of the city as a place of flows, movement and circulation. The body and the city were quite literally at one, most notably perhaps in terms of the water closet. Sitting on this distinctively nineteenth-century invention involved directly coupling the natural functions of the body and the vital economy of the city, so that in this 'hydraulic city' of modern sanitation the environment was no longer an 'exterior', but part of a grand socio-hydraulic design. Materially and mentally the body and the city were as one, nature infusing the self and the self nature. Anonymous drains, sewers and pipes functioned as the material embodiment of a political division between public and private, establishing

> the sanitary integrity of the private home, without recourse to direct intervention. What was at stake was not just a Victorian fetish for cleanliness, but a strategy of indirect government; that is of inducing cleanliness and hence good moral habits not through discipline but simply through the material presence of fast-flowing water in and through each private household.[11]

The conduct of conduct did not need to come into play as material change directly shaped the possibilities of conduct that were open: the home and the family were simply left to themselves. This material inculcation of privacy is a further instance of how the state 'subsisted in' material forms into which certain kinds of agency and knowledge are 'engineered'.

Hamlin's account of the politics and practice of public health in the age of Edwin Chadwick enables us to consider something more of what can be understood as liberalism here.[12] The new notion of 'public health' emerged out of deep conflicts within contemporary medicine, so that governmentality can be read not as drawing upon already firmly established bodies of knowledge, but as located in the formative processes creating these bodies. There was no unitary modern science, or 'modernity', serving as the bedrock of governance: modern science itself, since its inception, was deeply inflected with different views of its own procedures and of the natural world.[13] In the politics of public health, an older, more holistic and client-centred notion of health and disease was eclipsed by a new disease-centred notion, so that instead of disease being the absence of health, health became the absence of disease.[14] This represented a victory of analytical over individualist medicine.[15] In this new, Chadwickian view there was a physiological parity between individuals, an equality or universality in the medical sphere with clear connections to a liberal universalism made up of the sum of individual persons. There was also a clear displacement of political concerns from persons to places, the locus of disease now being found in the places of the city, in the details of its streets and the inner recesses of its houses. The city took on a new salience. In fact, in terms of a Foucauldian 'genealogy' it has been argued that in the eighteenth century, in respect of the science of 'police', the city was not the target of governance but rather the territory of rule as a whole. In liberalism the city was no longer simply a metaphor for good government but its privileged site.[16]

The new public health involved a concentration on lack of sanitation as the real cause of disease, and not work, poverty, diet or other factors in the social and economic situations of workers and the poor. It also involved a concentration on men, to whom women and children were seen as appendages, unlike the situation that obtained earlier, and was to obtain again later in terms of the family some half a century on.[17] This concentration on sanitation can be thought of in terms of the 'naturalisation' of poverty, whereby disease was 'de-pauperised'.[18] In terms of contemporary discourse about sanitation, particular diseases could mask the natural process of disease in the body: diseases could be either preventable or natural, and if preventable, amenable therefore to good urban government. Poverty was therefore purified from the distortions of disease, and by getting rid of 'easily preventable disease', sanitary regulations would serve to separate sickness that was a natural consequence of poverty or biological 'fate' from that which was simply a consequence of bad urban government. In the process the 'natural' relationship between poverty and economic activity could function without distortion.

Hamlin's account explores the means and extent to which Chadwick's view won out. And win out it certainly did, not completely but extraordinarily quickly, so much so that by the time of the Irish Famine the idea that poverty caused fever had almost completely faded, in England if not in Ireland.[19] The centrality of sanitation in public health ideology and legislation was evident for at least half a century after Chadwick's time. The sanitary idea lent itself to policy at the central level, in terms of the Home Office, and to policy in the locality in terms of the needs and interests of municipal authorities. It was, as Hamlin says, 'the only game in town', the only argument with sufficient coherence and clarity to function as *public* policy. How this was achieved involved the active 'selling' of sanitation, especially by Chadwick and the General Board of Health Inspectors, something also evident in the operations of parliamentary commissions, and the reports and other interventions these highly interested parties produced. The inspector himself was a critical figure. The towns were invited to see themselves and their interests in the mirror of the inspector, the cosmopolitan and neutral 'outsider'. One may utilise Hamlin's work to understand how the inspectors themselves can be seen quite clearly to be performing the truth of their reports, and of themselves, in the inordinate length and fact-laden nature of the reports, and in particular the presentation of these 'facts' in terms of the 'discovery' of what were called 'real' conditions and 'abuses', such conditions and abuses simply waiting to be unearthed by the patient work of the inspectors and the patient action of their facts.

The truth of themselves as impartial observers was present not just in the rhetoric of fact and discovery, but also in terms of the presentation of themselves as moral beings: the rhetoric of disinterested fact and moral revulsion were inseparable in this respect. For what is striking about the inspectors' reports are the paroxysms of moral outrage that mark them, a revulsion that the inspectors felt was almost impossible within the bounds of decent language to give expression to, so that the very reason and coolness of facts can be understood as stabilising the rhetoric of moral outrage, while at the same time this rhetoric imparted to the facts the *frisson* of moral self-righteousness. In the reports one can in fact see the inspectors working through a real revulsion at the manners and values of the poor, the reports being in part 'diaries of experiences and efforts to explain things to themselves in a way that would allow them to make a cogent case'. Going beyond this formulation, however, one can also see in the discourse of the reports the performance of the state in the sense of the inspectors struggling with their own moral outrage, struggling too with their direct experience of conditions in the localities they visited, experience which indeed sometimes involved them in rough treatment at the hands of the poor. As well as making a cogent case, they were making sense to themselves in what was a moral struggle to govern.[20] I shall return to this question of the ethics of governance in the next chapter.

The pure milk of Chadwickian Benthamite sanitation was eventually watered down, not least in this 'selling' of sanitation to municipal authorities. In the 1850s Chadwick came into conflict with the civil engineers, who objected not so much to his doctrine as to his being doctrinaire. There developed a conflict between what was seen as abstraction, system and theory, on the one hand, and the concrete instance, need and circumstance, on the other, one played out in terms of a new professional ethic, that of civil engineering. The conflict took a direct technological form in terms of the 'pipe-and-brick sewers war' of 1852–5, the self-scouring pipes of the true-liberal Chadwickian technology being pitted against the brick sewer linings of practical men.[21] By the time of Sir John Simon, the nation's Chief Medical Officer from 1858 to 1871, the view was established that the technological aspects of engineering were no part of central government, so that state administration took on a more political and diplomatic character, setting parameters, minimising errors and avoiding breakdowns, rather than engaging in direct technological involvement.[22] However, this did not mean that technology was now beyond government.

Quite the contrary, in that from at least 1800 civil engineering had emerged as a major, largely unacknowledged, arm of government, for instance in Thomas Telford's massive projects in Scotland and England. (Chapter 5 will consider aspects of this effort in terms of road systems and modes of movement in the city.) Unacknowledged as state policy, and indeed as political at all, Telford's practice-based, experimental and rational forms of project organisation presaged many of the techniques of the 'scientific' public administration of the Benthamites. Similar developments were to be found in Ireland at the same time. The Chadwickian revolution itself ensured that sanitation became an engineering question, one of water engineering. The Health of Towns Commission of 1843–5 itself served to establish this engineering solution. The 'black boxing' of sanitation as a matter of science and technology, separate from the political, took a new turn: the term is taken from the work of Bruno Latour, and it denotes the place of scientific procedures and material objects in framing solutions in durable forms.[23]

Something similar to this case of mid-nineteenth-century Britain can be seen in late eighteenth-century France.[24] French state military engineers attempted to produce functionally identical artefacts in developing the state projects of the time. Encountering the resistance of merchants and artisans, military engineers defined these artefacts with instruments such as technical drawing and tools that would themselves create tolerance in the finished, manufactured part, a tolerance designed to accommodate resistance. Military engineers then refined these initiatives in increasingly rule-bound ways to forestall further subversion. These standards of production can be be understood, at least in part, as resolving the conflicts that gave rise to them, and doing so in material forms which, like the engineering solutions to public health which I have been talking about, appeared to become 'objective'.

The creation of manufacturing tolerance in the production of artefacts reflected and gave material form to the emerging political 'toleration' of the French state for its citizen-producers. In this period, the state's rules regarding the invention, production and consumption of artefacts came to be defined in formal terms, rather than in terms of particularistic privileges granted on an individual basis. More generally, economic relationships between the state and its citizen-producers were henceforth defined in public terms, and not as a matter of private law or the moral obligation of subjects. These developments were of a piece with the emergence of manufacturing tolerance as a way to define the boundary between the state's need for commodities and the right of its subjects to make an economic livelihood. The juridically limited state and the decentralised capitalist order which emerged at the end of the eighteenth century ended the particularistic legal status which both persons and artefacts had enjoyed under the old regime. As Alder says, one might even say that henceforth objects could in some sense be considered 'objective'. It is precisely this 'objectification' of power and social relations that I am considering in this chapter.

This evacuation of the political helps our understanding of the modern state in general, and liberalism in particular. Liberalism, as a variant of governmentality which sought to secure interventions in conduct which were neither arbitrary nor direct, like indeed the agency of running water in the Victorian home, would seem in particular to have depended in high measure upon this separation of the political from the supposedly 'objective', from the material, and from the technological. One can think of these and similar material arrangements as the conditions of possibility of liberalism, or, in a stronger sense, as themselves liberal infrastructure, with nineteenth-century urban infrastructure being in this sense political infrastructure. Interventions in the supposedly objective 'material' world of urban infrastructure therefore permitted the 'social' to operate freely, and according to its own equilibrium as a natural system. They also defined a space in which individual volition, and consequently the moral self-regulation of the individual, could work naturally without undue interference, particularly in this context bodily interference. The process of 'naturalisation' considered in this chapter can thus in large part be seen to turn upon the creation of an ontologically discrete world of objects in which the non-human was severed from the human. Material objects, and the networks that brought them into action – such as sanitary systems or lighting systems in the urban infrastructure – can therefore be said to mediate society, rather than society being understood as simply permeated by such networks.

In terms of contemporary sanitary discourse and practice, as well as water the atmospheric environment itself can be understood as mediating between nature and the social, and between humans and the object world, and therefore as something that could be shaped in order to induce humans to behave 'normally'. It was the very imperceptibility of both that helped in their involvement in the process of naturalisation, just as it was in the case of so much urban infrastructure, buried in sewers, pipes and cables under the city or carried in insulated forms over and through it. Later on in this chapter, in terms of the blood of the city, I want to consider the market as the site of similar kinds of mediation, or as what Latour would call a 'hybrid' of human and non-human agency. The 'liberalism' of environmental solutions themselves can be understood precisely in terms of their capacity to extricate governmental interventions from accusations of bodily interference, as the work of Christopher Otter shows in revealing detail in relation to the history of light.[25] Establishing and 'black boxing' technosocial solutions that would have political import thus depended on imparting durability to them, so that they could become normal and irreversible in their technosocial operation. Durability would therefore seem to have a technopolitical role generally, and, akin to that of imperceptibility, particularly so in relation to liberalism. The technology of urban infrastructure rapidly developed means of making materials themselves durable, and Otter has dwelt on the importance, for example, of encaustic tiling, glazed bricks and water-resistant paint in municipal construction as instances of this. Something similar to this emphasis on securing the auto-regulation of matter is also evident in terms of the inspection of urban infrastructure, which developed enormously in the second half of the nineteenth century. This involved ruling at a distance, connecting the remote corners of the city to offices and laboratories, by means of procedures of inspection designed to secure the self-correction of material systems themselves.

How difficult this task was is amply apparent. Drains broke, pipes leaked and roads had continually to be dug up in order to be fixed. The very attempt to create a city of free circulation might be its own undoing. The task of clearing and cleansing the city was constant, and in a sense self-defeating, for the more elaborate systems of infrastructure became, the more susceptible to breakdown they might be, despite the most sophisticated systems of maintenance. In this sense 'liberal infrastructure' was of a piece with liberal political reason, both constantly creating problems for themselves in the very acts of their operation, so that liberal political reason, in order to govern, forever had to create 'problems' and 'questions' around which governance might be thought and prosecuted. In respect to technopolitical governance, therefore, materiality itself might usefully be considered not as an essence, but as an ongoing process, potentially reversible as well as achievable. Durability was therefore an *effect* of maintenance and the fight against decay, so that what is social about the material can in important measure be seen to inhere in the temporary stabilisation of this inherent instability or volatility of the material.

The processes of naturalisation I have been considering thus always concern processes of temporary stabilisation. It is in this spirit that one might approach governance in this dimension, and indeed in other dimensions as well. So much is evident in this account of the 'hydraulic' or 'sanitary city', which emerged at this time as a dominant social imaginary of the city upon which governance was based. As will be apparent, such a view of the city can be regarded as a stabilisation of existing arguments within medical and other expertise, a view achieving its stability by adapting itself to the diverse needs of central and local government, not least through the complexities of the performance of governing. In this process, even if it was 'the only game in town', the message of the sanitary city became diluted and reformulated in all manner of ways, not least its diversion into technosocial, engineering solutions, which themselves were always unstable.

None the less, the sanitary city and, more broadly, the 'civic toilette' achieved a marked salience between the early and late nineteenth century, and before turning to the blood of the city I shall give a brief account of this development, in which the civic and the personal toilette went hand in hand. Corbin provides an account of this process in France,[26] which indicates that in the last two decades of the eighteenth century public health activities were increasingly centred on the great cities. In the following decades what was new was the political coherence of these policies, now even more centred upon the city, and their extension into the mass of society. One significant difference between European states was the considerable lead of Britain in so many of these developments. France was often behind Britain, and frequently copied developments there. For instance, the new pavements of Paris in the 1780s were based on the London example, and mains drainage came from England only towards the end of the nineteenth century, in emulation of the great engineering feat of the London sewers of the 1860s. England was recognised as the home of hygiene and of privacy, just as of the engineer (always relatively few in nineteenth-century France) and of the 'modern' dwelling. As Dominique Laporte eloquently argues in his *History of Shit*, the modern state since its earliest inception was predicated on acts of purification central to which was the transformation of the most repellent form of waste matter, namely human and animal faeces. Laporte cites James Joyce's *Ulysses* in confirmation of Britain's modern world leadership in this regard, Joyce's professor Mac Hugh speaking out against the 'foreign invaders' thus: *'The Roman, like the Englishman who follows in his footsteps, brought to every new shore on which he set foot (on our shore he never set it) only his cloacal obsession. He gazed about him in his toga and he said:* It is meet to be here. Let us construct a water closet.'[27]

The hygienisation of the city was accompanied by processes making for the individuation of the self, ones which, if distinct from governance, none the less were often linked to it. Hygiene involved creating spaces around and between bodies, protecting them from others' contact and smells, and it thereby brought people into a new encounter with themselves. This individuation was, however, pioneered long before the nineteenth-century civic toilette. Its laboratories were to be found in the eighteenth century, for example in soldiers' tents, in hospitals, prisons and asylums – and in ships: Captain Cook's ships have been described as the first hygiene city in miniature.[28] The cultural history of the bed also has its place in this history. The privatisation of sleeping appears to have begun towards the end of the sixteenth century. People began to wear night shirts. In bed private reverie became possible (but also other private activities that were not so permissible). In France the individual bed eventually became integral to notions of the Rights of Man, finding its way into political reason in this form: a decision of the Convention of 1793 in France ordained that state institutions such as hospitals and asylums should provide individual beds as a natural extension of the Rights of Man.

In the nineteenth century attention turned particularly to the home, at first very much the homes of the well-off. Within the home rooms ceased to be interconnecting and new possibilities were opened up for privacy. Use of domestic space became specialised and carried with it new routines and observances, not least in the spaces set aside for the toilette. In public Richard Sennett has described what he terms a 'bourgeoisie' which was 'preternaturally aware' of distinctions of dress, deportment, behaviour and the body.[29] Respecting the bodily senses, in France Corbin notes a shift in the history of olfaction from the biological to the social.[30] Social distinctions became classified in terms of smell, the poor becoming identified by their 'stench', and the respectable by the refinement of their (preternatural) senses, in particular their sense of smell (this is in fact one aspect of the history of social 'disgust', as opposed to an earlier fear

of smells as the source of infection). This became especially evident in the
second half of the century. The material embedding of the senses so as to
obviate the effects of sensory proximity became particularly evident in the
third quarter of the century, not least in urban infrastructure, but also
more widely in urban building, with the use of plate glass, asphalt for
roads, and of upholstery, to separate the senses and patrol the boundaries
between them. The widespread belief that the physical had direct material
agency on humans, especially through the sense of sight, was reflected in
the idea that the poor, most of all, were morally degraded by their
physical experience of exposure to sex, death, dirt and the other horrors
of poverty.[31]

The spread of the message of the hygienic self was a complex affair,
developments outside the sphere of governmentality obviously working
both with and against the development of new forms of political reason.
Corbin traces a resistance to this message in France, especially in the
countryside, where 'the idea of individuation was not yet pertinent'. There
was in fact a belief in the positive value of dirt and indeed excrement,
what might be called a popular economy of the body, marked by a
concern with comfort and release, over and above the restrictions of
hygiene. It was only after the 1860s, and then slowly, that the majority in
France and elsewhere became exposed to the practical consequences of
theories of hygiene. In France the dissemination of Pasteur's theories, the
effect of mass education and the influence of conscription all had their
place. Even then, clean clothes were the priority, rather than clean bodies,
and relatively few could take even regular baths. None the less, the war
against filth went on, particularly in Britain, which was in the van of
change. Even here, however, progress was gradual. This is apparent if we
take the water closet as a guide: only by the mid-1880s were these in the
majority in Newcastle-upon-Tyne, for example, and in Birmingham only
by 1901.[32] Manchester saw the real shift, from the dry conservancy system
(using the pail and closet), after the mid-1890s.[33] If we consider running
water in the home, in the 1840s in Newcastle less than 10 per cent had
access to this. By 1914 nearly all had, change being rapid from the 1880s.
However, bathrooms were scarce everywhere before 1914. The civic
bathhouse in part made up for this lack, as did philanthropic provision,
particularly by employers.

The more intimate the part of the toilette performed, the more
anxiously it was governed. The inevitable tension between the public and
private evident in public provision for intimate, private functions went
right to the heart of liberal governmentality. Perhaps this contradiction

explains something of the slow spread of public facilities. Intimacy, and therefore anxiety, were particularly apparent in relation to gender. WC provision for women was slow in coming: in Manchester it was not until 1890 that the first public toilet for women was provided. This was denoted by the sign 'women', 'ladies' being expected to find their own provision in the shops and restaurants of the main thoroughfares, and in the rail stations (places that working-class 'women' were less likely to frequent). Once again, the formal equality enshrined in liberal rationality was contradicted by inegalitarian gender and class factors. Even for men provision was slow. In 1900 there were still only eight public toilets in Manchester. In the London of the 1880s the only public toilet was in Covent Garden, and this had no facilities for women.[34]

The first of the public conveniences were sunk in the ground, and this long continued to be the case, removing all bodily activities from view.[35] Urinating was more easy to govern than defecation, and men's urinating more than women's. The number of public urinals in Manchester in 1900, ninety, reflects this (urinals should be distinguished from the much more elaborate new public toilets). Changes in the law in 1855 made it possible for the London vestries to spend on urinals, though most of them were slow to do so. A Parliamentary Act of 1844 gave the city of Manchester the power to regulate public behaviour in these respects, and stricter sanitation laws after this provided for urinals in public houses and eating establishments, and prevented men urinating against the walls outside pubs, though the understanding that urinating should be a strictly private affair seems to have been long in establishing itself. It was said that until 'the end of the horse-drawn era' drivers 'by custom' urinated against the wheels of their standing carts and wagons in the street. The clearing and cleansing of the city were, however, in other respects very highly developed, and constituted a contemporary 'science' carried forward on an industrial basis by the municipal authorities in British cities, whether based on the water closet or not. The Manchester Municipal Code of 1893, for example, decreed that owners of houses had to keep privies and ashpits in repair, and for new housing it established strict standards for sanitation. One's privy, the site of a peculiarly significant form of privacy, was in the end not one's own.[36]

The blood of the city

The 'civic toilette' was also about controlling the inevitable passage of time so that it might be endured; above all, time in the face of death. It was therefore intrinsically concerned with the regulation of the physical manifestations of death, and of the passage of life into death, in the form of a profound anxiety about blood, excrement, secretions of all sorts, rotting and dead matter, all the manifestations of corruption and decay. The blood of the city therefore helps us understand something of the deep anxieties of governing. It also helps us understand how contemporaries separated what they understood to be natural from what they regarded as social, so that it helps us approach the history of the social from another perspective, that of the symbolic and anthropological. This is how John Hogg described the streets of London in 1837: the streets of the city were completely blocked two or three three times a day, sometimes for an hour at a time, by traffic, people, filth, animals, and by the results of their constant need of maintenance. Even the widened streets were blocked. Matters were made worse by the large number of narrow and irregular streets and courts, with streets often terminating abruptly without crossing other ones. Proprietors of land in London had no control in projecting new streets. Building size was regulated but the building line and street width were not.

This city ran with blood, and Smithfield animal market was at its bloody heart: within one year well over a million sheep and a quarter of a million other beasts went there on their way to be slaughtered throughout the city. This all contrasted unfavourably with other European cities, which had suburban abattoirs. The human dead were also buried in the centre of the city. The middle of London was likened to a medieval charnel house, the dead piled upon one another in the over-used churchyards, so that the dead were constantly present to the living, in the most disturbing forms. The suburban cemetery of Kensal Green had only been opened in 1833, and for some time was the only new city cemetery.[37] This was the city that had to be reformed. In fact, the dead had been buried in this way for several centuries, without it being a cause for concern, or even interest.[38] What was new was the awareness that all this was now 'intolerable'.

Let us dwell on this matter of death and blood, first the animal bodies of Smithfield and their death. The 'vitalisation' of the city can be seen to have involved making the natural social, and in the process taming and controlling nature, even as a sort of genuflection was made to the natural. The transition from animal to edible,[39] the production of 'meat',[40] represented in the most powerful of forms this negotiation of the social and natural. 'Meat' is thus a 'natural symbol' of human control over nature,[41] and therefore of human identity, in short a means by which the social imaginary is created. Slaughter was and is at the centre of these symbolic operations, hence its highly ritualised character in societies including our own (we only eat meat killed by humans, and killed in a particular way; we do not eat all animals, or drink blood, usually, and so on). What happened in the course of the nineteenth century was that death, and the corrupt and decaying bodies of the dead, and this goes for the human as well as the animal dead, were finally rendered invisible and anonymous. The slaughterhouse, in the words of its anthropologist, became 'a place that was no place'.[42]

This was the case in France before it was so in Britain. The 'abattoir' had been exiled to the margins of towns and cities in the Napoleonic reorganisation of slaughtering and butchery, and removed from everyday life, where it was still situated in Britain. Slaughter now took place in anonymous buildings in anonymous places, and death itself was an anonymous and private thing, paradoxically private in that abattoirs were public institutions. In this process, as later in Britain, slaughter became monitored, controlled, hygienised and punished if it did not measure up to its new 'science'. Slaughter also became 'humane'. In the process it also became large scale and 'industrial'. Something of the invisibility of the slaughterhouse is conveyed by the use of the euphemism for slaughterhouse, 'abbatoir', which in its origin in French means to cause to fall, as trees are caused to fall. The word appeared in 1806, at the same time as the new slaughter regime, and rapidly entered English.

Considering the history of blood, in Paris this blood might be human blood,[43] but the blood of London as opposed to the blood of Paris was usually animal blood, and the everyday horror of London was to do with animals. This is how Smithfield was described in 1837:

Not only are these myriads of animals collected, to the great hinderance of all other business in the surrounding parishes and streets; but the scene of filth caused thereby, the overpowering miasmata, the savage conduct and exclamations of the drovers, the cursing and sweating of the men and the lowering and bleating of the frighted, parched and exhausted animals, goaded into narrow folds, and panting even for air. . . . Confusion and riot among the hosts of butcher and salesman attendant in the adjoining public houses and streets, and all this occurring for the most part in the night. . . . Then comes the morning, and with it the dispersing of the same herds and flocks all over London; the disorder and confusion . . . now spreads to every street (the great thoroughfares are completely blocked, the animals rush to the filthy gutters to drink, and often do they drop and die in the streets from ill usage, or exhaustion, and frequently are they crushed and destroyed by the wheels of heavy-laden vehicles.[44]

The animals then dispersed to be slaughtered in the city (though many were slaughtered in the environs of Smithfield). The flatness of its terrain meant that blood did not drain away easily. Only one in twenty butchers had more than a cellar under his shop for the keeping and killing of animals. In the circumstances the sights and sounds of suffering, slaughtering and death were an everyday occurrence. Reminiscences of London in the 1850s and 1860s speak of slaughterhouses and shops not closing their doors, so that children were free to see everything that went on.[45] At this time there were over a thousand inner-city slaughterhouses.[46] Animals were still driven through the streets, and horror at their treatment was still commonplace: the daily sight of sheep being pushed down the steps into basement abattoirs close to St James's church in Piccadilly was a cause of great upset at the time. None the less, the reorganisation of the animal and meat markets in the city by then meant that this experience was soon to be a thing of the past. Copenhagen Fields in Islington was opened as the new animal market in 1855. (The old meat market in Newgate, right in the heart of the city and a similar sight of bloody congestion to Smithfield, was condemned in 1861.)

The new Smithfield opened in 1861 as the great meat market of the city. By the 1860s large amounts of meat were arriving in the city by rail, though a great deal of slaughtering of animals was done at Copenhagen Fields. After 1876 US meat was being sent directly to Smithfield. Smithfield by then was the hub of a considerable railway network, produce coming into the market by underground rail. In fact the railways made a crucial contribution to the process by which the blood of the city was made invisible and the business of slaughter was made industrial. The regulation of all these markets was the concern of the Corporation of the City of London. Far from being a hangover of the *ancien régime*, as is sometimes thought, the City Corporation was a pioneer of the modernity so apparent in the new order of slaughter. In Paris, Baron Haussmann was a similar pioneer, the presiding genius of the great La Villette meat market, opened in fact a little after Smithfield, but perhaps the greatest European symbol of the new regime of slaughter. The intensified industrialisation of slaughtering, as opposed to what has been called the handi-craft slaughter of La Villette, became quickly evident in the Chicago stock yards, the Union Stock Yards opening also in the 1860s.[47]

In this respect the market can also be understood in the terms mentioned earlier, as a mediator or 'hybrid' between the non-human and the human worlds, the natural and the social, something that could be 'objectivised', like the environment, in order to induce humans to behave 'normally'. However, this could occur only as a result of the negotiation of people's deepest fears about matter, death and what was human. Although the sight of slaughter was dispersed beyond Smithfield alone, the market symbolised for nineteenth-century Londoners the horrors of the old order. It did so because it meant so much in other respects too. This is how James Stevenson Bushnan, Member of the Royal College of Surgeons, and Senior Physician to the Metropolitan Free Hospital, described Smithfield in 1851 (Bushnan was the very type of the medical reformer we have so far met, in this case one active in the fight of the City Corporation against the vested interests of the meat trade): the neigh-bourhood of Smithfield was made up of a series of 'objectionable locali-ties' and 'doubtful shops', such as 'bladder blowers', 'horse slaughterers', 'cat and rabbit fur dressers'. These abounded in immorality and offensive-ness, and were full of noxious fumes and 'death-bearing gases'.

He conducts the reader into a dustyard which is what he terms

> the receptacle of the offal of the neighbourhood; while under the shadow of its mountainous heaps, may at night be discovered half-savage men and women, carousing and blaspheming around cauldrons teeming with unblessed food. Some miserable habitations, of uncertain and ambiguous character abut upon this yard; and, turning the corner, the dustyard again branches out into another large neighbourhood, affording a refuge for foreigners of the lowest class, who here vegetate, and hold their so-called *fraternal* assemblies.[48]

He leads the reader further on into the labyrinth of Smithfield: 'From Smithfield, and extending to Victoria Street, are numerous slaughter-houses, presenting the most revolting scene, drenched with blood and other abominations. . . .' He enters a fur dresser's in Garden Court and there sees a naked human being 'red as a Cherokee Indian, jumping in all sorts of attitudes. . . . While between the rows of denuded humanity women were passing, pursuing their loathsome calling.' In the middle of this neighbourhood there is a 'full and reeking churchyard, so full that the parish has abandoned it'. He then goes on to describe in some detail what he calls 'the death-bed agonies of the withered prostitute'.

The account is something like a vision of hell and of evil, one of a witches' sabbath, of cauldrons and unblessed food, of humanity less noble than the animals that are slaughtered here. It is a vision of the unnatural sexuality of the prostitute, and the dangerous foreigner. The Corporation will get rid of this entirely. It will build washing houses, baths and fountains, so that the air itself shall no longer be poisoned. It will pave this poison into oblivion, not least the reeking churchyard. Smithfield itself was one of the old neighbourhoods of London, that of the Old Bailey another. Smithfield in fact was the neighbourhood of Cloth Fair and according to Bushnan was a relic of a disreputable old London, remaining much the same as it had been since before the Great Fire. These areas were 'famous in the history of crime'. What Bushnan and his like were doing was in fact attempting to destroy this old city, transforming the unknowable and the disturbing into the knowable, the rational and the governable. Much the same sort of thing was happening at much the same time in Haussmann's Paris.

How can the evident horror of this description be explained, a horror akin to that fear of stasis so apparent in urban reformers' veneration of progress in the contemporary literature on the city? It is a horror also evident in the reports of the inspectors of the General Board of Health, which, as has been seen, were marked by outrage and incomprehension. Hamlin goes so far as to claim that the public health movement was a product not of statistics or medicine but of revulsion. The inspectors, but others in the movement too, while divided politically and in their under-standing of medicine, were united by their belief that the poor were so blunted by their habituation to poverty that they were sub-human, incapable of responsibility. It is the people and not the conditions which they found incomprehensible. The reports are incapable of imagining the humanity of the people whose conditions they described. While revulsion was certainly a technique of governmentality, in terms of constructing reports that would persuade, there is no doubting the great contemporary psychological force of this revulsion.

Perhaps Bushnan's horror has something to do with the complex meanings of Smithfield, meanings which, like the conditions viewed in the inspectors' reports, summoned up a similar revulsion? In particular there was a sort of historical horror of the capacity of the old order to still subvert progress. Smithfield had been a place of death since at least the sixteenth century, when it was the scene of the burning of some two hundred martyrs during the Marian persecution of Protestantism.[49] It was also a place of disorder and misrule. Cloth Fair was in fact Bartholomew

Fair, Wordsworth's 'Parliament of Monsters', and for centuries the greatest of all the meeting places of the London multitude. Wordsworth
described it thus – 'What a shock / For eyes and ears! what anarchy and
din / Barbarian and infernal, – phantasma,/ Monstrous in colour, motion,
shape, sight, sound!'[50] This sacred site of the London crowd was instituted
each year on 25 August, the day of St Bartholomew, the patron saint of
butchers. Quite clearly, Smithfield was charged with the most powerful
meanings (butchers were themselves still slaughterers, men of blood).
Charged with such meanings, touching the deepest levels of thought
about the social, its reform had great urgency.

This reform was inseparable from reform of fairs, which involved the
reform of human misrule, as opposed to the bloody animal chaos of the
old Smithfield. Saint Bartholomew Fair was finally repressed in 1855, just
a little earlier than the old animal market itself. The abolition of the old
town and city fairs was evident throughout Britain – Manchester's Knott
Mill Fair was suppressed in 1876.[51] Dublin's famous Donnybrook Fair
ended the same year as Saint Bartholomew,[52] though not without a fight.
Roman Catholicism and nationalism do not appear to have made much
difference in this particular instance of urban liberal governmentality at
work; indeed the Catholic hierarchy itself led the the way in the reform of
wakes and fairs of all kinds, country and town.[53]

The power of Smithfield itself is to be understood in terms of the
symbolic nature of both markets and fairs. Markets are liminal places,
spaces of transition, places which occupy a position on a boundary, but
which also partake of both sides of this boundary. They are intermediary in a literal sense, in that they are places of exchange. They are
immensely sensitive markers of boundaries and distinctions. They mark
off buyers and sellers, and – traditionally – country and town, as with
Smithfield and the other great food markets of the nineteenth-century
city. Markets and fairs may occupy the (communal, sacred) spaces of
urban centres but also the places where town and country meet, for
instance the outskirts of urban settlements (as with many of the great fairs
of the nineteenth century, for instance Knott Mill in Manchester and
Donnybrook in Dublin). Donnybrook was set up on the fringes of the
city jurisdiction in 1172, as well as being situated at the place of a river
ford.[54] The power of markets was compounded by other factors too. They
often had a certain religious significance (marked by market crosses, or
by the immediate proximity of places of worship). They often had strong
associations with punishment, as places where, for example, pillories
were positioned, or where in some cases executions were carried out.[55]

The symbolic potency of markets as liminal spaces is evident in their functions as fairs as well: even when not explicitly accompanied by fairs, markets were occasions for a good deal of human mingling. As locations of perceived and real misrule and disorder, fairs were places where boundaries were threatened, and therefore places where the social order was threatened in a very palpable form, that of 'social' human interaction itself.

The food market in particular is an exceptionally sensitive location of the liminal, or, from another perspective, the mediator or 'hybrid'. Mary Douglas' understanding of how 'matter out of place' threatens cultural categorisation enables the market to be understood as a place where the social meanings of pollution are especially apparent.[56] The food market is a place of matter prior to and after decomposition, a place of flows, rot, deliquescence. It marks the transformation of matter from one state to another, when it becomes threatening because out of its fixed place. This seems especially the case for living matter, in the sense of animal matter, so that places of slaughter mark the decomposition of life itself, the passage of matter to death. The market can be said to regulate life and death therefore. It is also the case that, as the place where what is outside, namely food, becomes what is inside/eaten, or what will soon become so, markets address the most sensitive of all locations of boundary and categorisation, the body itself understood in terms of the bodily contour defining what is inside and outside, and therefore what is body and not body, and what is natural and human. In food markets boundaries come in question, and anxiety is marked, where matter erupts, leaks, runs, for instance as blood or offal, or as the faeces, urine and sweat of terrified animals. There is also the rot and stench of decaying vegetable matter.

In terms of meat markets and slaughterhouses, the propinquity of blood and water is characteristic: blood, the evidence of life, but also the sign of death, is perhaps the most sensitive instance of matter out of place and threatening. Water is invariably kept nearby for fear of this aberrant matter.[57] It is the places where what is inside and outside meet that are particularly significant, the orifices of the body, animal and human. These regulate whether matter will be out of place or in place, hence anxiety about control over such orifices (as, in human terms, in the nineteenth-century 'civic toilette' in all its forms). Social, and racial, boundaries of all sorts are defined, and patrolled, by such control over the orifices of the body, a process of 'erasing corporality', in both the human and the animal body.[58] In the liminality of markets, therefore, and involving an anthropological sense of societal 'freedom', in which the very nature of the social order is in question, one may see how these situations of blood, death and disorder brought into the sharpest focus the practice of liberal freedom. This liminal dimension of freedom denied and subverted, yet also agitated into practice, the operations of political reason. One can begin to understand how the market could summon such horror in men like Bushnan and Hogg, and why the reform of markets was such a priority. The nature of the social order was threatened.

The old Smithfield can be compared with the new (the dramatic nature of the contrast is apparent in Figures 2.1 and 2.2). The former was open, porous, a place where on market day crowds of children could be seen running in and out of the market cruelly taunting the animals.[59] The new market was closed, a place, according to its architect, where 'full command' could be had.[60] Smithfield was part of an integrated system of markets in the city centre, designed by the Corporation's architect Horace Jones.[61] Jones designed Leadenhall Market (1881) and Billingsgate Fish Market (1875), as well as Tower Bridge. The Smithfield site was itself made up of other markets designed by Jones, including markets for flowers and for fruit and vegetables. Along with Sir John Simon, the Corporation's Medical Officer of Health, Jones indicates again the modernist credentials of a purportedly archaic City Corporation. Smithfield was a highly controlled and closed environment.[62] Its hours of opening and routines of functioning were minutely regulated: porters were licensed, its tolls minutely ordered and its spaces meticulously planned.[63]

The blocks of shops within were all identical, with hygienised washing, eating and WC facilities.[64] The shops should have no blockages, projections or hanging goods impeding the free circulation of goods and people. Hawkers and all other interlopers were expressly forbidden. The specially designed roof allowed light without glare and ventilation without rain. Nature was carefully controlled, at all times permitting the free flow of the elements. At the same time Smithfield recalled the design of a French Renaissance palace. However, as with Victorian modernism more generally, an eclectic historicism involved the 'casing' of a severely functional interior[65] (as is evident in Figure 2.3). The great gates of the Market exemplified its symbolic meaning, excluding the outside but echoing in their grandeur the aristocratic and royal palace, though now a municipal palace emblazoned with the insignia of the City Corporation, as well as representations of the other cities of the kingdom, called the 'principal' cities, namely Liverpool, Edinburgh and Dublin.[66]

Copenhagen Fields, Islington, the 'Metropolitan Cattle Market', was where the slaughtering of animals took place after the reform of

Figure 2.1   The old Smithfield: George Sidney Shepherd, *Smithfield Market* (1824)

Smithfield (Figure 2.4). This was another sort of palace. It cost £500,000, and its space accommodated 7,000 cattle, but also between 40,000 and 50,000 sheep, calves or pigs. As at Smithfield, its functions were minutely supervised: the killing of animals on a mass scale, and in what was very carefully designed as a 'humane' way, became a new science. What went on in London was evident throughout the country. Manchester was not alone in appropriating the name 'Smithfield' to describe one of its markets, though this was not a meat market. The 1846 Markets Act in Manchester was consolidated in the Manchester Municipal Code of 1893. Like the Smithfield regulations, all aspects of market activity were governed.[67] In municipal markets there was a ban on hawking, crying and noisy instruments, on poultry plucking, dogs, smoking and improper language. Manchester's Shudehill markets, one of which was Smithfield, became the type of the new market.[68]

This type was predicated upon severing the market from the streets and street life of the town and the city, and hence from the old symbolic associations of markets. The old markets had been part of the town, street traffic running through them. Some of these markets continued, but the aim of the new, covered, public markets of the nineteenth century was to break the association with the old urban milieu, which was seen as vulgar

Figure 2.2 The new Smithfield (exterior): Sir Horace Jones, *Metropolitan Meat and Poultry Market* (1868)

Figure 2.3   Interior of the new Smithfield Market (photograph taken 1970)

and demeaning, as well as architecturally uninspiring. The market halls of
nineteenth-century Britain represented a massive wave of moral intervention in economic life, one finding form in almost every British town and
city.[69] However, the market was only one facet of a widespread municipal
regulation of urban space. Something of this regulation was evident in
the eighteenth century. The Court Leet records from Manchester, detail-
ing the clearing and cleansing of the eighteenth-century city, indicate
considerable activity.[70] In this, however, the regulation of consumption
seems to have been more important than the control of public space, and
the extent of the measures regulating the city are minuscule by comparison with the vast Municipal Code of 1893.[71]

The Code takes us into a different world. (It is a compendium of all
laws then obtaining in the city, from earlier in the century, the most
important of which date from 1844.) It anathematises anything that
prevents free circulation: 'standing', 'loitering', 'remaining', all of these
are prohibited, as are activities which involve those who, like street sellers,
'jolt', 'jostle' or 'annoy'. The setting down of people and goods has to be
close to the roadside. There are to be no projections into the road or into

Figure 2.4 Exterior of the Metropolitan Cattle Market, Copenhagen Fields, London: Anon, *Isometric View of the New Metropolitan Market* (1855)

the walkway.[72] The control of traffic was minutely regulated, also the driving of carts and carriages and the handling of goods, so that, for example, every commercial vehicle had to bear its proprietor's name and address and the description of their trade. Clothes lines and ropes should not obstruct streets (nor should the loitering 'Night Walker' or 'common prostitute'). Kites should not be flown or rubbish thrown. The list was endless. It can be summed up by item 113, dating back to an Act of 1851, which stipulated penalties for 'Every person who shall obstruct or incommode, hinder or prevent, the free Passage of any Carriageway or Walkway, or prejudice or annoy in any Manner whatsoever any Person travelling, passing, or going thereon'.[73]

In this city of free movement one had to be in control of oneself. The enforcement of direct moral self-control is everywhere evident in the Code, which was itself an instance of what was prevalent in Britain at that time. The Birmingham *Bylaws for Good Rule and Government* (1897) is a very similar instance of the same thing.[74] Above all it was drinking and drunken behaviour that were controlled, for at the time this was the most common example of not being in control of oneself in public. The

Manchester Code also governed 'riotous' and 'indecent' behaviour and language, particularly 'indecent exposure', also 'obscene, indecent and profane' books, language, songs and pictures, and bathing so as to expose the person. It prohibited women from cleaning windows which were higher than 6 feet off the ground. This control was exerted in a space which was rendered free of intrusion, divorced from all attributes that would interfere with its neutrality as a space where rational freedom could operate. This creation of a zone of separation around individuals can be regarded as a bodily, material precondition for the practice of freedom therefore, a governance of the air as it were. Direct moral intervention in behaviour was important, but this intervention depended greatly upon the creation of a shield or envelope around the self as it moved through the spaces of the city.

Self-mastery involved controlling one's animals. The driving of cattle was regulated. There was to be no display, feeding, cleaning, bleeding or dressing of animals in the street.[75] Animals were not to be mistreated. Bear-baiting and cock-fighting were among many older practices banned around this time. The Royal Society for the Prevention of Cruelty to Animals was formed in 1824 (some two decades ahead of its French equivalent).[76] In fact, the vitalisation of the city (or, from another perspective, the creation of liberal networks) involved the conscription of the animal world, so that this world was humanised and involved in similar disciplinary routines to the human one: for example, 'canine madness' was met not by the killing of dogs (as had earlier been the case) but by recourse to the disciplinary rehabilitation of the dog pound.[77] Rendering the unacceptable parts of the natural world invisible was accompanied by making the acceptable parts human (for instance, in the form of the pet). The undisciplined subject had an undisciplined dog, the disciplined one a pet. The pet was social, the dog remained in the natural world. Cats by contrast, endowed with intelligence, had a quasi-society of their own, so that the monitoring of cats was not required.[78]

As for other aspects of the everyday experience of new forms of free circulation for the majority, above all in the home, the historian Martin Daunton has coined the pertinent term 'social privacy' to describe the experience of space prior to the intervention of the municipality and the state in the provision of housing, which was seen with increasing effect after the mid-century.[79] The older cellular structure, in which the distinction between public and private was extremely ambiguous, gave way to a more open layout in which one thing was connected to another. Amongst housing reformers there was a dislike of the dead-ends of the old courts, situations where habitations were turned in upon themselves in their own social privacy. In the new order space became neutral and connective and therefore highly charged with the capacity for free circulation. In the 'bylaw housing' that increasingly marked the later nineteenth century, streets were regular in layout and width, with side streets at right angles, and parallel lines of back alleys.[80] The streets outside were (and are) surprisingly wide, in contrast to the narrow alleys behind. Such streets allowed a maximum of free passage. The street outside was public and 'communal'. The alley or lane behind was less socially neutral than the street, still rather secret. It was not a traffic thoroughfare for the public at large, being reserved for the immediate inhabitants, for the hanging of washing, and perhaps for the playing of football and other games. In between these public and semi-public spheres and the house within was the space of the yard at the back, which in contradistinction to the street was private and individual (if less so, potentially, than the house itself). These gradations of public and private were to be one school for the new democracy then slowly emerging. This was a school for the living. There was to be another school for this new society, that of the dead, in the form of the cemetery.

In reporting on the blocked and bloody city of London in 1837, John Hogg thought of Smithfield as at its heart, but also at its heart were the human dead, who continued to be buried in the city centre. Indeed, until relatively recently at that time, the dead had been buried within the walls of the church itself. From the late eighteenth century onwards the sense that these previously unnoticed and natural activities were now insupportable and had to be reformed grew powerfully.[81] The dead came to be seen as now poisoning the living. In 1842 a Parliamentary Bill at last banned intramural burial. The decline of the church as a place of burial was dramatically quick, the three decades after the new cemeteries of the 1820s being sufficient to see off this age-old practice.[82] What developed in place of the churchyard was the cemetery. The cemetery was accompanied by the growth of the belief that the death that was now to be feared was that of the other person, not oneself.[83]

The death of the loved one was not accepted, and from the late eighteenth century the tomb increasingly became a sign of the presence of the dead, a place where the dead could be visited, and where memory could thereby be kept alive, as opposed to the earlier practice of consigning the body into the care of the church itself, and sometimes into the physical structure of the church. The site of internment became also the property of the living, for the burial plot was purchased, and indeed purchased into perpetuity, the fact of ownership going on for ever. Memory could thereby also become eternal. Death could be conquered by property as memory. In visiting the cemetery one went to visit a place where memory inhered, as on going home one visited a similar shrine of memory (and another piece of property). The development of the new cemeteries was accompanied by the growth of the commercial funeral, and by new technologies of internment that enabled those with sufficient resources to purchase not only memory, but also privacy, security and a hoped-for measure of corporeal integrity after death, in dramatic contrast to the lowly grave and the highly uncertain fate of the body of the pauper.[84]

The new cemeteries of the early nineteenth century were therefore peculiarly private places, where the cult of memory could be practised in privacy, and where death could be endured. As with the abattoir, death was exiled to the margins of cities, and, if not quite anonymous, became located in a place abstracted from everyday life. Like the death of animals, the death of humans, and the bodies of the dead, became something to be avoided. However, as Philippe Ariès so brilliantly saw, the cemetery was also a public place,[85] and indeed one associated with the city itself, as well as with the idea of modern 'society'. As has been seen, society came to be understood in terms of the human body as a social body. But this social body now came to be made up of all bodies, the bodies of the dead as well as those of the living. The cemetery, as the city of the dead, was what Ariès called 'the intemporal image' of the society of the living. The cemetery and its monuments were the visible signs of the permanence of this new city of the dead. All cities and towns came to have cemeteries. They were seen as intrinsic and necessary to urban experience, their seeming permanence a sign of the permanence of the city itself, in death as in life. Their meticulous walks and rows of monuments echoed the 'improved' streets of the city. Very quickly, as early as the 1820s in Liverpool, for example,[86] their design reflected the architectural rhetoric of urban improvement (but also the idea of the rural, as in Kensal Green in London). As one facet of their new permanence in city life, they came to be an integral part of the overall design of the new hygienic city of the early and mid-nineteenth century. Therefore, one kind of society gave way to another, that of the pre-modern social of a more collective and anonymous burial within the old churchyard or the church itself, to the 'society' of the cemetery.[87] In this society communal and spatially specific parish rights of burial gave way to absolute and abstract property rights.

What is apparent here is another instance of the individuation of the human subject, in death now as in life. If the cemetery was in theory open to all, then this was a universalism of the individual subject. The relative hugger-mugger and confusion of the old churchyard gave way to the possibility of the individuation of the dead person, by means of the memorial and the deployment of clearly demarcated spaces.[88] One could really have eternal rest, instead of being dug up every few decades. The individual had his or her space in death as in life, the bed of eternal rest corresponding to that of nightly slumber. The cemetery was in this sense part of the history of abstract space charted in the previous chapter, because unlike the old churchyard it was portable. One could build a cemetery anywhere, and it would still be nowhere. However, it could still belong to everyone. It was therefore part of a whole new series of meanings given to the term 'public' at this time, meanings increasingly demotic, if only slowly democratic.

If the cemetery now belonged to everyone, the new cemetery society of this 'everyone' of abstracted individuals reproduced the contradictions inherent in this universalism. The cemetery was riven by class differences from the earliest days. These differences might concern the character of the propertied and respectable classes, for instance the differences that appear to have characterised the practices of French and British cemeteries.[89] In this instance the 'individualist and self-reflexive quality' of English cemetery design, and the *laissez-faire* policy of cemetery administration, have been contrasted with the uniform, dynastic and indeed more 'urban' characteristics of the French cemetery. The greatest contrast was, however, between the dead bodies of the wealthy and the poor. The new governance of death represented a massive assault on the culture of the poor. The corpse in popular culture was a metaphysical object, in its liminal situation between life and the finality of death a site of the most profound anxieties about the nature of the social. This was so for the governed, and for the governors. What exercised Edwin Chadwick most of all in burial reform was the rapid removal of the body after death, at the very moment when popular rituals and practices to do with the corpse were at their most significant.[90] Burial rituals and practices of great antiquity were in fact powerfully alive in Victorian Britain, and especially in Ireland.[91] In the early nineteenth century these beliefs were subjected to the most sustained assault, in terms not only of the corpse as a commodity, but most of all of the corpse as an anatomical object. The 1832 Anatomy Act allowed the bodies of the very poorest, often the unclaimed bodies of the workhouse poor, to be used for the purposes of medical dissection.[92] Death, as life, was medicalised, and in the process

the profound fear of the pauper's grave was engendered in British popular culture.

What is apparent here is also another instance of 'liberalism', only the
living now operated upon themselves through the medium of the dead.
The new cemetery in theory welcomed all comers. In Britain its organisation owed much to provincial religious Nonconformism, as opposed to
the statist traditions of France, the latter being especially evident in the
form of Père Lachaise in Paris.[93] With the exception of Kensal Green, all
early English cemeteries were in provincial towns and cities.[94] As in the
case of Manchester's Rusholme Road Property Cemetery in 1820, purported to be the first modern cemetery in Britain, the early pioneers were
strongly concerned with opening the place of burial to all, irrespective of
religious denomination. These early pioneers were, however, as keen
exponents of the new gospel of sanitation as any of their Anglican
counterparts, and their reforming attempts were as much concerned as
any others with developing the urban itself as a new site of the governance
of the dead. Their efforts coincided very closely with the move to make
the city now not only the site but also the engine of liberal freedom. The
Municipal Corporations Act of 1835 was one expression of this drive. It is
to the city as self-consciously an engine of governance that attention will
be given in the next chapter.

Another instance of this drive to directly engage the city itself as the
engine of freedom was the establishment of the Burial Boards of the
1850s, which put in place the system that has more or less continued to
the present day in Britain. No private cemeteries were set up after the
1850s. Power was vested in the locale, indeed in the parish, but this time
not the erstwhile hegemonic Anglican parish, but a 'liberal parish', as it
were, in which all who paid the poor rates were equal and had an equal
voice in the Boards themselves. As the historian of the early property
cemeteries argues, there was little difference between the outlook of those
involved in the 1820s and the 1850s, both groups being concerned to
develop voluntary, local and urban initiatives.[95] The Boards might also
appeal to the Privy Council if necessary, over the heads of the ecclesiastical
power, a decisive shift to civil power. In respect of the dead as of the
living, Edwin Chadwick's influence, if great, was once again considerably
diluted: a striking degree of national uniformity in the governance of
burial was achieved not by central means, including Chadwick's idea for
'national cemeteries', but by the permissive local act, and local political
initiatives. As will be seen, the local and the voluntary marked British
forms of governmentality greatly, and it is to the so far somewhat

neglected dimension of the political itself that I now turn in my consideration of the urban as self-consciously the engine of governance.

Notes

1. Michel Foucault, 'Space, Knowledge, and Power', in Paul Rabinow (ed.), *The Foucault Reader* (London: Penguin, 1986), p. 244.
2. See above, p. 4.
3. Graham Davidson, 'The City as a Natural System: Theories of Urban Society in Early Nineteenth-Century Britain', in Derek Fraser and Anthony Sutcliffe (eds), *The Pursuit of Urban History* (London: Edward Arnold, 1982). On Manchester liberalism in the early nineteenth century, see John Seed, 'Political Economy and the Antinomies of Liberal Culture in Manchester, 1830–1850', *Social History*, 7:1, 1982. See also C. Lawrence, 'The Natural System and Society in the Scottish Enlightenment', in Barry Barnes and Steven Shapin (eds), *Natural Order: Historical Studies of Scientific Culture* (London: Sage, 1979).
4. For Taylor, see W.H. Chaloner, 'Introduction', in *Notes of a Tour in the Manufacturing Districts of Lancashire* (London: Frank Cass and Co., 1968, first published Manchester, 1841).
5. W. Cooke Taylor, *The Natural History of Society in the Barbarous and Civilised State*, 2 vols (London, 1840). See also Patrick Joyce, *Democratic Subjects: The Self and the Social in Nineteenth-Century England* (Cambridge: Cambridge University Press, 1994), pp. 168–76.
6. Robert Vaughan, *The Age of Great Cities: Or, Modern Society Viewed in its Relation to Intelligence, Morals and Religion* (London, 1843). On Vaughan, see Andrew Lees, *Cities Perceived: Urban Society in European and American Thought 1820–1940* (Manchester: Manchester University Press, 1985), pp. 47–8.
7. Friedrich Engels, *The Condition of the Working Class in England in 1844*, ed. Eric Hobsbawm (London: Panther, 1969, first published in Great Britain, London, 1892).
8. Patrick Joyce, *Work, Society and Politics: The Culture of the Factory in Later Victorian England* (Brighton: Harvester, 1980).
9. Mary Poovey, *Making a Social Body: British Cultural Formation, 1830–1864* (Chicago: University of Chicago Press, 1995), p. 91; and see the two chapters on Manchester, namely 'Curing the Social Body in 1832: James Phillips Kay and the Irish in Manchester' and 'Anatomical Realism and Social Investigation in Nineteenth-Century Manchester'.
10. Alain Corbin, *The Foul and the Fragrant: Odour and the French Social Imagination* (Leamington Spa: Berg, 1986), chapter 6. See also his 'Backstage' in Michelle Perrot (ed.), *A History of Private Life*, volume IV (London: Harvard University Press, 1990).
11. Thomas Osborne, 'Security and Vitality: Drains, Liberalism and Power in the Nineteenth Century', in Andrew Barry, Nikolas Rose and Thomas Osborne (eds),

Foucault and Political Reason: Liberalism, Neo-Liberalism and Rationalities of Government (London: UCL Press, 1996), pp. 114–15.

12. Christopher Hamlin, *Public Health and Social Justice in the Age of Chadwick: Britain 1800–1845* (Cambridge: Cambridge University Press, 1998).

13. Ian Burney, 'Bone in the Craw of Modernity', in 'Roundtable on the Making of a Social Body', *Journal of Victorian Culture*, 4:1, 1999.

14. Christopher Hamlin, *Public Health*, chapters 1 and 2.

15. John V. Pickstone, 'Dearth, Dirt and Fever Epidemics: Rewriting the History of British "Public Health", 1780–1850', in Terence Osborne and Paul Slack (eds), *Epidemics and Ideas: Essays on the Historical Perception of Epidemics* (Cambridge: Cambridge University Press, 1992).

16. For this point see also Nikolas Rose and Thomas Osborne, 'Governing Cities', in Osborne, Rose and Engin F. Isin, *Governing Cities: Liberalism, Neoliberalism, and Advanced Liberalism* (Urban Studies Programme Working Paper No. 19, York University, Toronto, April 1998), pp. 5–10.

17. Christopher Hamlin, *Public Health*, pp. 3–7, 8–10, and chapters 2–3.

18. Mitchell Dean, *The Constitution of Poverty* (London: Routledge, 1991).

19. Christopher Hamlin, *Public Health*, p. 214.

20. Ibid., chapter 9, esp. pp. 278, 283, 285.

21. Ibid., chapter 10, 'Lost in the Pipes'.

22. Christine Bellamy, *Administering Central–Local Relations, 1871–1919: The LGB in Its Fiscal and Cultural Context* (Manchester: Manchester University Press, 1988), pp. 115–17, and Christopher Hamlin, *Public Health*, pp. 332–3.

23. Bruno Latour, *Science in Action: How to Follow Scientists through Society* (Milton Keynes: Open University Press, 1987); see also *We Have Never Been Modern* (Hemel Hempstead: Harvester Wheatsheaf, 1993) and *Pandora's Hope: Essays on the Reality of Science Studies* (London: Harvard University Press, 1999). On Ireland, see the forthcoming Patrick Carroll-Burke, *The Science/State Plexus: Engineering Culture and Modern State Formation 1650–1900* (University of California Press).

24. Ken Alder, 'Making Things the Same: Representation, Tolerance and the End of the Ancien Régime in France', *Social Studies of Science*, 28:4, 1998, and *Engineering the Revolution: Arms and Enlightenment in France, 1763–1815* (London: Princeton University Press, 1997).

25. Christopher Otter, 'Making Liberalism Durable: Vision and Civility in the Late 1870–1900 Victorian City', *Social History*, 27:1 2002, for a fuller discussion of these matters, and his 'The Government of the Eye: Light Technology and Liberalism in the Victorian City 1870–1900' (University of Manchester PhD, 2002).

26. As well as the works of Corbin cited above (note 10), see also his *Time, Desire, and Horror: Towards a History of the Senses* (Cambridge: Polity Press, 1995).

27. Alain Corbin, *The Foul and the Fragrant*, chapter 7 for developments in France. Dominique Laporte, *History of Shit* (London: MIT Press, 2000); James Joyce, *Ulysses* (New York: Vintage Books, 1961, first published 1922), p. 131.

28. Alain Corbin, *The Foul and the Fragrant*, p. 106.

29. Richard Sennett, *The Fall of Public Man: The Forces Eroding Public Life* (New York: Knopf, 1977), pp. 161–74.

30. Alain Corbin, *The Foul and the Fragrant*, chapter 9, 'The Stench of the Poor'.
31. Christopher Hamlin, *Public Health*, pp. 202–3.
32. Martin J. Daunton, 'Public Place and Private Space: The Victorian City and Working-Class Housing', in D. Fraser and A. Sutcliffe (eds), *The Pursuit of Urban History*, also *House and Home in the Victorian City: Working-Class Housing, 1850–1914* (London: Edward Arnold, 1983).
33. Alan Wilson, 'Technology and Municipal Decision Making: Sanitary Systems in Manchester, 1868–1910', (University of Manchester PhD 1990) and see Lawrence Wright, *Clean and Decent: A Fascinating History of the Bathroom and Water Closet* (London: Routledge and Kegan Paul, 1960); and Roy Palmer, *The Water Closet: A New History* (Newton Abbot: David and Charles, 1973).
34. James Winter, *London's Teeming Streets, 1830–1914* (London: Routledge, 1993), p. 127.
35. Thomas Burke, *The Streets of London through the Centuries* (London, 1940), p. 133.
36. Alan Wilson, 'Technology and Municipal Decision Making', chapter 3, 'Night Soil Disposal 1872–1895', and see *The Manchester Municipal Code, Being a Digest of Local Acts of Parliament . . . In Force within the City of Manchester*, 5 volumes, volume 1, 1894, section 3, The Sanitary Committee, (B.) Sanitary Conveniences. See also *Parliamentary Papers*, 1844, cxl, 571.
37. John Hogg, *London As It Is* (London, 1837), chapters ix–x.
38. Philippe Ariès, *Western Attitudes Towards Death: From the Middle Ages to the Present* (Baltimore: Johns Hopkins University Press, 1974).
39. Noëlle Vialles, *Animal to Edible* (Cambridge: Cambridge University Press, 1984).
40. Nick Fiddes, *Meat: A Natural Symbol* (London: Routledge, 1992).
41. Mary Douglas, *Natural Symbols: Explorations in Cosmology* (London: Penguin, 1977).
42. Noëlle Vialles, *Animal to Edible*, chapter 1.
43. Alain Corbin, 'The Blood of Paris', in *Time, Desire and Horror*.
44. John Hogg, *London As It Is*, pp. 219–20.
45. Alfred Rosling Bennett, *London in the 1850s and '60s* (London, 1924), chapter xix.
46. James Winter, *London's Teeming Streets*, p. 42.
47. Sigfried Giedion, *Mechanisation Takes Command: A Contribution to Anonymous History* (New York: Oxford University Press, 1955), pp. 210–11.
48. James Stevenson Bushnan, *The Moral and Sanitary Aspects of the New Central Market, as Proposed by the Corporation of the City of London* (London, 1851), pp. 15–16.
49. Thomas Gasprey, *The History of Smithfield* (London, 1852).
50. William Wordsworth, 'The Prelude', Book VII, in *The Poetical Works of Wordsworth* (Oxford: Oxford University Press, 1964), book VII, p. 546.
51. *Manchester Municipal Code* (1894), volume 1, appendix to part 1, 'Abolition of City Fairs'.
52. Seámas Ó Maitiú, *The Humours of Donnybrook: Dublin's Famous Fair and Its Suppression* (Dublin: Irish Academic Press, 1995), p. 20.
53. Ibid., chapter 3, 'Lent Victorious', for the history of the reform of the fair.
54. Ibid., pp. 9–13.
55. G.H. Rowbotham, *Ye Oulde Marketplace of Manchester* (Manchester, n.d.).
56. Mary Douglas, *Purity and Danger: An Analysis of the Concepts of Pollution and Taboo* (London: Ark/Routledge and Kegan Paul, 1984), chapters 6–7.

57. Noëlle Vialles, *From Animal to Edible*, pp. 17, 75, 80–2.

58. W. Anderson, 'Excremental Colonialism: Public Health and the Poetics of Pollution', *Critical Inquiry*, 21:3, 1995; Sudipta Kaviraj, 'Filth and the Public Sphere: Concept and Practice about Space in Calcutta', *Public Culture*, 10:1, 1997.

59. James Bushnan, *Moral and Sanitary Aspects*, p. 33.

60. W.J. Passingham, *London's Markets, Their Origins and History* (London, n.d., 1930s?).

61. Horace Jones, *On the New Metropolitan Markets* (n.d.), and on Jones see *Men of the Times* (London, 1887).

62. *Bylaws for Regulating the Metropolitan Meat and Poultry Market, Smithfield* (London, 1869).

63. *The Metropolitan Meat and Poultry Market: Descriptions of the Several Designs Sent In* (London, n.d.).

64. *A Description of the Metropolitan Meat and Poultry Market Smithfield* (London, n.d.). See also *Publications Relating to the Proposed Central Cattle Market and the Smithfield Market Removal Bill 1851* (London, n.d., 1850s); *An Appeal to the British Public, or, the Abuses of Smithfield Market, and the Advantages of a New Cattle Market Fairly Considered* (London, n.d., 1850s); C.J. Cuthbertson, *A Glance at the London Markets* (London, 1893). There is an extensive pamphlet literature on Smithfield Market in the Guildhall Library, Corporation of the City of London.

65. On Smithfield's design, see Horace Jones, *On the New Metropolitan Markets*.

66. *A Description of the Metropolitan Meat and Poultry Market, Smithfield*.

67. Roger Scola, *Feeding the City: The Food Supply of Manchester 1770–1870* (Manchester: Manchester University Press, 1992); *Manchester Municipal Code*, volume 1, 1894, part 1, 'As to the Markets Committee', also appendix to part 1, 'Second the Markets Committee'. See in particular (D.) By laws as to Markets, and (G.) Slaughterhouses and Meat.

68. See William Tomlinson, *Byways of Manchester* (Manchester, 1887), for essays on Manchester markets of different types.

69. James Schmiechen and Kenneth Carls, *The British Market Hall: A Social and Architectural History* (London: Yale University Press, 1999), especially part two, 'The Architecture and Design of the Public Market'.

70. *The Court Leet Records of the Manor of Manchester*, volume viii, 1756–86 (Manchester, 1888).

71. See, for example, the records for the meetings of 13 October 1756, 26 April 1757, 11 October 1786.

72. *Manchester Municipal Code*, part 1.1.B, 'Offences and Police Regulations Generally'.

73. 1.1.B., nos 32, 40, 44.

74. City of Birmingham, *Bylaws For Good Rule and Government* (Birmingham, 1897).

75. *Manchester Municipal Code*, 1.1.B., no. 28.

76. James Turner, *Reckoning with the Beast: Animals, Pain and Humanity in the Victorian Mind* (Baltimore: Johns Hopkins University Press, 1980).

77. *Manchester Municipal Code*, 1.1.B., no. 28.

78. Chris Otter, 'The Government of the Eye', chapter 3.

79. Martin Daunton, 'Public Place and Private Space', pp. 214–15.

80. For further information on municipal housing and nineteenth-century housing in

general see R.J. Morris and Richard Rodgers (eds), *The Victorian City: A Reader in British Urban History 1820–1914* (London: Longman, 1993).

81. Philippe Ariès, *Western Attitudes*, pp. 69–70.
82. Julie Rugg, 'The Origins and Progress of the Cemetery Establishments in Britain', in Peter C. Jupp and Glenys Howarth (eds), *The Changing Face of Death: Historical Accounts of Death and Disposal* (Basingstoke: Macmillan, 1997).
83. Philippe Ariès, *Western Attitudes*, p. 70.
84. Ruth Richardson, *Death, Dissection and Disease* (London: Penguin, 1988), p. 272. See also Peter C. Jupp and Clare Gittings (eds), *Death in England: An Illustrated History* (Manchester: Manchester University Press, 1999); Pat Jalland, *Death in the Victorian Family* (Oxford: Oxford University Press, 1996); and John Morley, *Death, Heaven and the Victorians* (London: Studio Vista, 1971).
85. Philippe Ariès, *Western Attitudes*, pp. 73–4.
86. Christopher Brooks, *Mortal Remains* (Exeter: Wheaton, 1989), chapter 9.
87. Thomas Laqueur, 'The Places of the Dead in Modernity'; paper presented to the ESRC workshop on a 'Rethinking the Social', Manchester, December 1998.
88. Ibid.
89. Christopher Brooks, *Mortal Remains*, chapters 9–10.
90. Ruth Richardson, *Death, Dissection and Disease*, p. 26.
91. Ibid., chapter 1.
92. Ibid., chapters 2–3 on the body, and see Ian Burney, *Bodies of Evidence: Medicine and the Politics of the English Inquest 1830–1926* (Baltimore: Johns Hopkins University Press, 2000).
93. Julie Rugg, 'The Origins and Progress', pp. 110–12.
94. Christopher Brooks, *Mortal Remains*, chapter 6.
95. Julie Rugg, 'The Origins and Progress'.

3

The Light of Publicity

Making Liberal Community

So far the account of liberalism has led into some rather strange places, into numbers, sewers and pipes, maps and markets. Clearly, political reason and its techniques cannot be mapped by orthodox means as the conscious implementation of clearly thought-out schemata of governance. If forms of power and human agency, and of bodily competence and of knowledge, are carried in the material world, and in the *use* of objects conceived of as practical epistemologies, then a narrative of liberalism as the term is conceived here would need to follow this strange and complex history of objects and material processes. Something of this history is already apparent, for example, in the often hidden, technosocial and seemingly 'objective' solutions that political problems sometimes took. At the same time, something akin to the liberalism that was shaped by, and shaped, the material world was also given clear discursive articulation. Groups and individuals did indeed put statistics and maps, sanitation and markets, into ideas and practices which formed social imaginaries of power, and into political programmes that gave expression to these imaginaries. It is in this more explicit and articulated sense of governance that I approach the city in this chapter. In terms of statistics, cartography, the civic toilette and the reform of markets, power, like the state itself, was diffused and ramified in society in complex ways; none the less, these various initiatives and departures do seem to have had a fair degree of coherence at the political level itself.

It is here that it is necessary to consider politics *per se*, politics conventionally understood as the more or less organised ground of differences about the disposition of state power. In terms of the relationship between governance and politics, in particular the contrast between liberal governmentality and what is usually called liberalism (understood as liberal thought, liberal party politics, and so on), it is useful to conceive of the 'political', like 'the social' and 'the economic', as from around the late eighteenth century increasingly taking on a more discrete identity, one which, again like the social, can be understood as becoming 'naturalised'. Liberal rule came to be prosecuted in terms of this new entity of 'the political'. In the British context, the emergence of the political in this way can be seen in terms of the separation of the political from royal authority, especially after the development, from the 1780s, of the notion that government was no longer 'the King's government', but was now rooted in Parliament, in terms of coherent government and 'opposition' groupings, and a nascent party system.[1]

With the shift in favour of Parliament, but away from royal authority as a source of political sovereignty, legitimacy was increasingly situated outside Parliament, and if the representative functions of Parliament had for long been important, then these seem to have become quite crucial from this time. The legitimacy of parliamentary sovereignty came increasingly to be centred in entities such as 'public opinion', 'the people', 'the democracy', eventually 'democracy' itself. A 'liberal polity', in a governmentality sense, can be seen in terms of the institutions and activities that permitted these entities to function best as free and self-regulating, in this case the city and town. Of course, these free political entities were not only identified in terms of *demos* or the popular, the pure rule of number really not achieving anything like a full realisation until after the First World War and the inclusion of women in the franchise. Representation was also understood in terms that often uneasily combined the idea of individual and communal or virtual representation (the landowner speaking for the community of his dependants, a husband as the virtual representative of his wife, for example). Whether narrowly or broadly conceived, the question of defining what entities should be represented might be as much a matter of exclusion as inclusion (inclusion being marked, for example, by the possession of reason, independence, the holding of property, and by male identity, among other definitions of the political nation). The struggle to define, and control, these new objects of political sovereignty was indeed central to nineteenth-century politics, and it was a struggle especially manifest in the case of the city.

Liberal governmentality can be considered as not only seeking to secure the city as a vital, auto-regulative entity. In line with the characteristic emphasis on identifying and implementing 'natural' systems and modes of their operation, it also sought to identify and facilitate forms of community through which it might 'rule at a distance' by allowing such communities to be as far as possible self-governing. We should not be surprised by this emphasis on 'community' in governmental liberalism, for the individual self and the community, the self and the social, always existed in relation one to the other in liberalism, though the relationship changed dramatically over time. Free communities and free individuals were mutually constitutive in liberalism, the sanctions of community guarding against the excesses of the individual self, and vice versa. 'Ruling at a distance' implied a particularly positive valuation of the local, but also a reconfiguration of the local and the national in terms of governmental organisation and power. In particular, it involved constituting the urban local as the source of political virtue by making it a true source of freedom, thereby bringing out its capacity for self-government, in this case in a quite literal sense.

Creating true freedom seems to have hinged very much upon creating the conditions of a political legibility and visibility which would entail full knowledge of the subject's self, and just as much of the subject's society. Political legibility was the condition for the true practice of freedom, for only when all were visible to each, and each to all, could freedom be properly practised. Only by making community transparent to itself by directing what I call the light of publicity could liberalism and liberal community be implemented. In turn, political legibility, and the proper practice of freedom, depended very much on the free availability of knowledge in general, knowledge of the self and the social being but subdivisions of this greater knowledge. In this regard the public library takes on a particular significance, and this chapter concludes with a treatment of the nineteenth-century library movement. The library exemplified the freedom of knowledge in general, and as a civic institution it exemplified the urban and local as the new engines of governance. In both guises it is therefore of particular interest. As much as any other institution, the public library was itself the light of publicity. However, in pursuing the significance of the local in the creation of liberal community and of a new and discrete political realm, seen here in terms of the municipal and its institutions, it becomes apparent that this business of *practising* or *performing* freedom seems particularly important. And this, and allied matters, require some more general comment before municipal and other sorts of politics are looked at.

If in one way defined as a realm marked by harmony, in the sense that rule would best be exercised in accordance with the naturally expressed, freely arrived at, tendencies of the polity, then conflict, for instance in the form of the political party, seems to have been intrinsic to 'the political' of liberalism in a way that does not seem to have been so pronounced as in other realms, for instance the social. For, if liberalism can be said to have invented modern politics, it did so in the sense that harmony could only be realised through the interaction and hence the potential conflict of political wills. Concerned as it was with the division of the spoils of power, the political realm was therefore open to contingency and chance, the raw material from which harmony might be made but also that which constantly threatened to undermine harmony. There was also a clear sense in liberalism in which the 'natural' aspects of the liberal polity were constantly undermined by fear of the taint of the political, the sense that government should be 'beyond' mere and often self-interested politics. The framers of the 1835 Municipal Reform Act itself at once identified the town as a potentially 'natural' political sphere, but also as a community that would best function free of self-interest and the party spirit of politics. By contrast, a characteristic way of talking about the social was to say that the freedom of its operation was only possible because it was outside the world of politics and the political. As a form of governmentality, liberalism had to be realised *within* politics, and one way of thinking of its ethics of governance is its realisation *in struggle*. If liberalism invented modern politics, then liberalism seems to have given birth to a Frankenstein's monster. This monstrous birth does explain something of the strengths and weaknesses of liberalism.

As has been suggested, as a form of rule that constantly questioned and contested the limits of rule, a certain agonistic quality seems central to liberal rule as an ethics of governance. As well as being realised *in struggle*, in the real world of the political sphere, it therefore had to be realised actively *as struggle*, as a mode of active, ethical being directed as much at the self of those who wished to govern as at the self of those who were governed. This distinction between liberalism *in struggle* and *as struggle* is one that informs this chapter. Here, as so often elsewhere, there were parallels between things and persons, non-human and human agency. In thinking about maps in chapter 1, their very volatility seems to have been involved in how we might consider them to be 'liberal'. Volatility, openness, complexity, all seem to mark the unprecedented level of detail in

mid-nineteenth-century maps, appear to be part of how maps projected
'subject positions' containing new levels of choice and freedom in their
use (but ones which also represented the excess of freedom that accompanied liberal freedom, exciting it into being but also subverting it). In
considering maps, it was said that liberalism might be in part defined in
relation to the very volatility and plurality it called into being, as an
attempt to recognise and embrace volatility. This embrace of freedom
indicates a certain audacity in the whole liberal project, a willingness to
risk that is the obverse of the desire to actively order behaviour through
freedom.

As a form of government that was at once an interrogation of government and of freedom itself, a certain tolerance of contradiction seems
evident in liberalism therefore, particularly the central contradiction of
ruling through freedom. But in practising freedom by constantly questioning it, an inherent instability also seems apparent. This tolerance may
explain the historical strength of liberalism. On the other hand, in
practising freedom by questioning it, liberalism seems constantly to have
been in danger of losing control over that which it can be said to have
created, namely Frankenstein's monster in the political world without,
and the liberal self set in the boundless world of freedom within. In the
political realm especially, as realised in struggle, in bringing about the
paradox of harmony achieved through conflict, liberalism opened itself
up further to the realm of contingency and chance which always threatened it. In seeking to describe the emergence and consolidation of a
liberal form of political reason in relation to the contingent world of
politics, and in relation to the parallel elaboration of an ethics of
governance, in what follows my emphasis is particularly on the ways in
which the practice of freedom as the performance of contradiction was
intrinsic to the *strength* of liberalism. (The emphasis on practice as active
and open becomes particularly apparent here, in the sense of practice as
in fact actively like *performance*.) This emphasis on the strengths of
liberalism is because a simple, and quite widespread, understanding of
liberalism as merely disciplinary power does not do justice to its subtlety
and its historical success. However, the *weaknesses* of liberalism will also be
apparent.

It must be said that in thinking about the relationship of governance
and politics, the existing literature on liberal governmentality is not a
great deal of help. This is because there is in this work a tendency to
reduce all politics to government. In turn, this perhaps owes something
to the historical method taken from Foucault, one in which contingency,

chance and the recognition of the embeddedness of forms of political reason in particular historical contexts and conjunctures, above all in politics itself, are relatively undeveloped, or at least developed in a different way and for different ends, ones related to a sensibility more theoretical than historical in nature. This literature does not say much on politics as a realm of the contingent and the conjunctural, though in fact a recognition of this is consonant with understanding liberalism as governmentality. So, while liberalism as a mode of governmentality clearly, and legitimately, cannot be equated with politics as conventionally understood, conventional understandings none the less illuminate liberalism in a way not always brought out in the existing literature.

In historical terms which for the moment go beyond the urban sphere alone, we may trace the consolidation of a more clearly delineated 'political' sphere back to the emergence of a recognisably modern form of civil service between about 1780 and 1830. In an analogous move to the separation of political power from royal authority, there was also a separation between the administrative and the political, the former itself increasingly taking on a discrete form. A clear distinction was made between governance and politics, governance being located in a separate 'administration', which, if ultimately having to operate in accordance with political power, had its own legitimate sphere of operation, sanctioned by the idea of its neutrality. The state in its administrative functions thereby became separated from 'the political', and in this process one can also discern how the political could come to have negative meanings, the civil service, like urban administration, for example, being 'beyond' politics.

The eighteenth-century civil service was neither civil nor a service.[2] Eighteenth-century state administration lacked the uniformity, hierarchy and corporate discipline to be a service.[3] It could not be considered such until appointments ceased to be based on patronage, which in fact, despite the importance of the 1780–1830 period, was not the case until well into the nineteenth century. If not a service, eighteenth-century administration was not 'civil' either, for there was no distinction between civil and political affairs, politicians doing what would later be called administration, and 'administrators' themselves having clear political functions and powers. Nor was the administration permanent. Officials might in effect be almost permanent fixtures but this was not systematic: the concept of permanence was meaningless outside the idea of a change of government, something only evident, as has been seen, with the demise of the idea of the monarch's government after the 1780s.[4]

On the national political stage, a strategy for governing through a minimal but regulatory state, in which freedom in economic, social and political spheres could be realised, was developed in a much more systematic and self-conscious way from the 1820s, in the shape of the reforms of liberal Toryism and Whiggism, and particularly in the figure of Sir Robert Peel.[5] In many ways eighteenth-century political structures were favourable to this nineteenth-century 'natural order' liberalism. The 'fiscal-military state' that developed in the century before the 1780s combined great strength with great flexibility.[6] This particular combination of attributes in fact marks out the character, and perhaps explains something of the relatively early emergence, of liberal governance in Britain, particularly in the early nineteenth century in the political sphere itself: the decentralisation of much of the eighteenth-century state seems to have been conducive to what came after. The eighteenth-century state was highly centralised in its military and fiscal dealings, yet depended on a bureaucracy that was amateur, if imbued with a strong sense of public duty.[7] Not only was this bureaucracy not professional; unlike its continental counterparts it was neither venal nor particularly sizeable, and it did not have a strong sense of its own corporate identity and interests. The central institutions of government, especially Parliament, and the activities of this bureaucracy were based on consent, however qualified this may have been. Beyond the fiscal and military functions of the state, and again unlike continental Europe, administration was highly decentralised, depending once more on amateur and in these cases voluntary and unpaid service, both elective and non-elective.

Considering rural Britain for the moment, rather than the towns, one historian of eighteenth-century government has spoken of the 'parish state'. The communal and participatory elements of this were important, but these went hand in hand with strong oligarchic tendencies. The parish state was in this respect a microcosm of the national one. However, it should not be thought that local government was not intensive government: the saturation of the political territory by governance that Foucault called 'police', which in eighteenth-century continental Europe was achieved by central government, in Britain was achieved at a local level. The parish itself was a very important aspect of this minute governmental regulation of everyday life. None the less, the reality of 'liberty before liberalism', as Quentin Skinner has put it, was real enough.[8] This particular blend of centralisation and decentralisation, of authority and liberty, can be said to have had roots in the relatively homogeneous and unified nature of English society, and after union with Scotland in 1707, what had become British society.

In one sense this was already governing through freedom, but this was very far removed from the positive and active governance through freedom that emerged in the early nineteenth century. Partly because of the relatively limited form of the state (though this was not how it appeared to eighteenth-century contemporaries), at least in comparison to some continental regimes, there was the lack of a strong sense of popular expectations about and support for the state. This anti-statism was to be a powerful force in the nineteenth century as well, including the popular classes. Earlier it had been linked to perhaps an even stronger sense, the sense of the popular and customary rights and liberties of the 'Free-Born Englishman', a sense shared to some extent at all social levels, not only among the poor. This sense was also firmly connected to Protestant religious traditions.[9] Nineteenth-century governance through freedom involved divesting the eighteenth-century state of the rights, indeed the liberties, that were intrinsic to it, for it conceived of these old liberties as 'pre-modern' accretions that had to be stripped away in order for natural order freedom to flourish.

In terms of the history of political concepts, Skinner has described this as the eclipse of liberty by what he calls the 'liberalism' of the nineteenth-century state, in the shape of eighteenth-century utilitarian thought. Whether we conceive of liberalism's subversion of liberty in terms of political thought, in social history terms of eclipse of the rights of the 'Free-Born Englishman', or in the sense of liberalism as understood here, the early nineteenth century in particular seems to mark an important transition in the form of the state. Therefore, if in some respects conducive to what came after, the eighteenth-century state was also a grave limitation. Liberalism in the governmental sense can be said to have indeed suborned liberty, though, as will be apparent, the relation between the two, which in fact can also be seen as in part that between governance and the political, was by no means as straightforward as this. Older ideas of 'liberty', and their subsequent transformations, were one part of the ground of politics in which political reason was embedded, qualifying but also supporting liberal governmentality.

Performing liberalism

The process of governing through a new sort of polity which was at once a new sort of political community was particularly evident in the cities and towns. Perhaps the central building block in this edifice of liberal community was the Municipal Corporations Act of 1835. The Act was of quite fundamental importance, as the basis of all subsequent urban local government. Of course, by virtue above all of its gargantuan size, London was in a different situation from the rest of Britain: as will be seen, London presented particular problems for governance, though very many dimensions of the urban experience were shared across Britain. In the short term the significance of the 1835 Act was not among these shared experiences. In fact, rather than in the ostensibly political sphere of municipal reform, it was its creation as a city of free circulation that actually defined London in governmental terms. For London, the developments seen in the previous chapter take on if anything an even greater importance when compared with elsewhere. As Lynda Nead has recently suggested, the 'conceptual machinery' (or 'social imaginary' in my parlance) which most defined nineteenth-century London for contemporaries was one shaped by the monumental mains drainage engineering works of the mid-nineteenth century.[10] Rather than the 1835 Act, and indeed based upon the prior creation of the sanitary city, it was the 1855 Metropolitan Local Management Act that really established London's 'first municipal government', the Metropolitan Board of Works. This acted as the main administrative organ of municipal government until the development of active political municipal self-government towards the end of the century.

In the country at large, in order to understand the meaning of the 1835 Act it is necessary to consider the character of urban government before then. Let us take the government of Manchester in the early nineteenth century.[11] If unusual in its strongly manorial elements, the city was characteristic of the patchwork of jurisdictions and institutions typifying urban government in the eighteenth century, comprising corporations, manorial institutions, but also a range of other forms, varying between county magistrates, parishes, Improvement Acts and voluntary societies.[12] The Manchester instance represented a quite extraordinary mix of different jurisdictions. These involved the manorial, centred on the Court Leet, the ecclesiastical, involving the Parish Vestry, the parliamentary, involving various Police and Improvement Commissions, and the juridical, involving the Justices of the Peace (JPs), some of whom were appointed by the Crown and some of whom, the municipal magistrates, were in fact locally elected. Within each jurisdiction there was a mixing of functions that would later be assigned to separate and distinct jurisdictions. At the same time, these jurisdictions involved sources of authority which would later be themselves strictly demarcated, particularly civil and religious authority.

The Parish Vestry and poor relief is a good example. As well as its more purely religious functions, the Parish Vestry was involved in the election of Churchwardens, who, along with the Poor Law Overseers (some of whom were appointed by the JPs), were responsible for raising and spending the Poor Rate. The administration of what would later be a 'social' domain, governed by civil, political authority, was therefore in part the concern of a religious institution supplemented by a politico-legal one. The quasi-feudal Court Leet, whose members were selected by the legal agent of the Lord of the Manor, mixed together a wide range of administrative and legal functions. It elected the Constables, for example. However, in the 1830s, while the Court Leet was responsible for the Day Police, the Night Police were entirely under the jurisdiction of the Police and Improvement Commissioners, as constituted by a Parliamentary Act of 1792. Not only were forms of jurisdiction mixed, therefore, but institutions, like the police, that would later have a clear jurisdictional remit were divided between different jurisdictions, themselves with very disparate functions.

Under the Police Act of 1792, the meaning of 'police' extended far beyond later notions of the term, embracing the older meanings of 'policy'. It involved, for instance, matters of housing regulation and street maintenance. The activities of the JPs, as is evident, themselves extended far beyond juridical matters: for example, they could order outdoor poor relief, against the authority of the workhouse. If jurisdictions overlapped and combined, qualification for membership of these various bodies varied greatly, for example between the often rather democratic, residence-based, form of the Parish Vestry, the property-based franchises of the Commissions, and the nomination of the Lord of the Manor.[13] Election itself might be direct or indirect. The period of elected authority itself varied greatly. Election did not necessarily mean accountability: those elected by the Parish Vestry were not in their year of election accountable to those who elected them. In all of this, there was no clearly defined political subject. The 'political subject', as it were, was splintered between these different jurisdictions, functions and franchises. At the same time, there was no clearly delineated public sphere, just as the civil was incompletely separated from the religious and the political. The general emergence of an autonomous political sphere is therefore evident in this area too. The Municipal Corporations Act intervened upon this situation with a relentless, liberal logic, in part the product of Benthamite thinking.[14] There was a radical simplification of political subjecthood, and a clear delineation of a discrete civil, political sphere.

Under the provisions of the 1835 Act Manchester was incorporated in 1838. By the Act it was intended that the municipal corporation be restored to its original meaning as the legal personification of the local community. The community itself became, therefore, the *raison d'être* of the Act. Voting was to be equal and direct, and simplified on the basis of a ratepayer franchise, with three years' residence. To be a voter one had to have occupied rateable premises and to have actively paid rates, so that property became even more the sign of a stake in the community than it had been in the eighteenth century. This renewed emphasis on property in the franchise characterised the redefinition of the political nation that occurred so widely at this time, at the parochial, county and parliamentary levels, as well as the civic level.[15] The old public parish vestries, as with other aspects of the old, unreformed order, were in fact often more representative and participatory than the reformed system that followed them. This redefinition of the political nation was also importantly a legal one – the public parish vestry, for example, did not exist in law before 1818, that is to say, it was regulated by custom and the common law, not by official statute. As at parliamentary level, the municipal franchise was restricted entirely to men. However, as property was itself in large measure gendered as a male preserve at this time, the restriction was in a sense superfluous (the reform of the law regarding women's property later on in fact meant that as ratepayers women were included within the municipal electorate way ahead of other sectors of political representation).

Therefore, property, law and gender were defining elements in a new liberal, political subject, and in the more uniform and discrete kind of polity then emerging.[16] As part of this emergence, the terms of the 1835 Act themselves decreed that justice be strictly separated from municipal government. In effect the franchise created voters who were technically equal and identical, composed of the same substance (masculinity, property and membership by residence of a single urban, political community), unlike the multiple political subjectivities of previous times. Again, the relationship to 'modern abstraction' is evident, for these new political subjectivities could only be imagined when realised in terms of 'repetitious actions; reproducible products; interchangeable places, behaviours and activities'. The Act can therefore itself be considered as a crucial intervention in what might be called political epistemology, clearing away the conceptual clutter of the old order.

Existing municipal institutions, as described in the First Report of the Royal Commission of 1833 that preceded the Act, were considered to be closed, secret and corrupt.[17] The ethos of community was therefore complemented by the idea of openness. There was a marked emphasis, in the Act and the Report, on town government being open government, for instance in terms of municipal meetings and the auditing of municipal accounts. Government, like justice, was to be seen to be done. The open was here equated with the public, and both with the notion of accountability. This new emphasis on the open and the public was also an emphasis on the visual, and on a sort of political visibility. The advocates of municipal reform, above all Richard Cobden, who led a national campaign from Manchester, and who promulgated the gospel of corporation in his pamphlet *Incorporate Your Borough*, dwelt on the enemies of incorporation as mired in the dark of their own corruption. Seen as the 'booby squirearchy' of Toryism, and evincing the 'feudal insolence and slavish servility' of the Court Leet, closed government was equated with everything that was the opposite of the open, the clean and the illuminated (also the free). The enemies of incorporation are characterised by stupor, dirt, dark and hidden places, and by an attachment to the slavery and dependence of a feudal past.[18]

The connections between technologies of light and forms of surveillance that depended on illumination, especially policing, are striking. The first public gas burner in Manchester was that above the Central Police Station in Police Street, in 1807. As Foucault saw, social discipline amounted to a 'political economy of detail', a mobilisation of visual technologies designed to secure scrutiny of the entire surface of the body politic. This scrutiny was panoptic, in the sense of the one seeing the many, but in the nineteenth century this political economy of detail can be understood as increasingly oligoptic, the few seeing the few, and eventually omnioptic, the many seeing the many. Light in its interaction with police surveillance was central to all these stages. The Commissioners of Police, and not only in Manchester, owned and ran the lighting of the town. It was not until 1851 that the City Council took over from them. Street lighting grew rapidly, and as early as 1823 in London there were 215 miles of street lighting, provincial cities catching up with this level of provision in time. Light became central to the government of the city, therefore, materially as well as rhetorically.

It would not do to exaggerate the impact of gas lighting, however, as until the end of the century street lighting still tended to be tied to the rhythms of natural light, and many town authorities turned off street lighting after midnight or when there was a full moon. The quality of light in gas street lighting was not constant, and therefore insufficient for monitoring detail sufficiently. Gas produced shadows as well as illumination, pools of light that brought the surrounding darkness even more into prominence. It was electric lighting from the 1880s onwards which marked the most dramatic change, with its even and intense illumination.[19]

If not from the sanitarians' point of view as important a determinant of personal and social health as water, light very quickly became a municipal concern in provincial Britain, though London largely remained in the hands of private gas companies, as was to be the case with electricity as well. Elsewhere, following the 1848 Public Health Act, gas and eventually electric lighting became municipal concerns. The contrast with the eighteenth century is clear. Then housekeepers whose house or gateway was next to the street had to provide lighting on dark nights. Power therefore shifted from the person and local commune to the municipal state, in that the individual light carrier or provider was robbed of power, whether one conceives of the latter as the watching, and lighting, inhabitant of the town or the constable of the old watch. One was lit but did not light. One was identified but did not identify.

The police of the eighteenth century, accurately called 'the watch' because that is what they did, simply watched, largely in the dark, over private premises in order to secure property (chiefly the property of the wealthy). These are to be differentiated from the nineteenth-century police. The latter secured public space in the interests of law and order: the difference was fundamental. The technology of the old police, in the relative absence of street lighting (relative to the better-lit parts of continental Europe that is), was the padlock.[20] The technology of the new police was the police 'beat', the organised *passage* of the policeman through the streets of the city, streets increasingly illuminated by artificial means (the old police certainly went on their rounds, but the systematic patrol was new). The central aspect of the beat was that it was repeated in the same form, and known by the inhabitants of the city to be repeated in this form.[21]

The disciplinary potential is clear enough – it was of course a means of surveillance, but more subtly than this of self-surveillance, because the very possibility of observation ensured the citizen's circumspection. Circumspection was not subscription to the law of course, and what seems to have been more significant than any internalisation of the law was a series of understandings, in effect nods and winks, that grew up between the police and city dwellers.[22] The outwardness of circumspection as a form of social discipline was, however, still some distance away from the agonistic operations on the self I later want to consider. The consequences of these new policing initiatives, if somewhat slow to unfold, were in the end hugely significant, especially in the increasingly clear distinction between public and private space, the former now being regulated by police authority. Hitherto, for instance in the industrial districts of the north of England, a sort of communal policing by local communities continued strongly up to about 1850 (and, in fact, resisted the new police strongly for a time). This involved rights to and claims upon space which enunciated a very different, older sense of 'public'.[23] New public space became a neutral medium which one simply moved through (in line with the spatiality of the mapped city in fact). Indeed, the 'moving on' of those who dallied in the street, and the attendant and novel concept of 'loitering', were extraordinarily powerful irritants to those first exposed to the new police.

These new police forces were greeted with dislike and suspicion not only by the poor, but by the better-off as well. In the name of the Free-Born Englishman, in the name of liberty and independence, Tories as well as Liberals, rich as well as poor, disdained the military overtones, for instance the uniforms, of the new police. These were evidence of an overweening state. In Manchester, for example, these anxieties produced much conflict within the municipal authorities themselves, before the government stepped in, in 1847, and ensured control over the police by the borough corporation.[24] Indeed, it took some time before the police pulled back from the public order and 'domestic mission' functions they had in the early days, and established the subtle reciprocities that enabled 'policing by consent' to operate (reciprocities which might indeed involve bending, even breaking, the law, as well as upholding it). Public order and morality also gave way to a concern with 'criminal' groups, and to the science of criminality. Liberty could indeed resist liberalism, but in the process what eventuated was no simple rejection of liberal modes of rule, but the idea of the involvement of citizens in their own policing. Liberal governance became situated within a particularly English idea of liberty, therefore, and reshaped and in many ways strengthened in the process. The best example of this English style of policing was the Metropolitan

Police of London under the leadership of Richard Mayne, which proudly differentiated itself from the despotic police of continental Europe.[25]

If the practice of policing was different from the rationality that informed it, this applied to municipal government too, where the intractability of the liberal polity was often evident. The Municipal Reform Act itself, as with all other reforming initiatives then and later, was realised in a political sphere, increasingly one of party struggle, and therefore governance can be here understood in the sense of its realisation *in struggle*. There was much that was *parti pris* in the Act, for instance in the attempt by the Whigs to dismantle Tory power. Change in the municipal sphere was subsequently temporally and geographically uneven. Municipal authorities were riven by political differences within, by differences between themselves and the central state, and by the constant arguments of local groups and interests. The reform of the cities took a long time to reach the counties: until 1888 the latter were controlled by the unelected Quarter Sessions, and the model of the cities was not followed until 1894 in the case of the Parish Councils. It was only after 1870 that a more coherent and uniform shape was given to the earlier proliferation of authorities, particularly after the Local Government Boards of 1871 and the County Councils Act of 1888.[26] Although the central state had the final authority, given the devolved nature of much of this power, a lot depended on the initiative of particular towns and cities. For example, the municipal reform currents evident in Manchester in the first half of the century only began to develop rapidly in Birmingham after about 1870, with the advent to power of Chamberlainite Radicalism.

On the centre stage, historians of government have pointed to how between the 1820s and the 1840s politicians were genuinely unsure of the way ahead, and their search for appropriate governmental agencies between the central and local levels was ongoing. None the less, agreement about the positive and active deployment of freedom as a mode of governance seems to have been widespread and increasingly consensual. This appears above all to have involved the growing dominance of the administrative state over the legislative one. If we return to the notion that these years saw the acceleration of the division between politics and administration, we can situate an understanding of governmental liberalism in terms of this division. It is precisely in the demarcation of administration as a sphere which would be itself self-sufficient and self-regulating that we can understand liberal governmentality. Akin to the emergence of technosocial solutions to political problems, for instance evident in the engineering outcome to the problems posed by the sanitary city, there seems to have been a parallel emergence of political problems as themselves technical. In chapter 1 I referred to other aspects of this in regard to the emergence of statistics as part of a 'technicisation' of the political. Political questions and problems became increasingly the concern of administrative experts. The level of local government is in fact a good instance of this, for if in the eighteenth century the local state was a partner with the central state in the generation of information about governing, by the time of the Municipal Reform Act it had become the object of reform itself, that which information had to be collected *about*, in the form of parliamentary committees, themselves increasingly dominated by what came to be regarded as a form of administrative expertise autonomous from the political.[27]

On the other side of the divide, it is in this separation of the political and the administrative that we can also situate the identification of the *political* as itself a discrete sphere. This separation was achieved by some of the means already considered, for instance those evident in the performance of statistical and social knowledge as neutral and objective, these characteristics being evident not just in numbers themselves but also in the persons, activities and institutions that, as has been seen, actively *performed* neutrality and objectivity. It is in this performance of how administration differed from politics that we can in fact again think of the achievement of liberal governmentality as something realised *in struggle* with the political, a messy struggle always to define what was the province of technical, administrative expertise and what was not, namely the political. And this struggle to 'technicise' power was about carving out ethical personae and codes that would legitimate this notion that governing was technical. Therefore, it was a moral struggle, an active human operation upon the self of governor and governed, so that the sense of liberal governance *as struggle* is evident, and its inseparability from the achievement of governance *in struggle*. Having opened up the question so far of the urban as a site of liberal community in which the conditions of political legibility and visibility might secure the active performance of freedom by the city's inhabitants, I now want to turn more directly to the performance of liberal governmentality as an ethics of governance.

However, before doing so it should be noted that the achievement of the administrative state was secured by other means than the governance of the will that I now wish to address. It depended upon identifying and implementing governance as not just technical but indeed as a sort of self-correcting machine – rather like the self-acting mule in the cotton-spinning factory of the 1830s and 1840s, and indeed like the factory itself as a giant machine. One can see this, for instance, in the institutional structures and procedures that followed the Poor Law legislation of 1834, in which the old negotiated authority of the parish officers and magistrates was replaced by workhouse tests, uniform provision for workhouse inmates and systems of increasingly professionalised and paid inspectors and boards, in short all the means of a 'self-acting', bureaucratic structure. There were spatial analogues of this institutional reconfiguration too, for instance the new governmental territories of the Poor Law Unions, which cut across older political and administrative boundaries, and which added a spatial reality to the institutional machine. This all amounted to a sort of political infrastructure, evident at the municipal level as everywhere else, which was parallel to urban infrastructure, and like it can be called from the present point of view 'liberal'. The test of government increasingly became efficiency, and a major test of efficiency was economy.

Liberal government was also economic government. The liberal state's attempt to rule through freedom and the natural order was implemented not merely in social but also in economic terms. Gladstonian finance, for instance, in particular the taxation system, was aimed at encouraging the belief that all groups in society had a responsibility for sanctioning and financing government activity, and therefore they should have an incentive to keep it under control. Subsequent implementation of the liberal state, especially that of Gladstone himself, should not be seen simply as that of the amoral market. In the third quarter of the century, as the apotheosis of the developments being described here for the first half of the century, Gladstone's economic version of the liberal state represented a form of individualism based not upon greed and self-interest but upon probity, self-control and a sense of duty and Christian morality. If government was free of an economy that was seen as self-regulating, then it would also itself be free from the influence of powerful economic interests.[28]

In considering the birth of a liberal ethics of governance, the figure of John Stuart Mill seems particularly important in understanding liberalism *as* struggle. As both a political thinker and a 'public moralist', Mill straddled the worlds of politics and thought and the personal and the political, the worlds of the private and the public. In short, he encompassed liberalism both *as* struggle and *in* struggle. If the Municipal Corporations Act was in measure Benthamite, then Mill's writings on liberty and on representative government can be regarded as an attempt to relate Bentham to the Britain of his time, the 1850s, and in particular to soften Bentham's rationalist message by attending to the lessons of

Romanticism, particularly the lessons of Coleridge and Carlyle. As the historian of local government Redlich put it in 1903, Mill did for democracy what Chadwick did for administration, namely he moralised and 'Anglicised' Bentham, relating his thought to moral considerations and to the world of affairs. In this process, one becomes aware of Mill as an important component of the realisation of mid-Victorian liberal political reason in terms of mid-Victorian liberal politics. Redlich is in fact representative of a widespread understanding of the Englishness of Mill as central to his great reputation:[29] for all his fear of public opinion, in the third quarter of the century Mill enjoyed enthusiastic support amongst working-men radicals, as well as wide influence in governing circles.[30]

The influence of Mill, and of 'public moralists' like him, upon the machinery of government was very considerable, particularly in the Social Science Association.[31] Such 'public moralists', greatly significant for British cultural and political development, represent a different trajectory to the European figure of the 'intellectual'. Both figures can be understood as of great importance in the generation of thought about government, the British variant often being more directly involved in actual government than in many European cases, partly through the agency of the educational system, as will be evident, but also in institutions like the Social Science Association. From the 1850s to the 1880s, this 'social parliament' served to link intellectual 'experts' to policy-making in a direct way, resulting, for example, in the fashioning of several Royal Commissions. Liberal, Tory and eventually socialist politicians, as well as intellectuals, leading businessmen, professional people and radical working men, all came together in what was decidedly the most significant intellectual engine of liberal governance at the time. If Liberal Party members tended to dominate the institution, there is no clearer example of how liberalism understood as governmentality can be seen to embrace all strands of political opinion.

In the mid-century years the Association both looked back to Owenism and utilitarianism, and looked ahead to Christian Socialism and radical forms of political positivism, transacting the relationship of these different influences in such a way as to create a continuously productive means for ideas about government to be translated into the practice of government. Its role in moralising notions of government was quite crucial: by the time of Mill the Association saw political economy as 'reductive, narrow, abstract', and social science as 'expansive, synthetic, and embracive'. This comment from 1861 understood social science as being constituted precisely because political economy had no sense of moral duty and purpose. Mill and the Social Science Association were therefore examples, important ones, of the gradual deepening of that active governance *through* freedom which has been seen to emerge in the 1820s and 1830s. This positive governmental embrace of freedom transcended the limitations that older forms of liberalism presented for governing in a burgeoning democracy, particularly Benthamite utilitarianism with its overtones of eighteenth-century 'police' governmentality.

Although Mill cannot be regarded as an architect of municipal government, his writings enable us to understand the reshaping of community within liberal modes of rule (Mill in fact was hugely influential in the Social Science Association). In terms of Mill's thought, these modes can be said to have involved the 'discovery of the state', in that in Mill and others of his generation there was a new interest in the actual processes of government as carried out by civil servants. Mill was concerned with how to direct a state which had developed in spite of all political efforts to prevent it. An older concern about the functioning of the constitution receded before a recognition of the potential of the administrative apparatus for carrying out reform. For Mill the state was not an abstract idea but a tangible entity possessing the machinery for intervening in society and changing its direction. The loss of liberty involved was compensated for by the state's new-found ability to educate and improve its subjects. Again the importance of Mill is evident, above all his contribution to reshaping the forms of liberal community that this discovery of the state now made both possible and necessary. The urban was a central element in this recasting of community.

Mill's thought on 'local representative bodies', in his *Considerations on Representative Government* of 1861, takes up the relationship between the centre and the local in government.[32] There is a clear distinction between the two. The law is laid down for the guidance of the local official, and the centre superintends and compels the law. Metropolitan public opinion is of a higher grade than local opinion. The authority most conversant with principles, the centre, should be supreme in the matter of principle. 'Power may be localised, but knowledge to be most useful must be centralised.' As Mill also says, 'It is a poor education that associates ignorance with ignorance', and 'What is wanted is a way of making ignorance aware of itself . . . accustoming minds which know only routine to act upon, and feel the value of, principles'.[33] Things could hardly be clearer. The local is in a position of subordination, and 'principle' dominates over execution. However, at the same time the local is one of the principal means by which the state can be used to reform society.

Making ignorance aware of itself was indeed central to liberalism in its nineteenth-century forms, political and governmental. This is why the library was such a central institution in the operation of liberalism, in both senses of the term. In terms of political liberalism, and more particularly early kinds of liberal politics for Cobden the political agitator, two decades before Mill, the newly incorporated towns would be 'little democracies', calculated 'to afford useful lessons of equality, teaching the haughty few to respect the many', 'and, which is of greater value still, they tend to impart to the multitude the elevated feelings of self-respect'.[34] The *raison d'être* of nineteenth-century liberalism (particularly when understood as governmentality) would in fact appear to have lain in the active creation of liberal subjects, in the sense that there seems to have been something like a *compulsion* to proselytise and educate, and to remake the political self. It is here that the relationship between political thought, municipal government and intellectual life in Victorian society needs to be considered in some detail.

The relationship of political thought and intellectual life has been charted in terms of the transition from an eighteenth-century language of 'Virtue' to a nineteenth-century language of 'Character'. There was a move from an emphasis on maintaining an existing order, by speaking the language of governmental virtue, to the notion of progress as an open-ended future. The new language of 'character' was in contrast to the backward-looking and cyclical conception of history evident in the old language. The one was ordered by a fear of corruption, the other by a fear of stagnation. As Collini suggests, the passage from Whiggism to Liberalism in figures like Mill, Bright and Gladstone was one powerful consolidation of the language of character, a language which in the form of these figures can immediately be seen to have had a resonance with the cultural and social worlds in which contemporary intellectual life was embedded. There was in this regard a close connection between 'high' political discourse and the development of popular forms of politics, and, as Collini argues, between this discourse and the Evangelical 'moral psychology' that was so important in the language of character.[35] This psychology itself permeated all spheres of Victorian life, even those in which which Evangelicalism was renounced.[36]

In terms of 'the culture of altruism' and 'the language of character', features of Victorian political intellectuals and many others too, what was involved in this change was the legacy of Evangelical Protestant revivalism.

This brought to the language of character an intensification of the sense of inward struggle. Within Evangelicalism itself there were divergent strains, a voluntarist one but a very strong deterministic element too. Romanticism, and even religious agnosticism itself, also contributed to a widespread moral psychology in which the problem of adequate moral motivation was the central issue. There was a marked belief in the ingrained, and dangerous, power of 'habit' (habit took physiological and psychological forms as well as moral ones). In many respects this was a highly pessimistic view of human nature, one marked by the *necessity* of struggle. As students of liberal governmentality have noted, particularly in the case of the government of the will, for example in the control of alcohol, the category of 'habit' seems of particular importance for liberal governance, in that it mediates between desire and compulsion, making it possible to conceive of political subjectivity as embracing both change and stasis – habits *are* ingrained in nature, but can none the less be broken by the power of the will.[37] This 'culture of altruism' was dominant until the late nineteenth century, when it encountered more 'psychological' and 'social' (as opposed to moral) understandings of individual and collective motivation and behaviour. 'Laws' outside individual moral control were now perceived to operate.[38] Something of this will be considered in the next chapter under the heading of 'the social city'. None the less, the older 'religion of humanity', in its concern with struggle and character, continued to be a very significant influence after the turn of the century as well. It was central to the twentieth-century British Labour movement, as once it had been to the Liberal Party before it.

In considering the language of character, it is apparent that in order to overcome the potentially vicious force of habit, humankind had constantly to exercise the muscles of the will. One exercised these muscles over others, so that the educative role can be seen to be central but also in a sense compulsive, and one exercised them over oneself as well. Therefore there was something like a moral imperative to educate oneself into citizenship. If we consider Mill's *On Liberty*, this sense of the active exercise of freedom is very apparent.[39] While liberty is essentially defined in terms of the pursuit of one's own interests, so long as they do not clash with those of others, none the less 'the permanent interests of man as a progressive being' are essentially determined by the capacity and indeed the necessity to make choices. The best protection of individual freedom is the most widely dispersed sense of altruism and fellow feeling. The more dispersed the better, so that choice itself would have the biggest possible range of material to work upon. In echoing Humboldt on how 'the permanent interests of man as a progressive being' are only fully realised in terms of a richness and diversity of choice, Mill also rejects what he took to be a powerful contemporary Calvinistic ethic of 'Christian self-denial' in favour of 'Pagan self-assertion'.

Mill was asserting the sense in which the exertion of the will against the force of habit was central to the development of the self. It was also quite central to the development of society, and there is a clear sense of an historical threshold over which some cultures have crossed, but over which most have not (especially those of the East, with which of course in the shape of India and its government Mill and his father had a great deal to do). In fact, the greater part of the world had not yet reached this stage and were immured in 'Custom'. There was a strong sense of the destructive force of Custom, associated with stasis, over which, through the exertion of choice and the encouragement of the greatest diversity, Progress might in the end triumph. By choosing choice, as it were, one could overcome stasis and habit, and so realise 'the permanent interests of man'.[40]

To combat the enervation of selfishness one had to be active. Activity was only of value if it was pursued voluntarily, because only thus, in freedom, in action, and indeed in struggle, might the will be exercised. And this voluntary action was in turn only meaningful when performed in public, as in order to be judged as freely forthcoming it had to be opened to inspection and be seen to be done. Therefore the so-called 'public sphere', which emerged into such political importance in the first half of the nineteenth century, especially in the city, seems to have been rooted in widely dispersed contemporary notions of the self and of the social order, from which it drew its strength. 'The public' was therefore in this sense something that was *performed*, as part of the only fully meaningful display of the self. The notion of the performance of political reason is clearly central to how I understand the operations of power in this book, but in this instance performance takes on an even greater salience as the active performing of the self. Again, the parallels between human and non-human agency seem important: as scientists seek to create knowledge and 'capture' material agency by repetition, routine and discipline, typically in machinic forms, so one can think about the creation of political knowledge and action in terms of a similar capture of human agency. Towards one end of a spectrum, the more material end, human agency is captured in water closets, sewer markets, but also in a slightly different sense in the administrative machines such as the one then coming into being in the British state. Towards the other end, the constant training of the self, of oneself and others, that is required to master habit involves similar processes of routine and discipline to those in the material world, where matter is configured in such a way as to 'perform' agency in particular ways. Habit must counter habit, and in chapter 6 something more of the learned, 'automatic' dimensions to behaviour evident in spheres of urban governance will be considered.

Character, though it was also exercised in private, had to be possessed and enjoyed in public view too, therefore. In contrast to eighteenth-century notions of the cultivation of sociability and 'social man', there was a premium on inward sincerity, which was now, however, to be on outward display – as the next chapter will suggest, the built forms of the city echoed and reinforced this outward display, or performance, of power and the self. This cult of sincerity, owing much to both post-Romantic assertions of authenticity and a Puritan taste for austerity, also involved the notion of 'Reputation'. Reputation only meant something if it was possessed and enjoyed in public. The idea of reputation was therefore strongly informed by the importance of being open and above board, lacking pretence. Again we return to the notion of openness and 'publicity', which is clearly so crucial to the implementation and articulation of liberal modes of rule. This emphasis on the rejection of pretence involved also a rejection of privilege, for privilege was a sign of the inauthentic, of a reputation that was given and not earned or struggled for.[41]

In thinking about the Englishness of Mill in relation to his writing on the educative role of municipal government, the emphasis on active citizenship was absolutely central. Mill's thoughts on municipal 'sub-parliaments' emphasised the citizen who was trained by his own activity because he had a stake in his own locality (unlike, for example, mere newspaper readers, who were part of a passive 'public opinion'). Because the citizen is active, he is therefore responsible.[42] Mill's advocacy of women's rights aside, the dominant form of this new, agonistic liberal self was highly masculinised, in that performance in the political sphere was almost entirely a male preserve. Local interest meant above all local involvement, and participation is the essential element, for with participation there comes a citizen who is politically educated. The markers of participation are indeed property and gender, but these are in the end only the basis of a political education which depends on participation. The fear of *demos* was central to the construction of the democratic citizen: the mass produced social breakdown, but a 'well grounded opinion' depended on face-to-face knowledge, the essential domain of which was the local, in this form the civic, but also all the other imagined communities of liberal political thought and Liberal politics.[43] This face-to-face knowledge can in fact be regarded as forming a sort of 'reciprocal censorship' (Mill's term) in which the citizen watched other citizens, and in the process evaluated his own political contribution, in effect watching himself as well, in oligoptic and omnioptic forms. However, this sort of ethical rule, if encouraged in others, was to be practised on the self of those who sought to rule as well.

The sphere in which the liberal subject was located, and in which it was 'naturalised', was therefore itself unstable, and indeed agonistic. In this understanding, there were no easy options, for the necessity of self-correction had always to be striven for and was not simply given in the order of things. However, a liberal *agon*, if in some sense unstable, had its own stability too, namely the figuration of the world as the site of a drama of moral struggle, a struggle which did not guarantee Progress but one which with the right moral action might bring Progress about: in terms of popular politics, heavily moralised narratives of struggle were greatly important in popular Liberalism.[44] This dimension of moral drama will be taken up in more detail in the next chapter, on the design of the city. Moral action, in terms of a rationality of government, seems then to have turned crucially upon the idea of 'publicity'. In fact, the public sphere, so-called, which, as we have seen, can be understood as an arena for the performance of the self, may also be considered as the end result of a set of institutions and practices which can be called 'political technologies' of publicity. Ruling at a distance, therefore, ruling through 'the local' and through 'community', took the essential form of the deployment of technologies of 'publicity', for instance the public library. The practical and mundane details of democratic politics themselves can indeed be regarded as elements of just such a political technology of publicity, for example the many procedures ensuring open accountability in election and representation.

It is in this light that the development of the public examination for the civil service has been approached. The examination was central to the reform of government at home and abroad precisely at this mid-century time.[45] Understood as a technology of publicity, the civil service public examination can also be seen to have a close connection to the agonistic dimensions of liberal political reason. This is evident in the mid-nineteenth-century formation of the civil service, a formation that has indeed shaped the subsequent character of the civil service down to the close of the twentieth century. In this process of formation the

consolidation of governmental liberalism is clearly on view. It is apparent
first in the political laboratory of the colony, above all India. The
Northcote–Trevelyan Report on the civil service, of 1853–4, was inspired
by the example of Macaulay's reform of the Indian civil service, which
involved the use of competitive examinations as early as 1833.[46] Sir Charles
Trevelyan himself, author of the Report, was educated at the Indian civil
service college of Haileybury, and was Macaulay's brother-in-law. The
creation of a new governing class as well as a new ethic of government is
evident in these sorts of family and educational connections.

Gladstone himself was crucial to this particular ruling circle, linking
Oxbridge to a new sort of governing class, one that was made up of a now
moralised upper class. As well as sponsoring university reform, Gladstone
commissioned the Northcote–Trevelyan Report. The idea implicit in the
move for civil service reform was that the reform of Oxbridge education,
centred on the study of 'Literae Humaniores' or 'Greats' (involving
political philosophy, ethics and metaphysics), would prepare the new
Guardians for the task of rule. The Guardians of Plato's *Republic* were in
fact a model for these public school men of England, men who, in youth
separated from their parents and raised in Spartan conditions, would aim
to subordinate personal desires to securing the greatest possible happiness
for the community as a whole.[47] Benjamin Jowett, of Balliol College,
Oxford, was a close friend to both Macaulay and Trevelyan, and a notable
Plato scholar, renowned for his decided views on the place of a classical
education in teaching hard work and self-mastery. It is clear that intellectual excellence, above all that gained at Oxford and Cambridge, was *ipso
facto* moral excellence. Those who did best at intellectual work would
prove to be 'superior men'.[48] Sir Stafford Northcote, from Eton, and a
Balliol contemporary of Jowett (both had firsts in 'Greats'), was Gladstone's private secretary at the Board of Trade.

The Report itself, through the means of the examination, aimed at
making promotion dependent on merit alone, so encouraging industry
and fostering a 'service' ethic. Reform also created a clear divide between
'mechanical' and 'intellectual' labour, one fostered by the public moralists' (especially Mill's) sanctification of intellectual labour. Lowe's Civil
Service Order of 1870 introduced the intellectual–mechanical distinction
across the whole service, also the examination, and with the expansion
of the civil service (to a quarter of a million in size by 1911) the organisation of the state was increasingly modelled on the machine, something
evident, for example, in Haldane's *Report on the Machinery of Government*,
of 1918.[49] There is an instructive contrast between the anonymous,

bureaucratic, late nineteenth-century 'mechanical' and the eighteenth-century public service at the lower levels. Then the exciseman was involved in a careful self-fashioning public performance designed to shore up the rationality of the national level of government, in distinction to the local, which was perceived as corrupt and venal.[50] Beyond the 'mechanicals', and this particular 'machining' of agency, Gladstone saw Northcote–Trevelyan as a deliberate attempt to strengthen ties between administrative power and the existing upper classes, whom he understood as at best evincing a 'natural ability' which, irrespective of book learning, amounted to the 'insensible education' of 'gentlemen by birth and breeding'. Essentially, one was born into the upper civil service. The contradiction with the elevation of merit and the advocacy of university training will be evident. This contradiction tells us something about the relationship of old and new kinds of political reason, the old based on patronage and privilege, the new on merit. So too does the apparent contradiction between the light of publicity and the upper civil service code of 'honourable secrecy'. The new was embedded in the old, the real contradictions involved creating difficulties for the new but also novel possibilities. While Gladstone's invention is apparent, the contradiction of merit and secrecy continued to mark the subsequent history of the civil service.[51]

The ingenuity of contemporary solutions to this clash of patronage and merit was none the less considerable. As a technology of publicity, the public examination fabricated an ethical persona for the administrator of government. 'Publicity' worked via openness to secure the victory of merit over patronage. A supposedly neutral persona was created, independent of politics, which would enable not only merit but also accountability to manifest itself. This supposed neutrality was synonymous with liberal toleration, and was an 'ethic of distance', so that ruling at a distance also meant ruling *through* distance in the sense of the ethical disengagement of those who governed. Accountable government was in contemporary discourse about civil service reform also 'economical' government, for only with accountability could the best service be had for the best price. However, replacing nomination with examination in the civil service also introduced profound difficulties. How could relations of trust be built up when face-to-face knowledge and contact were gone, and when what appeared to many as amoral intelligence threatened well-bred toil?

Mill's sanctification of intellectual labour was one answer, the emergence of the compromise of 'honourable secrecy' another. This was the compromise of old and new kinds of governmental reason, one worked out in the conflict between civil service reformers and their opponents.[52] Modernising the existing gentility of the senior civil service brought the agonistic quality of liberal governance into the open, above all the need for this quality to be performed in the light of publicity. The performativity of honourable secrecy, and thus of the contradictions of liberalism, is evident above all in the protean shape of the gentleman. It was through this figure that 'political truth' was performed. By these means, as in the other instances of the performance of political truth so far considered, performance depended upon the mobilisation of many cultural resources. Centred on the gentleman, these resources can be seen to have involved all the sources of social prestige supporting gentility, for example the standing of an increasingly revitalised public school and university system.

Performance also drew on widespread notions of what a 'gentleman' should be, ones evident in the stream of gentleman's etiquette books published at this time. The purpose of the education of the (new) gentleman was seen to be the inculcation of tact and reticence. The paradox of the public performance of reticence represented the paradoxical nature of the new governors, their strengths and weaknesses in the public eye. As Vincent argues, the contradictions of honourable secrecy were in part managed by the public presentation of the secret keeper not as arrogant but as enduring a sort of 'administrative purgatory'. The new 'administrative culture' of the time, in which honourable secrecy was embedded, implied that control over state secrets was a function not of the powers of the state but of a private community that had sacrificed its comforts for the good of the country. One aspect of the public performance of this new civil service code was the role of the politicians themselves: the bureaucrats swapped the right to go public for a silence protected by ministers and politicians, who defended the civil service from parliamentary and press attacks, in the process publicly promulgating the new administrative culture of the time.[53] Of course this invention of the non-bureaucratic bureaucracy also drew on all the considerable historical capital attaching to the idea of a non-political class of public servant, an idea, as has been seen, embedded in eighteenth-century British political history.

This emphasis on 'publicity' has been traced by Keith Baker to some of the roots of modern democracy in the French Revolution.[54] The revolutionary technology of power involved a process of the greatest possible differentiation of those elements which were to be ruled over, elements known as 'individuals'. The sum of these differentiated elements was also to be the legitimation of rule, a sum that took the name of 'the people',

among others. This emphasis on differentiation as individualisation therefore simultaneously involved a process of the universalisation of the
relations between these individuals. There was therefore, first, a process
of differentiation, which involved legal changes, among them the abolition of an existing legal apparatus that distinguished between subjects on
the basis of their status within a corporate social order. But this process
extended far beyond legality itself – what Baker calls a technology of
transparison was also involved, a making transparent.

> To achieve the total individualisation and universalisation of the subject, social
> and political life had to be made entirely transparent. Each had to be opened
> to all. Hence the critical importance in the Revolution of such instruments of
> transparison as the press and the popular societies and clubs. However these
> instruments of transparency continuously produced new obscurities to be
> dispelled – in the same way as the disciplines of penality, in Foucault's analysis,
> continuously produced criminals to reform.[55]

As chapter 5 will indicate in more detail, rather like the effect of gas
lighting itself, the other side of technologies of light, publicity and
transparency was the darkness, closedness and obscurity that summoned
these technologies into being and constantly threatened them. In considering the Revolution, 'public opinion' was none the less intended to be
transparent, universal, objective and rational. In fact it was a social
imaginary with roots before the Revolution, but what was different after
1789 was that this opinion was now to be actively realised in terms of new
sorts of political interventions, interventions which we can call technologies, such as the press.

  In terms of technologies of transparison, the newspaper press in mid-
to late nineteenth-century Victorian Britain was especially important,
particularly the local and provincial newspaper press.[56] This took on
distinct political colorations, Tory on the one side, Liberal on the other,
but was also liberal in a governmental sense in crossing party lines. The
local press was extraordinarily important in reconstituting the town and
the city as a community which both politics *and* governance could work
upon.[57] It articulated the various other communities of liberalism around
itself, especially those of party political Liberalism and Conservatism,[58]
presenting the town as a universe of voluntary and religious associations
in all the range of their many local activities. These it reported on as
elements in the life of a single entity. This entity was, through its
representation in the newspaper, constituted as one and transparent. In
fact, the form and use of the newspaper itself, as well as its representation

of the urban, actively *performed* the transparency that was central to governmental liberalism.

   This was apparent in the material form of the newspaper, the layout of news, for example, and the material act of reading, which, as Benedict Anderson has shown, was essential to the performance of political identity in the nineteenth century.[59] In terms of representation transparency was performed by means of the content of the news: reports, for example, were exhaustive, detailed and relied heavily on supposedly verbatim accounts of what was said, especially accounts of 'eyewitnesses'. The whole *raison d'être* of the liberal newspaper in fact centred upon transparency: only by being truly 'public' and open could it be liberal in the first place. However, while the instruments of politics, like the political party and the local press themselves, can be pursued for their governmental functions as political technologies (the press is pursued in chapter 5), it is the new municipal institutions of the reformed urban, liberal polity that I want to emphasise here, institutions around which new valuations of the local as the focus of liberal community took form. It is to the public library that I shall turn for this municipal dimension, for the library was an institution uniquely concerned with bringing about the conditions of perfect transparency, in this case the transparency of knowledge which was essential to all other transparencies.

   Before this, however, the theme of the local in the creation of liberal community needs some further elaboration. From the early to the late nineteenth century one can discern the movement from what might be called rational to moral models of community. In the case of Manchester, early attempts by propertied reformers to develop educational institutions for the poor were followed by attempts to develop 'visiting' societies, as it became apparent that the former were failing.[60] In the 1820s and 1830s an ultra-rational political economy and Unitarianism, with their asocial and ahistorical models of community, gave way to these new societies, which attempted to reconstitute the social bond at the level of personal contact. The model was very often that of the parish.[61] The concern with the local in these visiting societies is very clear. The influence of Thomas Chalmers was widespread. Chalmers' attempt to moralise political economy around the model of the parish involved encouraging 'emulation' and 'watchfulness'.[62] His influential *Christian and Civic Economy of Large Towns* (1821) dealt directly with what he called 'the influence of locality in towns'. The encouragement of moral visibility by means of the operation of the local was to lead to another sort of visibility, namely the capacity of people to see into each other's hearts. Putting ourselves under the roof of the poor man made the poor man himself for a time superior, in that we are under his protection. This 'proud and peaceful' 'popularity of the heart', got by being with the other, for example with the poor man on his deathbed, opened heart to heart. Chalmers was concerned in this work to educate the philanthropist and the clergyman, so providing a new sort of expertise for those who were now to be 'experts' in the human heart.

This emphasis on the reconstitution of the social bond by means of the local and the personal was even more strongly evident after Chalmers' time, and most often took the same strongly religious form even if the character of this religion was to change. So much is apparent in Birmingham, which from the 1870s developed as the primary focus of new visions of the city as a community. These visions involved an emphatic, and self-consciously provincial, re-Christianisation of the city. The influence of German idealism, of Carlyle and of Ruskin was again much in evidence. But it was here taken up specifically by key Nonconformist clerics like George Dawson and R.W. Dale, whose aim was to avoid religious dogmatism and what was perceived to be the moral impoverishment of the economically minded municipal Rate-Payer Associations.[63] Dale and Dawson, like Chalmers before them, were preaching, and practising, a sort of ethical work upon the self, in this case the selves of those who they hoped would promulgate what became known at the time as the 'civic gospel'.[64] In this view, the state had in fact a Christian character, and, as Dawson put it in 1884, 'Civil authority is a Divine institution'. The service of the great town was considered to be a form of divine service. 'The solemn organism' of the town, as Dawson went on, 'through which flows the truest ends of a man's moral nature', was to be the site of an emphasis upon conduct itself, as opposed simply to faith.[65] This pragmatic Evangelicalism emphasised 'effective moral action'. There was an emphasis not simply on conduct, in the sense of comporting oneself in a respectable and rational manner in the world, but upon conduct as action, on conduct as being seen to be conduct – in short, upon conduct as a public performance of duty, a duty rooted in a conflict of good and evil.

By 1890 the Birmingham view was said to have become something like the national orthodoxy.[66] It was evident in London, in the form of the London County Council. 'New Liberals' took it up, as did many among the intellectuals of the new Labour Party, who were to be found in some number on the London County Council. The influence of the Birmingham reformers on the so-called 'New Liberalism' of the late nineteenth and early twentieth centuries was in fact very considerable. It was also felt in other cities, not least in Manchester, where E.D. Simon's inaugural address as mayor in 1921, 'A Citizen and His City', was directly indebted to the earlier Birmingham example. There were close links between reforming city regimes like that of Simon, and New Liberal and Labour intellectuals. Simon dedicated his works on what was called 'The Science of Public Administration' to Graham Wallas and Beatrice Webb.[67] The religious intensity of Wallas was in turn evident in his introduction to Simon's 1926 account of city government. This was imbued with religious feeling, the work of the city administrator involving what Wallas called 'meaning intensely' and 'meaning good', so that the practice of civic government could bring about what he called 'The City of God'.[68] By this time, however, for all the continuities, the model of liberal community that was most in evidence was less the moral one than what in the next chapter is called the 'social city'. Nine years after Simon's address on the citizen and his city an enormous new public library was opened in the centre of the city, the Manchester Central Reference Library. If this reflected new views of the city as a community, these views, like those of Simon himself, were powerfully shaped by the Victorian years, and it is to these that I now turn.

The light of the library

The Public Record Office was founded in 1838, and still proclaims itself as 'the treasure house of the nation's memory'.[69] The British Museum, with its Reading Room, preceded the Public Record Office in 1753.[70] Although they were theoretically 'public' archives, access to both was in various ways limited. The Public Record Office itself, while allowing free public access in the new Office building of 1851, in fact represented a narrowing in definition of what constituted a 'public record' as time went on: at the start of the century the term applied to legal documents embodying the rights of individuals, and though the 1838 Act referred to this, from the 1840s 'public record' meant in effect state records rather than material which was about and created by the population at large.[71] It was the mid-nineteenth-century public library which more fully consti-tuted a public in this sphere. Although there was much activity before 1850, the Library Act of 1850 instituted this 'democratic' archive. It first took form in the laboratories of British liberal democracy, the great provincial cities, particularly Manchester, where the Manchester munici-pal Free Library was set up in 1850 (Figure 3.1).[72] Edward Edwards, who

Figure 3.1 Manchester Free Library, illustration made 1855 (originally a 'Hall of Science', built 1840, and used by the Free Library from 1852)

was its first librarian, is widely regarded as one of the co-founders of the library movement. (John Stuart Mill was in fact a great influence on Edwards and many in the movement generally.)[73]

The idea of the *free* library was central to the creation of a new sort of public, one constituted in a civic, urban public sphere. Prior to 1850 existing libraries were not funded from the public purse, and had an attachment to different groups, communities and organisations.[74] New meanings of 'public', which were developed through the idea of the free institution, meant not only public funding (however limited at first) but above all the idea of a subject which was not attached to different (private) bodies, or to the market, a domain in which earlier notions of the public were indeed highly developed. The civic public of the library was to be opened to each and everyone, and was to be free to use. Open, and therefore transparent, in membership, transparency was also the key to its particular function as one variant of liberal community. It was a community of knowledge users, transparent to one another, formed around the idea of the openness or transparency of knowledge itself. Indeed, contemporary discourse spoke *ad infinitum* of knowledge as itself light.

Edwards, for example, was consumed by the idea of the open library, concerned to reach out to the people, by means of an accessible cata- logue, and by the use of assistants who would make it their express business to go among and initiate the new library users. W.E.A. Axon, of the Manchester library, and a major publicist for the library movement, in fact spoke of this new reaching out as the creation of a 'public domain', which would include all classes.[75]

The library created the liberal citizen in large measure through the fostering of self-help and self-culture, both of which involved self- knowledge.[76] In fact, this was a constant operation on the self that directly represented the moral self-address that has been seen to be intrinsic to a liberal ethics of governance. The principles in the legislation behind the library involved the use of voluntary action, voluntarism thereby shaping the ethos of the library. (Municipalities would themselves show self-help in setting up the library.) Self-help was not only individual, therefore, but also collective and communal, so that knowing one's society was a pre- requisite for knowing oneself. Knowing one's society, amongst other things, involved knowing the statistics that enabled one to know its true form. Those involved in the library movement were keen compilers of and advocates for statistics. Axon and Edwards were members of the Manchester Statistical Society, and were adept at deploying statistics in furthering the cause of the library. Knowing one's society involved know- ing about what increasingly became understood as its 'social' condition, and its social problems, particularly those to do with capital and labour. It also involved knowledge of its habits and its mores, and this form of the public archive of a liberal society was from the earliest days heavily involved in collecting information about the cultural or ethnographic as well as the social condition of 'the people', as exemplified in its customs, local history and language, particularly dialect.

This information was in turn closely related to the idea that the library should represent the identity of the local community. Given the intimate link between the library and the town, the community that liberalism most shaped itself around in this respect was the urban one. However, while the local was crucial, it was always in relation to the national, just as liberalism was itself about the balance of the local and the national state. The centre was always an important model for the organisation of the public library: the British Museum library was regarded as the ideal type for other libraries, and there was always a good deal of commerce between the centre and the provinces (as in the case of Edwards in fact). The municipal library frequently echoed the British Museum: local collections were balanced by the aspiration to universality, to cover everything, which marked the national collection. This aspiration to a universality of knowledge was of course an age-old one; however, liberalism gave it a new shape in the mid-nineteenth century by relating it to the idea of human progress.[77]

How did the public library itself actually function as a sort of technology translating these governmental aspirations into action? In part, as has been seen, by means of the catalogue. The old catalogues were of use only to those versed in their arcane ways. Whether Panizzi at the British Museum or the municipal librarians, all were concerned to make knowledge open by means of the catalogue. The results of this belief in openness were somewhat different to the aspiration, however: despite the efforts of the early pioneers, it was not until the last two decades of the nineteenth century that books were put on open access for readers with any regularity.[78] Sunday opening, essential for workers, did not occur until 1878 in Manchester, and the great provincial cities were in advance of London in this respect. Constraints of lighting also limited use – the British Museum library seems the first to have been electrically lit, in 1879. Provision was also geographically uneven – Glasgow, for instance, had no free library as late as 1886.[79]

None the less, the passionate advocacy of publicity in the third quarter of the century bore fruit in the final quarter. By the 1890s the Dewey System of decimal library classification had begun to be adopted quite widely. Manchester was in fact the first library of any size in the United Kingdom to use the system, in 1894. The system itself enshrined a certain tradition of universal liberal learning. It was based in its broadest dimensions on Bacon's chart of human learning, and at the middle level on nineteenth-century concepts of how knowledge should be organised.[80] Thus, the catalogue fostered self-help, as did direct access to library materials. William Ewart, the political arm of the library movement, Edwards being its professional one, commented on this public use as creating 'a kind of public police by their presence, which safeguards the collection'. Through the second half of the nineteenth century a system of library use was worked out which differed radically from the one that preceded it.[81] In terms of use the idea of a 'public police' was actively fostered by the design of libraries.

The social psychology of the library owed much to Enlightenment ideas, as these were developed in utilitarianism. This involved the view that the physical environment had a direct impact on perception and behaviour. There was therefore a premium on organising space so as to

Figure 3.2 Interior of Reading Room, Rusholme District Library, Manchester, opened 1892 (photograph taken 1940)

affect behaviour. The 1850 Act in fact provided money for buildings and not for books (the latter were often assembled from earlier collections, or donated by the well-to-do).[82] The internal decoration of the library often figured busts and pictures of the heroes of self-help, among them those of liberal learning and literature, for instance John Milton. This amounted to a commemoration of the glorious tradition of English learning and liberty, and the indissoluble link between the two, in fact to what was a kind of English Enlightenment. The liberty of the press was part of this tradition, a tradition evident in the design of library newsrooms (see Figure 3.2). These newsrooms were an important part of the early libraries, and are still sometimes evident today. They were of palatial design, each newspaper having its own stand, table space or reading slope. Space and light were generously provided, such lit spaces being in effect individuated, in terms of the person who read and the newspaper that was read. The aim was to give maximum expression to each view. In this way, through the spatial production of a 'debate', the truth would emerge and the light of knowledge reveal itself (physical light thereby producing the light of knowledge and truth).[83]

The British Museum Reading Room of 1857 is evidence of a certain panopticism, with its raised central structure housing the staff and the supervisor of the Reading Room (who literally had vision over the whole room). Other libraries followed this ideal type, but more humble ones had a long issue desk at right angles to the book stacks so that vision was possible along them. After 1850 some libraries dispersed their newsstands around the walls of newsrooms, the better to facilitate central viewing. The contrast between the old and the new British Museum reading rooms is interesting.[84] The old reading rooms were located in Montague House, first built in 1674, and then rebuilt, both times in the manner of the aristocratic house. The model for the library itself was therefore the library as found in the aristocratic house. The Museum's collections themselves were assembled from the great collections of the wealthy, particularly royalty, and the aristocracy. In these rooms readers sat face-to-face with one another across reading tables. After the building of the British Museum itself, the reading rooms within the new structure for a time echoed the old, but the really significant departure was the magnificent, domed Reading Room opened in 1857 (Figure 3.3). This was designed by the man who was the Principal Librarian of the Museum, Antonio Panizzi, and it is striking how this custodian of the book took a direct role in the design of the new Reading Room.[85] The contrast between the new 'democratic'structure and the 'aristocratic' library was marked (even though there were many precedents for domed libraries); the great new, domed Central Library of Manchester of 1935 followed the 'democratic' British Museum example.

In the new Reading Room readers sat separated from one another and not face-to-face, with other readers to their sides. The library was designed therefore to facilitate privacy, as well as surveillance. But this surveillance was of a new kind, a self-surveillance that was also collective, one that constituted a community of the self-watching. The creation of the liberal subject in its new and increasingly democratic forms involved the many viewing the many, rather than the one viewing the many. The panopticon gave way to the oligopticon of the Reading Room. (The less bounded spaces of the omniopticon, in the form of the street, will be considered in chapter 5.) The (relative) few of the British Museum would view the few. There was also considerable attachment to the idea of all the books in a

Figure 3.3　Interior view of the new Reading Room, British Museum (date of illustration 1870?)

library being on open display, even though they were not available to public access until later in the century.[86] Eventually, of course, many books were put in store out of the public gaze. However, as in the British Museum library, there were numerous instances of books continuing to be put on display. This involved the books themselves returning the gaze of the reader in all the majesty and colour of their massed ranks. The book was therefore a form of ornament, but one with a didactic purpose, impressing the reader with the power of learning, and indeed acting as an eye which overlooked the reader, the reader's own eye returned to him or her in the form of the majesty of learning's light.

Provision such as that made by Panizzi at the British Museum fostered privacy, but of course the act of reading had for long been one conducted in silence and privacy, at least in libraries. As Corbin has shown, reading was part of the long history of the individuation of the self.[87] This was especially so as regards reading in silence, which was one of the arts of the library that had to be mastered by a number of its users in the early days, especially its poor and uneducated ones. Lest the democratic art of silent reading be taken for granted, it should be emphasised that silent reading in the elementary school room was frowned upon as late as the 1870s. The library was to encourage it, and with it the governance of *attention*: as the magisterial work of Jonathan Crary shows, from the 1880s across Europe new ideas of what perception was put a premium on the training of attention. Aspects of this will be taken up later in chapter 6.[88] The individuation of the user proceeded also by means of personal responsibility for the borrowing of books, the observance of rules, the paying of fines and the use of gates to ensure individual access to libraries. However, all this has to be set beside the users seeing themselves as a collective, as in the British Museum Reading Room, where the radial formation of the seating, while involving privacy, meant also the chance to view the giant structure of knowledge as a whole when using the room, and to walk around its vast, galleried spaces viewing this community of users going about its business in silence, order and diligence. The reader viewed and was viewed, and the self was re-created in terms of the social transparency of this great library's everyday commerce.

The local dimensions of liberal community were most apparent in the municipal library. This was to be a library in the centre of the town. Hence the use, to this day, of the term 'Central Library'. This central library was the showplace of the other libraries of the town or city. In terms of library design it was felt that such libraries should be placed so as to be accessible to all in the town. They were to be separate and specially designed buildings, which were sometimes called 'landmark' buildings.[89] These were shaped by the interests of civic leaders, rather than the active proponents of the library, and were designed to exemplify civic identity and proper civic behaviour. In terms of their archival character, the local was exemplified in their collections, which were heavily marked by interest in the history, culture, institutions and current concerns of the cities and regions in which they were situated. Axon, for example, wrote about city history, compiled an annals of Manchester, produced commercial guides to the city, and wrote extensively about the great symbols of civic identity in the city, such as the town hall of 1877.[90] Figures like Edwards and Axon were also inspired by a kind of demotic antiquarianism, which drew upon the late eighteenth-century discovery of 'folk' traditions and 'popular' culture, a discovery which fed directly into the collections.[91] There was a kind of anthropologising of the archive, a deployment of the local which was central to the creation of a *national* liberal community which would embrace the working classes. (The anthropologising of the colonial archive is something I shall consider in the concluding chapter.)

This concern to embrace the worker was all the more the case in that men like Axon and Edwards were members of these 'working classes'

themselves. They were aided by figures like Panizzi and Andrea Crestadaro, who was the third Principal Librarian at Manchester.[92] Both Panizzi
and Crestadaro were ultra-liberals, cast in the mould of early nineteenth-
century romantic nationalism, with its own idealisations of the people.
(They were *émigrés* from continental Europe, Panizzi having had to flee
for his life after being sentenced to death for his activities in the
movement to liberate Italy.) What such men helped put together, and this
is particularly clear in the case of Axon in Manchester, are collections
which gave 'popular' culture, and therefore the working classes, a tradition, one which reached back into the past of the nation, but the past
of the nation conceived in terms of the specific identities of a local and
regional culture. This conjoined local, regional and national culture was
elaborated alongside conceptions of the nation's political development
towards the traditions of a liberal parliamentary system. Liberal institutions were part of British culture too, a culture that in fact preordained
liberalism. And, just as the nation's political development was seen in
Whig fashion as the result of natural and evolutionary developments, so
too was the culture of the people seen as the outcome of progressive and
evolutionary patterns of change which led from lower to higher states of
civilisation, the lowest state of course being evident in examples such as
the Indian colonial subject.[93]

The growing collections of Manchester Free Library were described by
Axon in 1877.[94] They illustrated the advance of the 'working class',
indicating in the process the history of manufactures, the development of
the factory system and the arrival in history of a 'working class' organised
around the gospel and the institutions of self-help. Axon conceived this
new library as 'modern', by virtue of this sort of interest, unlike the
traditional library. This historical arrival was also represented in the strong
history and literature collections in the library, in the sense of an *English*
national historical and literary tradition. History itself was presented in
the teleological form of the progress narrative, and was explicitly linked
to the formation of a mode of judgement which concerned the freely
acting individual, whose freedom could only be secured when knowledge,
and the information upon which knowledge was based, could attain the
maximum degree of transparency. The library was one spatial framing of
this understanding of history, an understanding in fact central to the
creation of liberal governmentality. This framing of history involved the
constitution of community at the national and especially at the local level,
as has been seen.

The visual representation of community in time, in history, took many

Figure 3.4 Didsbury Library, south Manchester, opened 1915 (photograph taken 1929)

forms, most notably perhaps in the nineteenth century the gothic. I will conclude this chapter with a photograph (Figure 3.4), pointing forward as this does to the extended treatment of gothic that follows in the next chapter. As will be seen, the gothic exemplified the local within the national, but also what might be called the local within the local, for after the opening of the central libraries of the time, branch and sub-libraries opened too, each held to represent the spirit of communities *within* the city. In its very late version of Victorian gothic, Didsbury Library, in south Manchester, represented its community, as indeed did the Rusholme branch library pictured earlier. It is therefore to the governance of time as well as of space that I shall now attend.

Notes

1. Henry Parris, *Constitutional Bureaucracy: The Development of British Central Administration since the Eighteenth Century* (London: Allen and Unwin, 1969), pp. 27–8.

2. Ibid., chapter 2; see also Norman Chester, *The English Administrative System* (Oxford: Oxford University Press, 1981); R.A. Chapman, *The Higher Civil Service in Britain* (London: Constable, 1970); J.E. Pellew, *The Home Office 1848–1914: From Clerks to Bureaucrats* (London: Heinemann, 1982).

3. Henry Parris, *Constitutional Bureaucracy*, p. 22.

4. Ibid., pp. 22–7.

5. Pat Thane, 'Government and Society in England and Wales, 1750–1914', in F.M.L. Thompson (ed.), *The Cambridge Social History of Britain 1750–1950*, volume 3 (Cambridge: Cambridge University Press, 1990), pp. 12–13.

6. John Brewer, *The Sinews of Power: War, Money and the English State 1688–1783* (London: Unwin Hyman, 1989).

7. Ibid., pp. 14–21.

8. David Eastwood, *Government and the Community in the English Provinces 1700–1870* (Basingstoke: Macmillan, 1997), pp. 9–10, chapter 2; Quentin Skinner, *Liberty before Liberalism* (Cambridge: Cambridge University Press, 1998). For a long-term view of the history of British state administration see José Harris, 'Society and State in Twentieth-Century Britain', in F.M.L. Thompson (ed.), *The Cambridge Social History of Britain*, volume 3.

9. E.P. Thompson, *The Making of the English Working Class* (London: Penguin, 1968), and 'Eighteenth-Century English Society: Class Struggle without Class?', *Social History*, 3:2, 1978.

10. See Lynda Nead, *Modern Babylon: People, Streets and Images in Nineteenth-Century London* (London: Yale University Press, 2000), pp. 17–20.

11. Arthur Redford, *The History of Local Government in Manchester*, 3 volumes (Manchester: Manchester University Press, 1939–40); Shena D. Simon, *A Century of City Government: Manchester 1838–1938* (London: Allen and Unwin, 1938), chapter 2.

12. Joanna Innes and Nicholas Rogers, 'Politics and Government, 1700–1840', in Peter Clark (ed.), *The Cambridge Urban History of Britain, Volume 2, 1540–1840* (Cambridge: Cambridge University Press, 2000).

13. Arthur Redford, *The History of Local Government*, volume 1, chapters liv–ix; see also volume 2, chapters xxi–xxix.

14. First Report of the Commissioners Appointed to Enquire into the Municipal Corporations of England and Wales, *Parliamentary Papers* 1835 (116), xxiii.i.

15. James Vernon, *Politics and the People: A Study in English Political Culture, c.1815–1867* (Cambridge: Cambridge University Press, 1993), chapter 1; see also B. Keith Lucas, *English Local Government Franchise* (Oxford: Oxford University Press, 1952).

16. This simplification of the political system did not, however, mean that government functions were no longer still fragmented between many different sorts of institution. See K. Theodore Hoppen, *The Mid-Victorian Generation 1846–1886: The New*

Oxford History of England (Oxford: Oxford University Press, 1998), chapter 4, 'The Nature of the State', especially section 2, 'Centre and Localities'.

17. First Report of the Commissioners . . . into . . . Municipal Corporations, pp. 32–5, 'Corporate Body'; see also Josef Redlich, *Local Government in England*, 2 volumes (London 1903), volume 1, part 2, chapter ii.

18. Richard Cobden, *Incorporate Your Borough* (Manchester, 1837).

19. Christopher Otter, 'Making Liberalism Durable: Vision and Civility in the Victorian City 1870–1900', *Social History*, 27:1, 2002, and on Manchester lighting see also John E. Wilson, *Lighting the Town: A Study of Management in the North West Gas Industry* (London: Paul Chapman, 1991), chapter 1. See also Christopher Otter, 'The Government of the Eye: Light Technology and Liberalism in the Victorian City 1870–1900' (University of Manchester PhD, 2002).

20. On continental Europe, see Wolfgang Schivelbusch, *Disenchanted Night: The Industrialisation of Light in the Nineteenth Century* (Leamington Spa: Berg, 1988).

21. On police procedures and beats, see Francis Dodsworth, 'The Institution of Police in Britain, c. 1750–1856: A Study in Historical Governmentality' (University of Manchester PhD, 2002).

22. On police history, see David Jones, *Crime, Protest, Community and Police in Nineteenth-Century Britain* (London: Routledge and Kegan Paul, 1982); David D. Howell and Kenneth O. Morgan (eds), *Crime, Protest and Police in Modern British Society: Essays in Honour of David J.V. Jones* (Cardiff: University of Wales Press, 1999); Eric J. Hewitt, *A History of Policing in Manchester* (Manchester: Morten, 1979).

23. Robert D. Storch, 'The Policeman as Domestic Missionary: Urban Discipline and Popular Culture in Northern England 1850–1880', in R.J. Morris and Richard Rodgers (eds), *The Victorian City: A Reader in British Urban History 1820–1914* (London: Longman, 1993).

24. Arthur Redford, *The History of Local Government*, volume 1, chapter iv and see part II *passim*; also volume 3, chapter xxx. See also Eric J. Hewitt, *Policing in Manchester*.

25. For Mayne, see Stefan Petrow, *Policing Morals: The Metropolitan Police and the Home Office 1870–1914* (Oxford: Oxford University Press, 1994), pp. 41, 55–6, 71, 279–80.

26. Derek Fraser, *Power and Authority in the Victorian City* (Oxford: Oxford University Press, 1979), and *Urban Politics in Victorian England: The Structure of Politics in Victorian Cities* (Leicester: Leicester University Press, 1976). K. Theodore Hoppen, *The Mid-Victorian Generation 1846–1886*, chapter 4. See also Derek Fraser, *Municipal Reform in the Industrial City* (Leicester: Leicester University Press, 1982), and E.P. Hennock, *Fit and Proper Persons: Ideal and Reality in Nineteenth-Century Urban Government* (London: Edward Arnold, 1973).

27. David Eastwood, '"Amplifying the Province of the Legislature": The Flow of Information and the English State in the Early Nineteenth Century', *Historical Research*, 62, 1989, and his *Government and Community in the English Provinces, 1700–1870* (Basingstoke: Macmillan, 1997), for this account.

28. For liberal governmentality as economical government and as the governance of the economy, see Peter Miller and Nikolas Rose, 'Governing Economic Life', and Dennis Meurat, 'A Political Genealogy of Political Economy', in Mike Gane and Terry Johnson (eds), *Foucault's New Domains* (London: Routledge, 1993).

29. Josef Redlich, *Local Government in England,* edited with additions by Francis W. Hirst (London, 1903), book 1, part 2, chapter iv, pp. 185, also 178, 184; and see also Stefan Collini, *Public Moralists: Political Thought and Intellectual Life in Britain 1850–1930* (Cambridge: Cambridge University Press, 1991), chapter 4.

30. E.F. Biagini, *Liberty, Retrenchment and Reform: Popular Liberalism in the Age of Gladstone 1860–1880* (Cambridge: Cambridge University Press, 1992), p. 166. See also his 'Liberalism and Direct Democracy: J.S. Mill and the Model of Ancient Athens', in E.F. Biagini (ed.), *Citizenship and Community: Liberals, Radicals and Collective Identities in the British Isles 1865–1931* (Cambridge: Cambridge University Press, 1996).

31. On the Social Science Association, see Lawrence Goldman, 'A Peculiarity of the English? The Social Science Association and the Absence of Sociology in Nineteenth-Century Britain', *Past and Present,* 114, 1987, and see chapter 1, note 28: also Patrick Carroll-Burke, 'Moralising Economics, Making the Social Scientific: From Political to Social Economy in the Early NAPSS', *Social History,* forthcoming.

32. J.S. Mill, *Considerations on Representative Government* (1st edition, 1861), volume xix of J.M. Robson (ed.), *Collected Works of J.S. Mill* (Toronto: University of Toronto Press, 1977), chapter xv. See also Josef Redlich, *Local Government in England,* book 1, part 2, chapter iv, pp. 178–83. On 'the discovery of the state', see Mark Francis and John Morrow, *A History of English Political Thought in the Nineteenth Century* (London: Duckworth, 1994), chapter 11, especially pp. 245–6.

33. J.S. Mill, *Considerations on Representative Government,* chapter xv, esp. pp. 544, 545.

34. W.E.A. Axon, *Cobden as Citizen: A Chapter in Manchester History* (Manchester, 1907), pp. 35–6.

35. Stefan Collini, *Public Moralists,* chapters 2–3; and 'The Idea of 'Character' in Victorian Political Thought', *Transactions of the Royal Historical Society,* 5th series, 35, 1985.

36. Patrick Joyce, *Democratic Subjects: The Self and the Social in Nineteenth Century England* (Cambridge: Cambridge University Press, 1994), p. 216. See also Boyd Hilton, *The Age of Atonement: The Influence of Evangelicalism on Social and Economic Thought 1795–1865* (Oxford: Oxford University Press, 1988).

37. Maria Valverde, ' "Slavery from Within": The Invention of Alcoholism and the Question of Free Will', *Social History,* 22:3, 1997, and *Diseases of the Will: Alcoholism and the Dilemmas of Freedom* (Cambridge: Cambridge University Press, 1998).

38. Patrick Joyce, *Democratic Subjects,* p. 223.

39. John Stuart Mill, *On Liberty* (1859), edited by Stefan Collini (Cambridge: Cambridge University Press, 1989).

40. Ibid., pp. 13–16, 158–9, 62–4, 70: and for these ideas on custom and progress in the context of Manchester upper-class society in earlier times see Patrick Joyce, *Democratic Subjects,* pp. 168–9. See also Maria Valverde, ' "Despotism" and Ethical Liberal Governance', *Economy and Society,* 25:3, 1996, on Mill.

41. On the language of character for this paragraph, see Stefan Collini *Public Moralists,* chapter 3.

42. See the discussion of Mill in Josef Redlich, *Local Government in England,* volume 1, part 2, chapter iv.

43. E.F. Biagini, *Liberty, Retrenchment and Reform*, chapter 6.

44. Patrick Joyce, *Democratic Subjects*, part 3, 'Democratic Romances: Narrative as Collective Identity in Nineteenth Century England', especially chapters 14–17; also *Visions of the People: Industrial England and the Question of Class 1840–1914* (Cambridge: Cambridge University Press, 1991), chapter 14.

45. Thomas Osborne, 'Bureaucracy as a Vocation: Governmentality and Administration in Nineteenth Century Britain', *Journal of Historical Sociology*, 7:3, 1994.

46. Richard Chapman, *The Higher Civil Service in Britain* (London: Constable, 1970), chapter 2.

47. Ibid., esp. p. 28.

48. Ibid., pp. 27–8.

49. John Agar, *The Government Machine* (London: MIT Press, forthcoming).

50. Miles Ogborn, *Spaces of Modernity: London's Geographies 1680–1780* (London: Guilford Press, 1998), p. 191.

51. David Vincent, *The Culture of Secrecy: Britain 1832–1998* (Oxford: Oxford University Press, 1998), pp. 50–65, and chapter 3, for continuing tensions and contradictions between secrecy and merit after the mid-nineteenth century.

52. Ibid., pp. 41–4, 46.

53. Ibid., pp. 44–5, 47–50.

54. Keith Michael Baker, 'A Foucauldian French Revolution?', in Jan Goldstein (ed.), *Foucault and the Writing of History* (Chicago: University of Chicago Press, 1994).

55. Ibid., p. 191.

56. Aled Jones, *Powers of the Press: Newspapers, Power and the Public in Nineteenth-Century England* (Aldershot: Scolar Press, 1996).

57. Patrick Joyce, *Visions of the People*, pp. 41–4.

58. E.F. Biagini, *Liberty, Retrenchment and Reform*, chapter 6.

59. H.C.G. Matthew, 'Rhetoric and Politics in Great Britain 1860s-1950s', in P.J. Waller (ed.), *Politics and Social Change: Essays Presented to A.F. Thompson* (Brighton: Harvester, 1987); Benedict Anderson, *Imagined Communities: Reflections on the Origins and Spread of Nationalism* (London: Verso, 1991). For a study of the role of the newspaper press in the constitution of the 'Irish problem', something that hinged upon the newspapers' creation of their own authority by diverse means, representational and material, see Mindy Silverboard, 'Ireland, the Newspaper Press and Liberal Governmentality: The Formulation of Expertise on the "Irish Question", 1880–1889' (University of Manchester PhD, in progress).

60. John Seed, 'Unitarianism, Political Economy and the Antinomies of Liberal Culture in Manchester 1830–1850', *Social History*, 7:1, 1982.

61. Mary Poovey, *Making a Social Body: British Cultural Formation 1830–1860* (Chicago: University of Chicago Press, 1995), pp. 98–106.

62. Thomas Chalmers, *The Christian and Civic Economy of Large Towns*, 3 volumes (London, 1821–6), volume 1 (1821); chapters 1 and 2 are especially revealing.

63. E.P. Hennock, *Fit and Proper Persons*, book 1, chapter 6 on Dale and Birmingham.

64. For information on Dale, Dawson and Birmingham, see ibid., part II, 'The Municipal Gospel'. See also Alex Ireland, *Recollections of George Dawson and His Two Lectures in Manchester in 1846–7* (Manchester, 1882).

65. Dawson quoted in E.P. Hennock, *Fit and Proper Persons*, p. 75, and R.W. Dale, *The Laws of Christ for Common Life* (London, 1884).

66. E.P. Hennock, *Fit and Persons*, pp. 173–6.

67. Shena D. Simon, *A Century of City Government*. See also Matthew Anderson (ed.), *How Manchester Is Managed: A Record of Municipal Activity* (Manchester, 1925).

68. E.D. Simon, *A City Council from Within* (London, 1926), p. xiii.

69. Public Record Office website, May 1998. See also Jane Cox (ed.), *The Nation's Memory: A Pictorial Guide to the Public Record Office* (London: HMSO, 1998).

70. Arundell Esdaile, *The British Museum Library: A Short History and Survey* (London, 1946); F.R. Harris, *The Reading Room* (London: British Museum, 1979).

71. David Vincent, *The Culture of Secrecy*, p. 41.

72. Alistair Black, *A New History of the English Public Library: Social and Intellectual Contexts, 1850–1914* (Leicester: Leicester University Press, 1996), chapter 4.

73. Ibid., pp. 50–8.

74. For an account of earlier library provision, see W.E.A. Axon, *Handbook of the Public Libraries of Manchester and Salford* (Manchester, 1877).

75. On Axon see *Manchester Faces and Places*, volume 3 (Manchester 1891–2), pp. 109–11.

76. Alistair Black, *A New History*, pp. 236–8 especially, but *passim.*

77. Thomas Richards, *The Imperial Archive: Knowledge and the Fantasy of Empire* (London: Verso, 1993).

78. Alistair Black, *A New History*, p. 247.

79. W.E.A. Axon, 'Sunday Opening of Libraries', *British Architect*, 19, July 1880. See also *British Architect*, 24, July 1885, pp. 52, and 25, 1886, p. 567.

80. *Encyclopaedia of Library Information and Science*, volume 7 (New York, 1972).

81. Richard Sims, *Handbook to the Library of the British Museum* (London, 1854), p. 8, for the rather less inclusive admission procedures of the national library.

82. Alistair Black, *A New History*, pp. 232–3.

83. Ibid., pp. 239–40, 245; W.E.A. Axon, *The Ideal Library* (London, 1911); Edward Edwards, *Free Town Libraries: Their Formation, Management and History* (London, 1865).

84. Arundell Esdaile, *The British Museum Library*, part 1; and Edward Edwards, *Lives of the Founders of the British Museum* (London, 1870), third part, chapters II–III.

85. Philip John Wemerskirch, *Antonio Panizzi and the British Museum Library* (London, 1981).

86. Alistair Black, *A New History*, chapter 2.

87. Alain Corbin, 'Backstage', in Michelle Perrot (ed.), *A History of Private Life*, volume IV (London: Harvard University Press, 1990).

88. Jonathan Crary, *Suspensions of Perception* (London: MIT Press, 1999). On public schooling, see F.H. Page, *An Inspector's Testament* (London, 1938), p. 51; also David Vincent, *Literacy and Popular Culture England, 1750–1914* (Cambridge: Cambridge University Press, 1989), pp. 79–91.

89. Alistair Black, *A New History*, pp. 238–9.

90. W.E.A. Axon, *An Architectural and General Description of the Town Hall Manchester* (Manchester, 1878). See also his *How to Succeed in the World: A Manual for Young*

Men (Manchester, 1883) and 'Testimonials for Axon' in Manchester Central Reference Library. The best way to approach Axon is through the catalogue of the Reference Library.

91. Patrick Joyce, *Visions of the People*, chapters 7–8.

92. N.K. Firby, 'Andrea Crestadoro', *Manchester Review*, 12–13, 1973–4.

93. H. Arslef, *The Study of Language in England* (London: Princeton University Press, 1967). For further details on the library and liberal governmentality, see Patrick Joyce, 'The Politics of the Liberal Archive', *The History of the Human Sciences*, 12:2, 1999.

94. W.E.A. Axon, *Handbook of the Public Library* (Manchester, 1877), esp. chapters XVII and XVI.

4

City Past and City Present

Building the Liberal City

Just as those who sought to govern cities imagined and operated upon them in practical and technical ways, so too did they in aesthetic ones. Indeed, given the scruples about direct political intervention that appear to have marked liberalism, the aesthetic took on a particular significance as a mode of indirect governance, and functioned in an analogous manner to engineering or sanitary solutions by presenting intervention as no intervention at all. Architects and artists were therefore as much involved as sanitarians and engineers. So much is evident in the transitions considered in this chapter, especially that from the 'sanitary city' to what I call the 'moral city', but also to the 'social city'. The ''sanitary city' has been described as a 'diagram' of government, a particular 'problematisation' of the city designed to make governance operable,[1] and these other characterisations of the city can be seen in a similar light. As has been suggested, in the nineteenth century the city became no longer a metaphor for government, as had earlier been the case, but a place where the problems and solutions of government were understood to be immanent to the city itself. The city had to be governed according to this immanence. Decisively from the early nineteenth century, the government of the city seems to have become inseparable from the continued activity of producing truths about the city, truths tied to novel practices of a distinctively spatial character.[2] However, this immanence and these truths were also historical and temporal, as well as spatial, though the existing literature has treated the city almost exclusively in a spatial sense.

The sanitary city involved a social imaginary of the city as a place of flows and movement, and as a site of free circulation. However, as chapter 2 suggested, the engineering and public health solutions arrived at for the problems of the sanitary city were often driven by powerful feelings of moral concern, and sometimes moral revulsion. The city was therefore also imagined, or diagrammed, as a moral space, one that, for example in the reform of markets, excited the most profound fears about the forms of social life emerging in the city. Sanitary reform, in the shape of the reform of the blood and water of the city, was therefore also a kind of moral reform. Yet the sanitary (technical and practical) answer was only one possible response, and in the built forms of the mid- and late nineteenth-century city one may see a most determined form of moral address to the city's inhabitants. The moral question could not be answered completely, could not be completely hidden underground, in drains and water pipes, successful as this way of governing was. Moral concern and revulsion were too strong. In the built forms of what I call the moral city, one may see the aesthetic and material implementation of the notions of governmental liberal community considered in the previous chapter.

The moral shape of the built forms of nineteenth-century cities seems to have been pre-eminently historical, or, more precisely, 'historicist'. The present here can be understood as that of the person and the nation, but also that of the city. As the historian of architectural theory Mitchell Schwarzer puts it in describing the German-speaking world, there developed in the early nineteenth century the idea that every historical phenomenon had an individuality and particularity in which the underlying moral and historical forces that governed the world could be found.[3] In thinking about and building cities, attempts to understand and harness these forces became a question of identifying the historical forms and styles which best expressed the character of the urban, but also the national character, which in this historical understanding of the world was so closely linked to understandings of the city. Something of this siting of the city within narratives of progress rooted in the nation-state will be evident from the preceding discussion of the public library. Realising urban character, however, was not a backward-looking activity but was actively modern: the historicism of the nineteenth century was not a retreat from the present, therefore, but a constant effort to express the new 'modernity' or '*Neuzeit*'. The historical was a way of being modern.

Essentially, in historicism the alterity of the past was domesticated by making it into a witness of the present.

Contemporary notions of history, reflected in historical writing at the time as well, embraced both the notion of anachronism, that the past was different from the present, and the notion that the past and present were formed out of a uniform temporality. Time was conceived as linear, uniform and absolute, in parallel with what was earlier called 'absolute space'. Enabling a separation from the past in one sense, linear time also connected one to this past, particularly through the means of the notion of the historical 'period', conceived of as a waystation on the path of progress that was historical time. Only because it was linear and uniform could time be chopped up into periods like this. It is striking that in England it was in the first half of the nineteenth century that architectural history developed strongly, and with it the appearance of the periodisation of styles, in particular English styles. Periodisation was central to what can in fact be understood as a naturalisation or objectivisation of time as history, just as we can talk about the naturalisation of space in the governance of the city around the same time. Thomas Rickman's *An Attempt to Discriminate the Styles of English Architecture, from the Conquest to the Reformation* (1812) and Edmund Sharp's *The Seven Periods of Church Architecture* (1851) categorised medieval architecture in particular, and were influential on the great advocates of the gothic and the medieval in urban architecture, Pugin and Ruskin.

Evidence for this historicism is apparent in the phenomenon of so much urban architecture, at least city centre architecture, being monumental, in the sense of the monument as something enduring that serves to commemorate, or to preserve in memory. But this commemoration, this preservation, does not seem to have been an easy matter. If the immanence of the city was now historical, it was none the less difficult to realise. The emergence of historicism in architecture, and the decline of the verities of the classical architectural inheritance, represented a movement from architecture as essence or ontology to architecture as epistemology, a transition from unchanging moral precepts to changing human events in which moral precepts had now to be located. Because the identity of the nation and the city were now understood to be rooted in change, the emphasis became one of becoming, not being, of an historical will to know in which the question became now one about what built forms actually meant for social relations, in a deliberate and continuous search for meaning.[4] This search for meaning is related to certain other characteristics of liberal monumentality, namely a quality of self-projection or self-representation in architectural historicism, a struggle to express inner meaning, a meaning that was understood to be immanent to built form and to building materials themselves, and to be realised through these. This quality of meaning can be contrasted with architecture as utilitarian. In fact utility and self-projection were at the time seen as complementary, and it was only modernism's subsequent construction of historicism which denied this utilitarianism.[5] Beside the will to know, there was, so to speak, a will, indeed a struggle, to represent. Because situated in change, the identities the built forms of the city attempted to represent were therefore something not easy to realise; hence the constant 'battle of the styles' that characterised so much of nineteenth-century architectural historicism. This struggle to represent can be related to the agonistic strain in liberal governmentality described earlier, itself something concerned with expressing, or performing, an authentic and inner moral identity in public.

As will be seen, mid- to late nineteenth-century city centres became empty or neutral spatial zones, places of free and, as it seemed to contemporaries, amoral circulation. The problem therefore became one of how to fill this empty space with time, a time which was a moral antidote to the shortcomings of free circulation. The role of civic authorities everywhere in this historical redesigning of urban space is apparent, the governance of the overground, as it were, alongside that of the underground (in sewers, pipes and wires). These new city designs were insistently moral, in Britain, particularly provincial Britain, perhaps more so than elsewhere. For example, many commercial premises had a decidedly didactic quality, as of course did religious architecture, so that this moralism was pervasive, especially in city centres. Of course there were many other built forms, pubs and music halls among them, which worked towards rather different ends. However, the very clash of these decidedly different institutions gave city centres a certain quality of a moral drama or moral struggle which seems also to have been conducive to social imaginaries of the moral city as the site of agonistic self-governance. As will be apparent, an important aspect of liberal political reason can be discerned in the attempt to marry authority and freedom, order and liberty, in this urban theatre of moral, self-regulating community.

The light of publicity, considered in chapter 3, represented a 'democratisation of the eye of power', in that what was once the one viewing the many now became the many viewing themselves, the panopticon giving way to what I have called the oligopticon, eventually the demotic omniopticon. The city became a place where one watched and was watched: in the public park, in the municipal museum,[6] in the public squares of the city, people were led to present themselves in ways that would be 'publicly' acceptable, and in presenting themselves to others, these others, in a reciprocal 'calculated administration of shame',[7] presented themselves in turn to them as but themselves magnified. Visuality was indeed essential to these strategies: as Simmel perceived, in the great cities of the nineteenth century there was a new premium on vision. In the greater anonymity and the 'objective culture' of the modern city the other senses gave way to sight as a means of knowing the world.[8] If many nineteenth-century city centres took on the quality of theatre,[9] the people and the city themselves became like actors on these stages. In pursuing these and related ideas, I shall turn first to Vienna and the Ringstrasse, where a distinctively liberal political regime, in the orthodox political sense, enthusiastically put history into political practice in the mid-nineteenth century, though the fact that it operated with earlier projections of the Ringstrasse emerging out of neo-absolutism indicates again the often tenuous link between governance and particular sorts of political regime.[10] After this consideration of the moral city, I shall in the second section of the chapter consider its eventual eclipse and replacement by what I call the social city.

The design of the moral city

This is how Carl Schorske described what can be called the politics of visuality evident in the Ringstrasse:

> Although the scale and grandeur of the Ring suggest the persistent power of the Baroque, the spatial conception which inspired its design was original and new. Baroque planners had organised space to carry the viewer to a central focus: space served as a magnifying setting to the buildings which encompassed or dominated it. The Ringstrasse designers virtually inverted Baroque procedure using the buildings to magnify the horizontal space. They revised all the elements in relation to a central broad avenue or corso, without architectonic containment and without visible destination. The street, polyhedral in shape, is literally the only element in the vast complex that leads an independent life unsubordinated to any other spatial entity. Where a Baroque planner would have sought to join suburb and city – to organise vast vistas oriented towards the central, monumental features – the plan adopted in 1859, with few exceptions, suppressed the vistas in favour of stress on the circular flow.[11]

Figure 4.1 The Ringstrasse, Vienna, photograph taken 1888

The Paris of Haussmann's massive redevelopment, contemporary with that of Vienna, is rightly seen as the epitome of the city of free circulation, but there is no better exemplification of the operation of the priority of free movement than the Ringstrasse itself. Nor is there any better example of the tensions which existed within the city of circulation. We can think of all these in terms of the tension between the horizontal and the vertical planes, the Ringstrasse itself revealing 'the enormous linear power generated by the street' (Figure 4.1). In the vertical plane, the great civic and state buildings of the city are 'subordinated to the flat, horizontal movement of the street'.

> The several functions represented in the buildings . . . are expressed in spatial organisation as equivalents. Alternate centres of visual interest, they are related to each other not in any direct way but only in their lonely confrontation of the great circular artery, which carries the citizen from one building to another, as from one aspect of life to another. The public buildings float in a spatial medium whose only stabilising element is an artery of men in motion.[12]

In Schorske's account these buildings expressed the desire to civilise and moralise circulation, while at the same time struggling greatly to achieve these ends. The great architects of the post-Ringstrasse period, Camillo Sitte and Otto Wagner,

> the romantic archaicist and the rational functionalist, divided between them the unreconciled components of the historicist Ringstrasse legacy. Sitte, out of the artisan tradition, embraced Ringstrasse historicism to further his project of restoring a communitarian city, with his enclosed square as a model for the future. Wagner, out of a bourgeois affirmation of modern technology, embraced as essence what Sitte most abhorred in the Ringstrasse: the primary dynamic of the street.[13]

There was, therefore, a tension in nineteenth-century urban historicism between space and time, just as between the vertical and the horizontal, a tension which in the following account is viewed in terms of circulation as space (and the horizontal) and history as time (and the vertical). However, though both Sitte and Wagner expressed the tension of 'historistic beauty and modern utility, they retained fidelity to one of the cardinal values of liberal bourgeois city builders: monumentality'.[14] Both were in the business of constituting the city as a liberal monument, and while both were greatly significant in developing what I later call the social city out of the tensions of the moral city, it is the continuity of these two city types which is also apparent.

In order to explore some of these tensions and continuities I shall turn a little later to another great liberal city, Manchester, for here was played out a particularly striking movement from the institution of circulation to its ordering; striking because, in Manchester, the commercial centre of the world's first 'factory system', it was a horror of circulation that was of particular importance, a horror bred by the recognition of the city as the epicentre of a new system of unbridled competition. The need to moralise circulation was particularly acute in this city. At the same time, over the longer span, from the eighteenth to the nineteenth century, it is possible to chart another transition, which can be understood as that from what I would call the 'display city' to the 'moral city'. One of the most persuasive accounts of the emergence of a public of private persons in the early nineteenth-century city, namely that of Richard Sennett, has spoken of how eighteenth-century notions of the public, and of character, were linked not to individual moral character (what Sennett calls 'personality') but to universal notions of human nature and 'natural man'.

For instance, in the eighteenth-century public of the fashionable spa and leisure town of Bath, it did not matter what kind of person one was inside (there was no inside), so long as one subscribed to the formal codes of polite society, governed by notions such as those of 'natural' or 'social' man. One was what one appeared. Display was everything. Sennett describes in great detail how 'personality' came to the fore, and with it a subject who was guarded, anxious, self-monitoring and concerned to read the signs of a private, interiorised self deploying itself in public.[15] 'Reading the signs' involved the search for order, indeed moral legibility, within oneself and in the world outside one. As Sennett indicates, this search for moral legibility in fact very often took the melodramatic forms of a person-alised struggle of good and evil, particularly in the political sphere.[16]

Following these accounts, and drawing upon those of urban and architectural historians as well,[17] it is possible to identify the 'display city' in terms of the built form of the eighteenth-century city, for instance the terraced house, the promenade and the assembly rooms, which expressed forms of sociability to do not with a moral interior but with the display of universal properties that depended for their realisation on their open, public exhibition. The nineteenth-century 'moral city' was the city of the private house, the suburb, yet also the highly specialised but highly transgressive city centre, where people met and mingled in greatly charged, greatly ordered, but always potentially disruptive city spaces. The ordering of these spaces, in terms of new codings of the public and the private, was carried forward by the attempted constitution of city centre space as now a 'neutral' medium; a place of and for ordered passage and free movement, but a place in which this freedom was to be morally shaped. City centres became places where reading the signs was every-thing. The architectural historian Mark Girouard conceives of the built form of the British Victorian city as being implicated in morality, unlike its eighteenth-century forebear. The eighteenth-century city and town were marked by consensus, by the polite, and by the understated. The moral city was marked by conflict and drama, *its* built forms and building materials embodying moral address, as they strove to moralise the city dweller in their different, and conflicting, versions of the truth.[18]

This drama of the Victorian city was evident in the materiality of its built forms, which were emphatic and assertive, the very opposite of the understated. The building as moral address was informed in its material shape by the bold, assertive line, the line of the building's overall form, and the emphasis in the line incised on stone. Design and ornament became in themselves a moral statement. It is this quality of vigorous moral address that seems to be new. Buildings were also big, costly and ornate, monumental in this sense too. The sheer wealth that went into public and especially municipal building needs to be appreciated: Burnley

Mechanics Institute, for example, was as imposing as any London gentle-men's club,[19] and the expense of the building of Manchester Town Hall was in contemporary terms staggering (almost £1 million).

Buildings were above all about meaning; they were symbolic. The outer design should represent the inner meaning of the building. This unity of inside and outside was especially evident in gothic architecture. For example, the Houses of Parliament in London were held to represent the Ancient Constitution, and the Law Courts in London the Common Law. Railway stations across Europe were decorated so as to represent the qualities of the regions of departure and arrival.[20] The seeming exceptions to this law of the symbolic in fact followed that law: the great glass buildings of Europe were not designed to express function, but were simply 'casings', objects of utility.[21] What was regarded as the pretence and artifice of older styles was rejected in favour of an emphasis on authenticity, sincerity and truth, virtues which were now given historical expression, so that one may see in this emphasis on sincerity an analogue of the language of character (and the 'light of publicity') which so informed mid-Victorian ethics of governance, including the ethics governors directed towards themselves.

This emphasis on authenticity was indeed reflected in contemporary historical writing itself. As Stephen Bann has put it, there was a move from eighteenth-century *vraisemblance* in historical representation to nineteenth-century *vérité*. In the old understanding, there was a separation between things and their meanings, but in the nineteenth century, historians attempted forms of representation in which there was no gap between the thing and its image, so that both were fused in terms of what 'actually happened'. This desire for the lifelike and the authentic in nineteenth-century historical representation extended from historical writing alone, to the museum, the pageant and also to architecture and city design.[22] In Vienna, for example, architectural historicism was evident in the way in which each public building was executed in the historical style that in its full historical authenticity appeared most appropriate to its function. The Rathaus was built in a massively gothic style to evoke the city's supposed origins as a free medieval commune, born again after the end of absolutist rule. The Burgtheater was conceived in early baroque style, commemorating the time at which theatre first joined together 'cleric, courtier and commoner in a shared aesthetic enthusiasm'. As an 'unequivocal symbol of liberal culture', the University was built in Renais-sance style.

Yet at the same time utility was of great importance, for public buildings always served a purpose. What was involved has been termed 'the aesthetics of practical morality'.[23] This architecture was designed to speak to the many and not the few. At first sight this may seem unlikely, given the often remarked contrast between the monumental city centre on the one hand and the uniform, architecturally impoverished streets of new housing, and the slums of the old city on the other. The contrast between eighteenth- and nineteenth-century town halls is, however, instructive: whereas the former looked like country seats, country seats in the nineteenth century looked like town halls. Architects in the nineteenth century were themselves involved with a much wider range of buildings than previously. Particularly in civic buildings they sought to moralise all those who lived in the city in terms of appealing to their *common* interests and identities as citizens.

As will become apparent, the city centre can be understood in terms of at least two socio-geographical axes, namely those of the centre and the new suburbs of the well-off, and the centre and the habitations of the majority, particularly the poor, which quite often ringed the immediate centre. In respect of the latter, and its attempt to elevate the ordinary, there was a sort of deliberate rule by aesthetic contrast. For example, as has been seen, the striking and elaborate public markets of Victorian Britain aimed to sever associations with the old, surrounding town, as vulgar, depraved and architecturally uninspiring. The contrast was with the old markets as well as the surrounding town, for the old markets were integrated into the surrounding streets, traffic and people passing through them. However, what was involved was not so much the denigration of the ordinary as its elevation. Good taste was to be devolved upon the masses by ennobling the mundane, in this case the mundanity of shopping. The aim, as expressed in the design and development of Glasgow, for example, was to surmount the plain and the utilitarian by moralising them. Ornamentation, in its application to common civic practices and identities, and to the ordinary practices of life, became something like an end in itself, something 'godly' by virtue of its simply *being* design – good design was seen as inherently moral.[24] The political institution of the ordinary, however, can be said to have reached new heights in the sort of city that began to emerge at the beginning of the twentieth century, what I call here the social city. Before discussing this I shall turn to some particular instances of the moral city.

Paris is often considered to be 'the capital of the nineteenth century', and other great cities, particularly London, have their claim too (in fact the modernity Paris sought was often to be found in London, the two cities aping and rivalling each other throughout the century). If we think of nineteenth-century modernity as defined by the city of circulation, then the claims of Paris are strong, especially the circulation that had to do with consumption and pleasure. But if we think of the city that has to do with production and distribution, then Manchester has its claims, if not to capital status, then to a peculiar sort of centrality. This was based on the widespread apprehension of Manchester in the first half of the nineteenth century as in a sense the pre-moral city of pure, as yet unformed, circulation. Manchester's claims are also evident in the city as substantially and dramatically a *de novo* creation of industry, despite having an earlier history. If we compare London and Manchester, despite the undeniable novelty of its unprecedented size, Victorian London was substantially a Georgian city in architectural terms, at least until the 1850s, when the City developed rapidly. Even then, its latitudinarian architectural style produced in the city what one of its architectural historians describes as the chaos and poverty of most of its public buildings compared to the British provinces.[25] In terms of commercial buildings, the grandiose, Renaissance-style warehouses of Manchester, and to a lesser extent Bradford, were pioneering a new sort of architectural modernity before London.[26]

Visitors to Manchester in the first half of the century decidedly saw it as circulation untamed, and in fact hardly a city at all. De Tocqueville and Engels are only the best known of many commentators on the city in the first half of the nineteenth century, but what is striking is the unanimity of these observers.[27] De Tocqueville wrote of the city as the outgrowth of the capricious, creative force of liberty: 'everything testifies to man's individual power, nothing to the directing powers of society'. In Manchester 'the human spirit affirms its complete development and utter brutishness'.[28] For the French observer Leon Faucher, writing at the same time as Engels, '[T]he town realises in a measure the Utopia of Bentham', and everything is measured by its results and by the standards of utility. The city is 'a great economy of both time and wealth in production'. Even Engels, who in some measure treats the city as a real city, in the end sees it as a spirit, the spirit of pure freedom, of circulation unconstrained by morality.[29] For him and others, this city was a place that was rough and raw in its built forms, or rather its *building* forms, for what observers were seeing in the 1830s and 1840s was the massive outgrowth of the city into unfinished streets and houses, new districts without seeming rhyme or reason. Manchester was to them irrational, inhuman, brutish, the 'shock city' of the age, as it has been called. The obverse of the coin of unfettered freedom was a moral and spiritual *disorder*.

The city from the 1830s and 1840s onwards would seem to be one of a moralised circulation, a 'sanitary city' concerned with securing the order felt to to be immanent to, if threatened by, circulation. But it was also a city marked by the ordering *of* circulation by direct moral intervention in the shape of the built forms of the city, so that, to echo de Tocqueville, things would at last testify to the 'directing powers of society', and not to 'man's individual power'. Engels misses this, in particularly illuminating ways. He talks of the 'old town' – the courts and alleys that made up not only the city centre, poor, residential districts, but large tracts of Salford too (which he compares to the medieval city of Genoa). The old town is a labyrinth, a place of caprice and disorder.[30] However, himself engulfed in the explosion of the city, he ran together in his mind the old city centre with the new 'working-class suburb' of Hulme, failing to discern in the latter the new moral ordering of circulation then emerging in its earliest forms.

This order was apparent in the streets of Hulme, in their order and regularity, and in the ordered spaces around but also within the houses. As has been seen, this ordering involved the eclipse of an older 'social privacy' by the spatial ordering apparent in the layout of streets and of what became known as 'bylaw housing', the municipal regulation of housing and the new ideology and practice of public health growing up together.[31] In Britain as a whole the development of 'self-contained' housing (flats and houses), the assault upon the old back-to-back housing (reformers abhorred 'backs' in their search for free circulation), and the development of piped water within houses all involved the governance of space. And, being 'self-contained', these new, internal urban spaces carried distinct potential for the sort of self-contained citizen liberalism wished to encourage. The Ordnance Survey city plan of Manchester in 1849, opening the labyrinth of the city centre to the gaze of power, was an integral part of this ordering. It was to be followed in the next half-century by the new moral design of the city centre, and of so many like it in and beyond Britain.

This process has recently been given exemplary exposition in the work of Simon Gunn on Manchester, Birmingham and Leeds between 1840 and 1914, work which indicates very strongly how Manchester was not only representative of change in Britain as a whole, but in many ways ahead of and initiating this change.[32] The sheer physical transformation of city centres should not be underestimated, nor should the enormous costs involved. Tens of thousands were displaced from city centres, and displaced furthermore often without any municipal re-housing. Disruption in London in the third quarter of the century was as great as elsewhere, perhaps greater, both overground and underground, given the vast sewering and railway projects in the city, including the new underground railway. It is important to emphasise that in cities like Manchester, and accompanying this building transformation, there was what can be thought of as a deliberate, collaborative project to reform the manners and the culture of the city populations (including the manners of the better-off themselves). City elites combined to pioneer an enormous range of educational, philanthropic and religious institutions and activities in the first half of the century, as will already be apparent.[33]

These innovations were led by socially similar, and relatively small, groups of reformers, chiefly leading businessmen but also clerics and men drawn from the professions, especially medicine. The influence of this kind of person was to continue. In what sense these comprised the Victorian middle class is open to question. Although styling his book 'the public culture of the Victorian middle class', Gunn recognises that what he calls 'bourgeois culture' was not synonymous with the middle class. As he says, the term 'bourgeois' in the context of 'bourgeois culture' has less to do with social origins than the development of a certain sort of 'social praxis', 'at least partly independent' of any simple social group or class.[34] Quite so, for it seems to me that this 'social praxis' can as well, or perhaps better, be understood as a question of the practice of political reason than as the expression of a class, though I think it did indeed provide the 'language' and cultural resources through which collective social identities of a middle-class kind could be articulated.

Around the mid-nineteenth century in Manchester the reformation of manners took a new turn. As Simon Gunn has shown, at this time in the city there began to develop a rather new sort of 'public sphere', one organised around the significance given to 'culture' in its now 'high' forms, particularly in the shape of the Hallé Orchestra, its concerts and its concert hall.[35] The creation of the 'moral city' was closely related to these developments, the place of the aesthetic being central to this. This new cultural sphere, and the 'public' that went with it, were now secular instead of narrowly religious, though religion still continued to frame the secular – classical music was in fact acceptable to northern Nonconformism by virtue of its secularised religiosity. In terms of the Hallé's music there was an emphasis upon feeling and sentiment, and a recognition of the limitations of the rational intellect. Classical music was elevating, its message one of aesthetic-moral aspiration, and its neo-romantic aesthetic one of the transcendence of the merely material and merely rational. It also involved, it should be said, the development of an *historically* framed musical canon from which the musical present was felt to have descended. Obviously, this development was a local manifestation of what was happening throughout Europe, in terms of the opera house particularly. The development of the Hallé Concert Hall occurred at much the same time as the great Manchester Art Treasures Exhibition of 1857, and the encouragement of what was later to be Manchester University, in the shape of Owens College.[36]

Building expertise itself developed in terms of an alliance between social reformers, political authorities and a new kind of expertise in governing city spaces, namely that of builders and architects themselves. This is particularly apparent in the case of the architectural journal *The Builder*, which spawned imitations in Ireland and the Empire. The *Irish Builder* of March 1880 featured verses which gave expression to the union of improvement and edification with what were termed the 'Building and Constructive Arts' – Catholic, nationalist Ireland was no less prone to this rhetoric of progress than the mainland:[37]

> *The Building of a Nation*
>
> If you want a School of Art,
> Build it up
> If you want a native mart,
> Build it up . . .
> Labour skilled can none degrade . . .
> School the lowly, labouring man . . .
> If for freedom you are fit,
> Build it up
> If a Senate makes her glad,
> Build it up
> First of all show moral power . . .
> Public spirit, stout as steel,
> Conquers for the Commonweal.

The technical, the aesthetic and the moral were inseparable in this advocacy of public buildings and amenities, one projecting fit housing for the poor and the erection of national monuments (as is evident also in the first number of the *Dublin Builder* of 1859, the forerunner of the *Irish Builder*).[38] They were also jointly evident in the advocacy of a professional ethic which defined itself in opposition to the 'jerry', namely everything that was shoddy, makeshift and impermanent. This emphasis upon the permanent and lasting was especially important in the colonial context of city design, given the depradations of climate.

Figure 4.2   Manchester Assize Courts, 1859 (photograph taken 1864)

In England the gothic represented only one of many historico-moral architectural possibilities, but it was a particularly revealing one, and I will concentrate on it here. The baroque or the neoclassical would tell the same sort of story, as is apparent from the cases of the Ringstrasse in Vienna or civic Birmingham in England later in the century. The trio of Manchester architects Alfred Waterhouse, Thomas Worthington and Henry Darbashire between them left a decidedly gothic stamp on their home town, as on a number of other British towns and cities, among them London (for instance, in the shape of Waterhouse's design for the Natural History Museum). After the 1850s the stamp of the gothic was widely apparent. (It was, for example, also the official style of the Liverpool municipal revival.) In the case of Manchester's Waterhouse, the influence of Ruskin's advocacy of the gothic was immense. Ruskin's lectures in the city in the 1850s and 1860s had a considerable local and national impact. His influence was felt most directly in Waterhouse's Assize Courts of 1859, which Ruskin in fact considered to be the best exemplification of his ideas so far in Britain (Figure 4.2).[39] Waterhouse was also the architect of Strangeways Gaol, built beside the Assizes shortly after, and he was also responsible for a number of other buildings and renovations, including the renovation of the Royal Infirmary.

Hospitals, courts and gaols, like mental asylums and workhouses, were elements in a range of municipal institutions built at this time in Manchester and in many other cities. Located towards the margins of the immediate city centre, and not usually in the centre itself, they formed a kind of institutional, disciplinary girdle around the centre, so that the splendour of the centre was offset by these exemplifications of order and discipline. However, these exemplifications of the disciplining of ordinary life were invariably as splendid as the buildings in the city centre. Again, the elevation of the ordinary can be seen at work. Like the architecture of Waterhouse, that of Thomas Worthington was a mode of social reform: Worthington was a member of the Manchester Statistical Society, and he, like Waterhouse, was responsible for the building of a whole range of reforming institutions, such as model dwellings for the poor, civic buildings like police courts, public baths and hospitals (Worthington had close links with Florence Nightingale).[40]

In terms of the design of the moral city, especially in its directly governmental forms, the best way to approach the meaning of the gothic, as of the range of other architectural styles employed, is by a consideration of the town hall. These had eminently practical purposes of course, as centres of council administration, and until the provision of specialised buildings later on the new services of the municipalities continued in many cases to be located in the town hall building, for instance the fire brigade, courts and prison cells, and even libraries.[41] The early emphasis on display was tempered by a greater attention to these utilitarian purposes in the last quarter of the nineteenth century. The meaning of the town hall was none the less highly symbolic, concerning the identity of the city as a whole, unlike the eighteenth-century town hall, which represented the Corporation and not the urban community.

Town halls were created by a process that itself represented the identity of the town in collective, public terms. Many town halls were created by a process of open competition between architects, a process overseen by leading local figures, but also one subject to intense discussion in the local press, which might indeed be highly critical of both price and design.[42] This process of ostensibly open, 'public' competition was directly related to the new mid-century cultural public sphere already considered, for example the Hallé which was not only a secular but also a public subscription-based institution, unlike the earlier semi-private music

Figure 4.3   Glasgow City Chambers, 1885

associations. It was also a professional rather than an amateur institution.[43] The public rhetoric of town hall design itself involved a passionate belief that the town hall was in fact the possession of the citizen: the architect of the Glasgow City Chambers (opened in 1885 and unlike many town halls not a neo-gothic building) considered the town hall to be 'not a state-aided institution, but the city's own, to be erected with their money, to be dedicated to their use, and to pass under their exclusive control' (Figure 4.3).[44] The City Provost of Glasgow felt the goals of the citizen to be represented in the architecture of the town hall, namely high aspiration, magnanimity and purity. The moral character of this architecture is clear, above all the omnipresent emphasis on aspiration set in a distinctively Manichaean moral universe.

Despite this emphasis on openness, the semantics of design and use in these buildings turned upon a dialectic, indeed a tension, between openness and being closed. This can be understood as a direct representation of the troubled relationship between authority and freedom in liberalism. The grand, formal entrances to the buildings initiated a process of invitation which continued in terms of elaborate and ornate entrance lobbies, grand staircases (Figure 4.4), vast and impressive public

Figure 4.4 Manchester Town Hall, the Grand Staircase (photograph taken 1877, Town Hall opened 1878)

halls, often called 'Great Halls' in a deliberate echo of an older tradition of such halls, religious and secular. The mayor's parlour and reception rooms were equally ornate and impressive, and the council chamber itself, with its public gallery, continued the emphasis upon the invitation of the citizen into the building. Movement into, and occupation of, the building were designed to exalt both the visitor and the town or city.

However, these grand entrances were most often purely formal, the everyday work of the city being conducted through specialised, smaller entrances. The Glasgow building is a case in point: the front gates of the imposing public entrance were most of the time kept shut, and entry was via a guarded gatehouse. The public entered these to conduct municipal business, and movement within the building was closely controlled (for instance, to protect councillors from unwanted contact).[45] The dialectic of exclusion and inclusion continued in the actual use of the town hall for public meetings.[46] Access to council meetings was by invitation or advance arrangement, as were meetings with councillors. Public galleries in council chambers were usually small, the emphasis being more upon spectatorship than involvement.

However, public meetings in the town halls were consciously aimed at creating widespread use. In its year of opening (1858) Leeds Town Hall was used by a vast number of organisations for the 'teas' and other social events which were themselves the lifeblood of the vast array of voluntary organisations in these cities. None the less, use itself was a form of both inclusion and exclusion, for while town authorities were responsive to groups and organisations which could be construed as 'improving', those which were not were excluded. There was considerable argument about radical political organisations' use of the town hall, for instance. This emphasis on *use* is important, for involvement in the town hall 'tea' was itself to experience being improved, the great room and building which surrounded one actively teaching their lessons. Use is particularly apparent in music, for it was through classical and sacred music that the town hall often came into its own. Bodily practices, involved in the sensory, aesthetic negotiation of these grand and unfamiliar spaces, were also involved in music, the practice of the ear being allied to the practice of the eye. Learning to negotiate the spaces involved the bodily *performance* of liberalism, literal performance in musical terms complementing this. Many town halls had salaried organists, and in the case of Huddersfield, for example, town hall sponsored choral music itself became in the end perhaps a greater symbol of the town than any town building.

The play of exclusion and inclusion continued in the great, highly ritualised celebrations that accompanied the laying of foundation stones, and the opening of the town halls.[47] In 1878 the opening of Manchester Town Hall was marked by a great procession through the town of some 44,000 trade and friendly society members. The inclusion of the trades and societies itself involved its own process of exclusion within the ranks of labour in favour of the skilled (and, of course, non-society and non-trades union men and women also suffered exclusion). The societies of the numerically dominant cotton factory workers were greatly under-represented on the day, and women were not represented at all, even though they made up an enormous proportion of the textile workers. Liberal governmentality constructed its claims to universality, as such claims are made, through a series of *exclusions*. The exclusions concerned with labour were compounded by other exclusions too, and this was the case for civic life in general as well as this celebration, for example the exclusion of Jews, of the Irish, of women and of so many of the 'unres-pectable' poor.

The procession also included the police, the military and contingents from the various municipal departments, as well as civic dignitaries and the paraphernalia of civic identity. The 'leading citizens' of the city, at this time the most wealthy businessmen, as was usual in the civic and ritual public life of cities, had the most prominent position. The trades and societies marched accompanied by the symbols and banners of their organisations. The idea for this trade and friendly society involvement came from the trades themselves, and was meticulously planned in meetings with the mayor, the police and the military. The stonemasons' banner, appropriately enough, showed the town hall, the free trade hall and the cathedral. The carvers and gilders carried the city arms in gold, and on the reverse the likeness of the town hall framed in gold. The mayor's likeness was carried by the bakers. The mayor, 'Alderman' Abel Heywood, the great force behind the town hall, was once a leading political radical but now a pillar of the Liberal establishment in the city. As a self-made man, he was himself an icon of moral and cultural improvement, as well as of a supposed liberal tradition that encompassed the radical past and the liberal present.

It is clear that while the trades were publicly expressing their various identities, and not simply paying homage to municipal Manchester, these identities were closely linked to the identity of the city as expressed in its new town hall. What seems to have been involved in this and similar public occasions was the ritual performance of social relations in the city in terms of notions of urban identity and urban community. Labour and other associational identities, the identity of the city and, at this stage and for some time afterwards, the social leadership of leading citizens were elements in this ritual enactment of the urban commune, in which voluntarism and independence, on the one hand, and hierarchy and authority on the other, could each receive expression, yet also coexist. The voluntarism of the parade, and its public visibility, served as an index and ideal of the self-regulating urban community policing itself through inherent codes of conduct (in the form of the tacit rules that regulated such ritual), as opposed to ones imposed from outside authority.[48] The parade was itself a witnessing of civility, with order, sobriety and, not least, dignity becoming manifest in terms of bodily self-discipline and the ordered disposition of the procession as a whole. The sheer size of the crowds attending these events is remarkable. In Manchester the number probably exceeded the half a million (out of a population of 700,000) who reportedly turned out for the foundation stone laying of Glasgow's City Chambers in 1885.[49]

The historicism of these public buildings, especially as exemplified in the gothic, can in the overall visual economy of the city be said to exemplify what was earlier referred to as a tension between historicism and rationality, time and space, and between the horizontal and the vertical. Arising from the tensions within the city of circulation, just as historicism and the horizontal strove to moralise rationality and the horizontal, so time can be said to have come to the aid of space. The gothic involved a special emphasis on time. Gothic town halls in particular echoed the town halls of what were perceived to be the free communes of medieval trading Europe. Gothic's emphasis on the national, the historical and the Christian involved in turn a particular capacity to express the local. For instance, in the great gothic town halls of the north of England, local history, local legends and local worthies were given special emphasis within this pan-historical frame.

In these cases as elsewhere, the creation of an urban imaginary through the means of the town hall involved the construction of a history for the city which, if by definition local, was always articulated with the national and the extra-national. In the external and internal structures and decoration of the town hall in Manchester, for example, above all in the famous murals of Ford Madox Brown in the Great Hall (Figure 4.5), a history was constructed around a past which stretched back to the Romans, and which turned since then upon the textile industry, the encouragement of commerce, the city's association with science and technology, also the Protestant religion, and with this the cause of liberty (which involved embracing the side of Parliament not the King in the Civil War). This unqualified association of the city with progress, particularly industrial progress, was also closely linked to Manchester as the centre of the world cotton industry, itself the greatest export industry in the world for much of the nineteenth century.

The deployment of the coats-of-arms of greater and lesser landowners in the area, and of other Lancashire towns, also linked the city to the past of the region and the county, such regional identities being particularly important in this period.[50] The town hall, in its construction of history, thereby also negotiated the various class differences that still existed within the wealthy inhabitants of the city and region, namely those between industry and land. This past was seamlessly part of a commercial and industrial present which was reflected in the ubiquitous presence of the symbols of the city in the external and internal decor of the building,

Figure 4.5 Manchester Town Hall, the Public (Great) Hall (photograph taken 1877)

symbols such as the industrious bee and the cotton plant and flower.[51] The gothic was of course also intensely romantic, and town halls frequently echoed the gothic castle of visual and literary imagination. This romanticism was linked to the evocation of old crafts evident in the actual design of town halls: Waterhouse in Manchester, following Ruskin and anticipating the arts and crafts movement, was a believer in the unity of the arts and crafts, and designed many of the fittings of the building himself.

The romantic and the historical were in turn fused with the spirituality of the Christian religion, and as well as a castle the town hall was a church. The town hall tower was at once a church spire and a castle tower. Christian didacticism was everywhere in these buildings, down to the last detail: the clock of Manchester Town Hall bore the message, 'Teach Us To Number Our Days', a didacticism given all the more point as there were no figures on the clock (it was marked by clusters of leaves at the appropriate locations of the hour). This didacticism was part and parcel of the art which at the time made a special appeal to the city fathers, namely that of the Pre-Raphaelites, in which a highly moralised painted content was frequently given added force by accompanying literary injunctions.

This didacticism worked through history in a particular kind of way. For architects of the time, the form of a building and history were linked together by a particular view of memory. Architecture could stimulate the mind and improve the character by a process of evoking associations locked away in personal memory. As Glasgow architects of the time put it, architecture could recall the stored-up treasures of the mind.[52] This understanding was part and parcel of the widespread view that mental processes had physical correlates, so that the visuality of built forms quite literally entered the mind, and directly stimulated memory so as to affect behaviour visually. In the Glasgow example, strongly influenced by Scottish Enlightenment ideas about the relationship between space and human behaviour, there was the idea that architecture and design could excite moral sentiment by *association* with what they represented in memory. Order and harmony in architecture could excite order and harmony in the beholder, so that there was a direct correspondence between architectural/moral order and political order.

In terms of the town hall, the particular style chosen was in fact subordinate to a visual economy in which the vertical of time was central. Therefore, it was in fact the tower which was most important. Neoclassical town halls such as that of Leeds had towers as well as gothic buildings like Manchester. There was a relative absence of domed town halls. In many cases the façades of town halls were not designed to be viewed, and even when they were, the façade was always subordinated to the effects obtained by the tower. Time came to the aid of space most dramatically in the form of the tower. This was a matter of the streetscape or cityscape (which will be taken up further in chapter 5), of the way in which the tower fitted into the experiential fabric of the town or the city. It was in terms of the visuality of the streetscape and cityscape that the town hall achieved its deepest impact perhaps. In the often closed, congested Victorian city the siting of the tower in relation to the accompanying street pattern created powerful visual effects, for instance closing off streets with the view of the tower (as with Halifax Town Hall, Figure 4.6).[53] When the town hall was sited in relation to accompanying, purpose-built squares, as with Albert Square in Manchester, the effect was more powerful still. Figure 4.7 is a view of Manchester Town Hall from the northeast corner of Albert Square, in 1900. Here, the setting is not congested, and there are, unlike today, no tall buildings to compete with the town hall. In the city there were no buildings higher than the town hall until the 1930s. Something of what may have been the contemporary visual effect of town halls is evident, not least the romanticism of the gothic. What is also evident, given the relatively small scale of Victorian and Edwardian cities, is the way in which the town hall tower secures the visual dominance of the building in the overall townscape.

In terms of the moralisation of the city, the central importance of aspiration here took perhaps the most powerful and emphatic of all its built expressions, the soaring tower and soaring aspiration as one, the gothic above all lending itself to this visual politics of the tower. It will also be apparent that the town hall was set in a purpose-built municipal square, Albert Square, in which were arrayed the statues of local and national politicians, in this case Liberal ones. In Birmingham, there was something similar, if on a much larger scale, in the neoclassical Chamberlain Place of the 1880s, in which were gathered together in one enormous square most of the leading institutions of the city. In many ways these places can be understood as shrines, the holy places of political and governmental liberalism.

The visual politics of the high temple of such shrines, the town hall, worked in relation to what was increasingly becoming the omnioptic city as a whole. Sir Charles Barry's conception of the ideal town hall, which he in large part translated into practice in the case of Halifax in the 1870s, envisaged the building in a central and elevated position.[54] It should have a tower and a clock that could be seen from all parts of the town, and from which all parts of the town could be seen. The tower should also have a balcony around it, from which the city could be seen. It was to be connected visually to all parts of the town, but also by the new system of 'electric wires', namely the telegraph. The citizen should at all times be able to view this emblem of citizenry, and in turn the citizen

Figure 4.6   View of Halifax Town Hall

should be opened to the view from the town hall. As the view from the town hall was in theory the view of the citizen, the citizen was both seer and seen. The town hall was therefore a sort of omnioptic machine of liberal political reason, virtual governmentality in fact.

Figure 4.7 View of Manchester Town Hall, 1900

This account of the built forms of the city has concentrated on a particular variant of historicism, and there were, of course, many such variants. The architecture historian Barbara Miller Lane has drawn attention to several phases within European historicism, the period after 1870 being particularly interesting in terms of the political dimensions of city design.[55] In the last three decades of the nineteenth century, in the construction of government buildings in European capital cities, an earlier deference to archaeological verisimilitude gave way to an historicist eclecticism in which architectural monumentality was given increasingly democratic forms. This has been related to architects' and city authorities' concern about the increasing illegibility of the city, given the ongoing battle of the styles. In the design of town halls, law courts and government offices, the purpose was to preserve dignity and grandeur, but to mute the effects of monumentality – amongst the examples with which Lane deals are the Law Courts in London, and the colossal and anything but muted Palais de Justice in Brussels. The aim of this generalised historicism was to finally break the link between the meaning of buildings and the possession of historical erudition, so that buildings became available to the mass of people, their ordinariness being thereby elevated. The internal dimensions of buildings were also reshaped in order to make government more accessible. After 1900 eclecticism in turn gave way to a more deliberate historicism, but one that was still based not on the idea of a true original, but on what were believed to be common architectural vocabularies, from which were selected variants that would have the widest popular effect. A simplified classicism in particular was thought of as the most universally understood style, the style in fact of 'democratic empire' in an age of democracy, imperialism and nation. This pre-war historicism took the two principal forms of a severe neo classicism and a national romanticism, both dominating a good deal of European government architecture down to 1945.

In both phases, before and after 1900, architectural form came to speak more for itself, and more in the present, if with an eye to the past, so that one may talk of architectural modernism emerging out of, and not against, historicism. The same can be said of the character of the particular styles used, the severity of this new classicism having much in common with architectural modernism (for instance, fascist modernism). This view of the continuity of the two is endorsed by Mitchell Schwarzer,[56] in that both modernism and historicism shared the view that they were the end-point of history, but modernism, as the *ne plus ultra* of historicism, imagined the impossibility of a future (for the future was now). Historicism, in its original move beyond eighteenth-century classicism, just as much as modernism, was self-consciously a way of being modern. Its supposed lack of attention to the functional and the utilitarian, and supposed lack of reference to the present, were qualities not of historicism itself but of the invention of it that modernism needed in order to create itself. And, as has been seen, in the shape of Camillo Sitte and Otto Wagner, two of the greatest influences on architectural modernism, the unresolved tensions of historicism itself – in its Ringstrasse form – can be seen to be at work in modernism also. In these two, the supposed traditionalist and romantic and the supposed rationalist and modernist were united in the belief that the city was a cultural artefact that evolved out of custom, use and habit. This modernist belief was also an historicist one, so that conventional notions of a simple transition from historicism to modernism seem unhelpful. Clearly, modernism evolved out of historicism, particularly these later phases with their simplified forms and their opening up to the popular.[57] This makes tidy periodisation difficult. However, it is still useful to think about change in terms of the creation of a new social imaginary of the city that seems to have emerged from the late nineteenth century onwards.

The social city

In their joint emphasis on custom and use, Sitte and Wagner pointed to the present as well as the past. Their concern with use meant thinking about the present of cities in a much more positive way than had earlier been the case. If in the moral city the ordinary and the mundane were elevated, this was because they were still treated with suspicion, and indeed sometimes with repugnance. In the new social imaginary of the city that seems to have emerged in the late nineteenth century, the social city, the present rather than the past was to be the primary locus of concern, and with this an increasingly positive embrace of this present. In architectural modernism the future was to be now, and the now was the means by which the future could be realised. Whether we equate the social city with architectural modernism or not, and the correspondence is only partial, city past gave way to a new emphasis on city present, the evident continuities notwithstanding. This new departure involved the eclipse of the architect by the planner, and often, as in the case of Wagner and Sitte, by the emergence of the architect as planner. As a sphere of governance, the moral city involved a rather limited view of what the city might be. Even though the centre was understood in relation to the suburban and the popular *quartier*, it was still the centre that engrossed the most interest. What became evident from the late nineteenth century were conceptions of the city as a *whole*, a new sense of the city as a totality that often embraced it in terms of its own larger, spatial 'environment'. This view called into being, just as it was also produced by, the new practice of *Stadtbau*, as it was called in German (the term was first used in 1890), and 'town planning', as it was known in English.

What seems to have been new was that the city was now to be planned according to the inherent characteristics of its inhabitants, which were seen not as repugnant and in need of reform, as in the 'sanitary city' and its above-ground analogue of the moral city, but as benign. It was the city inhabitants' inherent sociability which was now seen as the template for urban planning and design. With this there was a shift from a medicalised view of the city to a social, and indeed a cultural, one. There was also widespread rejection of material and mechanical views of the city, in favour of an emphasis on the ideal alongside ideas of the organic. In thinking about the social city I draw on Osborne and Rose's account of changing governmental 'diagrams' of the city, adapting it for my own purposes.[58] The social city they conceive of as the 'eudaemonic city', the city of 'social happiness'. There developed a sense of the city as potentially a 'contented space', a space which entailed the natural, immanent sociability of its occupants. The city was to be planned so as to elicit and maximise this sociability by means of 'an enlightened urban administrative imagination'. This administration was carried forward in terms of a new emphasis on both the importance of the social and the rationality and perfectibility of its administration.

These diagrams of the city as governable spaces, and as soluble 'problems', became apparent in a number of cases, for example the planning of cities in terms of their 'zoning', a zoning, as in the case of the planning of Chicago in the early twentieth century, based upon working *with* the sociability of neighbourhoods, and in this sense indeed magnifying, and transforming, the importance of the ordinary in governance.[59] Similarly, in the case of the internationally influential garden city movement of Ebenezer Howard, there was a desire to work with the grain of the social and cultural characteristics of city dwellers and their environments.[60] In these and other examples there was a deliberate reaction against the monumentality of the Haussmannisation of the city, which was believed to work directly against the grain of its sociability. This sociability was to be discerned by the 'social science' of sociology (as, for example, in the case of the Chicago School of urban sociologists). The new social of sociology was relocated from older locations to ones discerned within the patterns of association held to be intrinsic to social formations themselves, in this case the class, race and status formations of localities. The social in this view of the city became *sui generis*, something with its own laws of what was called 'society', a particular sort of reality to be known by social science.[61] The 'social' was now itself to do the explanatory work. Certain things came to be known to this science as 'social' things, and therefore different from anything else. In the process, the social question now became a sociological question, which, alongside the social state, it has remained until relatively recently.

This was one aspect of what was 'social' about this new view of the city, a view of the social which was of course far removed from eighteenth-century notions of the universal sociability located in the abstractions of Man and Nature. The social is also to be discerned in Osborne and Rose's depiction of the city as now a 'socio-administrative domain, with its own proper laws, characteristics and forms of life, these being understood as being amenable to a "social" administration'. This was a city for actively producing the social field rather than just a spatial milieu for already immanent social processes. It was, they say, a kind of 'social machine'.[62] On closer inspection, however, it seems that while the city itself was indeed now itself a sort of governmental tool, mechanical metaphors are in general less appropriate than organic ones. For Patrick Geddes, perhaps the most influential of all the British voices in town planning (which collectively were of great international importance), the city was a living entity. Because it was alive, to understand and shape it meant that tools had to be invented of such a nature as would realise the rhythm of this life. The life of the city had to be captured in order that the city might be active in its own government.

Therefore, in Geddes' work and in its wider influence, the idea of the plan as a 'living plan' was important. This living plan had several forms, most notably for Geddes what he called the Index Museum, which in the form of the Outlook Tower of his Regional Museum in Edinburgh was a means of presenting all the facets of urban development in such a way that they could be known experientially, through all the senses, and not merely the rational intellect. Not only this, but the experience of the plan was part of a process of involving people in the planning of the city. The 'Vital Revolution' spoken of so often at the time was for Geddes not a political revolution but one of recognition that the future depended upon creating the self-awareness and determination of the community at large in the development of the city.[63] This depended on the self-directed efforts of citizens, and on getting the consent of the whole community, with the aim of opening people's eyes to their biological nature, and treating with respect the interaction of the human and the environment. This aim was in fact highly prescriptive, despite the talk of consultation, and it involved a calculatedly scientific view of the subject of governance as a biological organism in terms of the need to create the right juxtaposition of stimulating environment with responsive organism. Geddes essayed a path between capitalism and socialism, but one may see in this attempt to harness the free acting person and community a new institution of freedom, and in the plan itself a technology of governing which was far more than a mere blueprint.[64] Involving the bodies and experiences of people, the plan projected but also in heuristic fashion enacted governance. These 'thinking machines', as Geddes called his living plans, would emphasise action above thought and get at the dynamic of change by working inside it, thereby harnessing the inherent sociability of the city.

Geddes' idea was that conscious and deliberate thought, unlike in previous times, should direct evolutionary change. 'Life' was to be brought into the centre of consideration, his emphasis being always upon practice, intuition and nature, as opposed to the material and mechanical. Planning therefore directed the '*élan vital*' so that the development of society could reach higher evolutionary goals.[65] Geddes' views distinguished him from the other great exponents of British planning, namely the utopian Ebenezer Howard, whose aim was to create a new city without reference to the needs, development and history of society at large, and Raymond Unwin, the 'practical town planner'. However, it was the Fabian Unwin, a believer in land nationalisation, who was among the first to actually implement the planned methodology of his friend Geddes, employing the latter's formula of 'survey, analysis, plan'. The influence of Unwin on the actual course of town planning was to be immense.

Geddes saw the trend of modern urbanisation as the evolutionary path of the future, so that his subject matter was 'the social life of the city'. The influence of the sociology of Le Play was crucial, particularly in terms of geography and cartography. Le Play's maxim for social studies – 'Place, Work, Folk' – was represented in the Regional Survey, another tool, another kind of governmental thinking machine. Geddes' development of his various thinking machines (the latter included the much-utilised machine of the summer school) represented perhaps his greatest impact before 1914, apart from his role in the foundation of the Sociology Society in 1903.[66] He caught the tide of the international exhibitions movement, which before the First World War did so much to promulgate not only town planning but the whole international development of the social sciences.[67] Indeed, it was as an international movement, rather than as a series of national ones, important as these were, that town planning established itself at this time.

In this transition to the social city there was also a new emphasis on the environment. Because the city's inhabitants were to be governed in terms of the sociability emanating from their interaction with their environment (physical and inter-personal), there was a corresponding movement towards identifying the environment as crucial. In earlier, 'moral', notions of the city, what was seen as 'habit' was viewed as a consequence of the reckless dispositions of the poor and of individual moral failing, but in the late nineteenth century this became gradually systematised, and to some extent removed from the individual, in terms of the determination of habit by the urban environment.[68] This systematisation of habit came to be viewed in terms of eugenics, the science that identified the degeneration of races and classes in terms of the environment. Degenerate habits were not learned but biological. There was a shift in emphasis from sanitation to housing, and from the open street towards living conditions within the home. It was in these new locations, within the family above all, that degeneration could best be tackled.

There was at this time also a general movement towards a scrutiny of the interior of houses. If in some respects it could be said that Britain was somewhat late in the town planning movement, in other respects its modernity was recognised and highly regarded in Europe and the United States. This was expressed above all in terms of the development of the single-family house, in relatively low population density form. The Town Improvement Clauses Act of 1847 and the Public Health Acts of 1848 and 1875 extended existing use of building regulations into the concerns of public health. After 1875 a model set of building bylaws had great impact, flattening out the variation between different towns and cities. In chapter 2 this external regulation of the spaces around the house, above all the spaces of the street, was considered in some detail.[69] It could be said that the British emphasis was on the street, as opposed to the city as a whole and the inside of the house, but in the late nineteenth century this was to change, as it did from 1890 throughout Europe.[70] The 'housing question' in Britain came to the centre of attention, and it was in fact this 'question' which did much to drive the actual practice of town planning, a practice somewhat slow to start before the First World War, as is evident in the rather piecemeal and timid Town Planning Act of 1910. Across Europe, the move to determine the internal life of buildings was, however, very marked, as was evident in the deepening concern with the size, function and layout of individual rooms in different town planning conditions.[71]

The emphasis of eugenics was on the inherited and the involuntary. This view of the environment, of course, ran counter to more voluntaristic understandings of the social. The latter were evident in terms of the development in intellectual and political circles in late nineteenth-century Britain of idealist notions which emerged alongside evolutionary, biological and organic ideas of a 'society' which was functionally adapted to its environment. The idea of society as based on inexorable natural laws to some extent gave way to one understood in terms of conscious will and purpose. Seen as natural, material and involuntary in one view, society in the idealist tradition was seen as mental and moral. In practice both traditions often coalesced, organicism and voluntarism cohabiting in terms of the view of an organic society which was rational and purposeful, rather than simply natural and predetermined.[72] Of course there was conflict between these perspectives, and indeed within each of them them, but in general they were compatible, not least amongst the Fabians, for example in the view that while mental ability was an individually possessed thing, the environment should be so planned that the possession of this ability would bear a close relation to one's social position.[73]

The state came to play a central role in this rethinking of the social. This involved the realisation that the state must work through the characteristics of society in a much more direct way than hitherto, constituting loyalties, obligations and rights which were to be much more collective than previously, even though the primary aim was the reconstitution of the individual self as the driving force in the regeneration of society. In Britain and in Europe the major consequence was the extensive 'social' legislation of the time, which laid the foundations of the twentieth-century 'welfare state'.[74] However, this 'social' city can in fact be seen to operate outside the remit of formally liberal regimes, and indeed of governmentally liberal ones too – as discussed in the concluding chapter, the 'social city' was evident in British and other colonial contexts. There it seems to have been aimed at creating hierarchy. One may think of the social city as it worked in other contexts too, for instance that of the Soviet city, where planning can be understood as aimed at equality, and does not seem to have attempted to elicit the free involvement of the citizen, either as an individual or as part of a free civil society. None the less, there is sufficient across these various versions of the social city to suggest important correspondences between political regimes usually seen as diametrically different. And this commonality can in certain of its characteristics be said to have 'liberal' qualities, so that again existing typologies are questioned. Thinking of modernity in this fashion may be useful, as Paul Rabinow shows in his book on architectural modernism and town planning in France.[75]

Also, international differences clearly emerge within what might be called governmentally liberal versions of the social city.[76] In the French case, it could be said that the aim was to rebuild the city entirely, and in the German case that it was to plan the extant city more, for instance employing extension planning. Although the latter was evident in Britain, the garden city movement points to a certain, and familiar, British ambivalence about the city.[77] One thinks of the long tradition, going back to Owenism, of forsaking the existing city for a new community in the country. Certainly, in the popular manifestations of the political Liberalism of the time the true home of the independence espoused by this politics was not the city at all.[78] The city was the place which threatened independence, and for liberal governance as well it was the big city that in many respects was the place where the 'reciprocal censorship' of governmentality was most at risk.[79] The anonymity of the city, its dissolution of the bonds of community, was contrasted with a whole range of alternatives, in popular Liberalism, for instance, the small-holding of the Scottish crofter, or the model of the town as an Athenian democracy.[80] In fact, in both governmentality and in politics (high and low), the city was often forced into the shape of the town, a shape that could be more easily idealised and worked with – this is evident in chapter 3, and not for nothing were town halls called such and not city halls, at least in England. None the less, in terms of the constitution of problems of governance, the city, more than anything else, was a 'permanent provocation' to government, its very intractability constantly defeating and engendering governance.

As for the political implementation of town planning, this was of most effect in the inter-war years. Then it became part of state practice in a very important way. Raymond Unwin was particularly significant in this. He helped establish the science and discipline of town planning, becoming a lecturer in town planning at Birmingham University, and across Europe as well as in Britain, town planning, or *Stadtbau*, generated its own journals, associations and experts. Unwin's *Town Planning in Practice*, heavily influenced by Sitte, was the most influential town planning manual in Britain in the first half of the twentieth century. Unwin in time became involved in the housing and planning bureaucracy in a major way, so that his influence, and that of his associate R. Barry Parker, was profound. It was felt by bureaucrats, at the highest levels of government, as well as being evident in architecture itself, his work shaping the design of much new state and municipal housing. In 1919 he became the chief architect and chief technical officer for building and town planning at the new Ministry of Housing. In 1919 the Housing and Town Planning Act made town planning compulsory, and between 1919 and 1932 almost two million houses were built under the auspices of the the new ministry, though by no means all came within the detailed regulations of town planning. The influence of town planning on what was often a very laggard central state occurred through the ways characteristic of liberal civil society, namely across many different political affiliations, and involving a myriad of local groups and associations. The role of municipal authorities themselves was crucial. Town planning was itself therefore a product of the increasingly complex and variegated civil society that governmental liberalism had ushered in.[81] Aspects of this complexity form the subject of the next chapter, in particular the complex relationship between power and resistance in the city. This I want to pursue first analytically, but mainly in regard to that most volatile of all arenas of liberal governmentality, which I call the republic of the streets.

Notes

1. Thomas Osborne, Nikolas Rose and Engin F. Isin, *Governing Cities: Liberalism, Neoliberalism, and Advanced Liberalism* (Urban Studies Programme Working Paper No. 19, York University, Toronto, April 1998).
2. Ibid., pp. 5–7.
3. Mitchell Schwarzer, *German Architectural Theory and the Search for Modernity* (Cambridge: Cambridge University Press, 1995), 'Introduction'.
4. Ibid., pp. 10–12.
5. Ibid., pp. 12–24.
6. Tony Bennett, 'The Exhibitionary Complex', in Nicholas Dirks, Geoff Eley and Sherry B. Ortner (eds), *Culture/Power/History: Readings in Contemporary Social Theory* (London: Princeton University Press, 1994); also Tony Bennett, *The Birth of the Museum: History, Theory and Politics* (London: Routledge, 1995).
7. Nikolas Rose, 'Towards a Critical Sociology of Freedom', Inaugural Lecture, Goldsmiths College, 5 May 1992.
8. George Simmel, 'Sociology of the Senses' and 'The Metropolis and Mental Life', in David Frisby and Mike Featherstone (eds), *Simmel on Culture* (London: Sage, 1997).
9. On the city as theatre, see Deborah Nord, *Walking in the Victorian City: Women, Representation and the City* (London: Princeton University Press, 1995), chapter 1.
10. Carl Schorske, *Fin-de-Siècle Vienna: Politics and Culture* (New York: Vintage Books, 1981), chap. II.
11. Ibid. pp. 31–2.
12. Ibid., p. 36.
13. Ibid., pp. 100–1.
14. Ibid., p. 101.
15. Richard Sennett, *The Fall of Public Man: The Forces Eroding Public Life* (New York: Knopf, 1977). See also his *The Conscience of the Eye: The Design and Social Life of Cities* (London: Faber, 1991).
16. Richard Sennett, *The Fall of Public Man*, chapters 4, 8, 10.
17. Mark Girouard, *The English Town: A History of Urban Life* (London: Yale University Press, 1990) and *Cities and People: A Social and Architectural History* (London: Yale University Press, 1985); Donald J. Olsen, *The City as a Work of Art: London, Paris, Vienna* (London: Yale University Press, 1986) and *Town Planning in London: The*

Eighteenth and Nineteenth Centuries (London: Yale University Press, 1964); Peter Hall, *Cities of Tomorrow: An Intellectual History of Urban Planning and Design in the Twentieth Century* (Oxford: Blackwell, 1988).

18. Mark Girouard, *The English Town*, pp. 190–3.

19. Ibid., pp. 196–7, 204–5.

20. Donald J. Olsen, *The City as a Work of Art*, pp. 69, 161–2, 171, 172, 177.

21. Susan Buck-Morss, *The Dialectics of Seeing: Walter Benjamin and the Arcades Project* (London: MIT Press, 1989), chapter 9.

22. Stephen Bann, *The Clothing of Clio: The Study of the Representations of History in Nineteenth-Century Britain and France* (Cambridge: Cambridge University Press, 1984), pp. 15–16.

23. John H.G. Archer, 'Introduction', in Archer (ed.), *Art and Architecture in Victorian Manchester: Ten Illustrations of Patronage* (Manchester: Manchester University Press, 1985); Donald J. Olsen, *The City as a Work of Art*.

24. James Schmiechen, 'Glasgow of the Imagination: Architecture, Townscape and Society', in W. Hamish Fraser and Irene Marer (eds), *Glasgow 1830–1912*, Volume 2 (Manchester: Manchester University Press, 1996). See also James Schmiechen and Kenneth Carls, *The British Market Hall: A Social and Architectural History* (London: Yale University Press, 1999), part 2.

25. John Summerson, 'London, the Artifact', in H.J. Dyos and M. Wolff (eds), *The Victorian City: Images and Reality* (London: Routledge, 1973).

26. Mark Girouard, *The English Town*, chapter 13.

27. J. Bradshaw, *Visitors to Manchester: A Selection of British and Foreign Visitors' Descriptions of Manchester* (Swinton: Richardson, 1987).

28. De Tocqueville, cited in ibid., pp. 34–5, from Alexis de Tocqueville, *Oeuvres complètes* (London: 1957), volume 5, pp. 78–82.

29. Friedrich Engels and Leon Faucher, cited in Bradshaw, *Visitors to Manchester*, pp. 37–42.

30. Friedrich Engels, *The Condition of the Working Class in England in 1844*, ed. Eric Hobsbawm (London: Panther, 1969, first published in Great Britain, London, 1892), pp. 78–96.

31. See above, pp. 88–9.

32. Simon Gunn, *The Public Culture of the Victorian Middle Class: Ritual and Authority in the English Industrial City 1840–1914* (Manchester: Manchester University Press, 2000).

33. Patrick Joyce, *Democratic Subjects: The Self and the Social in 19th Century England* (Cambridge: Cambridge University Press, 1994), pp. 164–6.

34. Simon Gunn, *Public Culture of the Victorian Middle Class*, p. 27.

35. Ibid., chapter 6.

36. Ulrich Finke, 'The Art Treasures Exhibition', in John H.G. Archer (ed.), *Art and Architecture in Victorian Manchester*.

37. *The Irish Builder*, 15 March 1880.

38. *The Dublin Builder*, 1 June 1859.

39. John H.G. Archer, 'A Classic of Its Age', in Archer (ed.), *Art and Architecture and Victorian Manchester*.

40. A.J. Pass, *Thomas Worthington: Victorian Architecture and Social Purpose* (Manchester: Manchester Literary and Philosophical Society, 1988).

41. Colin Cunningham, *Victorian and Edwardian Town Halls* (London: Routledge and Kegan Paul, 1981), pp. 214–20.

42. *Free Lance* (Manchester), 'The Opening', 14 September 1877; *City Jackdaw* (Manchester), 15 September 1877.

43. The *émigré* German Hallé can, in respect of the public sphere he helped initiate, be regarded as a musical parallel to a whole range of institutions and activities in the Victorian city. These, in the characteristic form of the 'voluntary society', with its new codifications of 'public' behaviour (in terms of its open criteria for membership, and for accountability), epitomised this new sense of the public body. Though still depending on voluntary effort, such bodies were part of a longer-term movement towards the secular and the professional. Their importance in the major Victorian city of Leeds has been documented in detail in R.J. Morris, *Class, Sect and Party: The Making of the British Middle-Class: Leeds, 1820–50* (Manchester: Manchester University Press, 1990). See also A.J. Kidd and D. Nicholls (eds), *The Making of the British Middle Class? Studies of Regional Cultural Diversity since the Eighteenth Century* (Stroud: Sutton, 1998), and their *Gender, Civic Culture and Consumerism: Middle-Class Identity in Britain 1800–1940* (Manchester: Manchester University Press, 1999).

44. William Young cited in Susan Paton Pyecroft, ' "Creating a City Chambers Worthy of Glasgow": The Social Meanings of an Architectural Process, 1878–1889' (Central Michigan University and University of Strathclyde PhD, 1995), p. 47. See also Thomas A. Markus, *Buildings and Power: Freedom and Control in the Origin of Modern Building Types* (London: Routledge, 1993).

45. Susan Paton Pyecroft, ' "Creating a City Chambers" ', chapter 3.

46. Colin Cunningham, *Victorian and Edwardian Town Halls*, chapter 11.

47. W.E.A. Axon, 'The Procession of the Trades', in Axon, *An Architectural and General Description of the Town Hall, Manchester* (Manchester, 1878); see also *Programme of the Trade Societies Procession*, also 'Grand Opening Song', together with illustrated reports in *The Graphic*, and the *The Illustrated London News*, also *The Penny Guide to the New Town Hall* (Manchester, 1877), all items in Manchester Town Hall Collection, Manchester Central Reference Library.

48. Simon Gunn, *The Public Culture of the Victorian Middle Class*, pp. 173–5.

49. Susan Paton Pyecroft, ' "Creating a City Chambers" ', pp. 42–8, and see *A Description of the Ceremonial Foundation Stone Laying* (Glasgow, 1885).

50. *Mural Painting in the Large Town Hall, Manchester* (Manchester: Manchester City Council, n.d. [1969?]), and Julian Treuherz, 'Ford Madox Brown and the Manchester Murals', in J.H.G. Archer (ed.), *Art and Architecture in Victorian Manchester*, see also description in W.E.A. Axon, *An Architectural and General Description*, and see Patrick Joyce, *Visions of the People: Industrial England and the Question of Class, 1840–1914* (Cambridge: Cambridge University Press, 1991), p. 182.

51. Charles Dellheim, *The Face of the Past: The Preservation of the Mediaeval Inheritance in Victorian England* (Cambridge: Cambridge University Press, 1982), esp. chapter 4.

52. James Schmiechen, 'Glasgow of the Imagination'.

53. Colin Cunningham, *Victorian and Edwardian Town Halls*, chapter 9.

54. R. de Zouche Hall, *Halifax Town Hall: An Account of Its Building and Inauguration* (Halifax, 1963). See also Mark Girouard, *The English Town*, chapter 11.

55. Barbara Miller Lane, 'Government Buildings in European Capitals, 1870s–1914', in Hans J. Teutberg (ed.), *Urbanisierung im 19. and 20. Jahrhundert: Historische und Geographischen Aspekten* (Cologne: Bohlau, 1983), and 'Changing Attitudes to Monumentality: An Interpretation of European Architecture and Urban Form 1880–1914', in *The Growth and Transformation of the Modern City* (Swedish Council for Building Research, Stockholm, 1979).

56. Mitchell Schwarzer, *German Architectural Theory*, pp. 12–25, 149, 167–8, 269.

57. On architectural historicism, see also Eve Blau and Monika Platzer, *Shaping the Great City: Modern Architecture in Central Europe 1890–1937* (London: Presel, 1999); Robert Van Pelt and Carol William Westfall, *Architectural Principles in the Age of Historicism* (London: Yale University Press, 1991).

58. Thomas Osborne *et al.*, *Governing Cities*, pp. 1–5.

59. On Chicago, see Christine M. Boyer, *The Rational City: The Myth of American City Planning* (London: MIT Press, 1983).

60. On Howard, see Peter Hall and Colin Ward, *Sociable Cities: The Legacy of Ebenezer Howard* (Chichester: John Wiley, 1998).

61. Patrick Joyce, 'Introduction', in Joyce (ed.), *The Social in Question: New Bearings in History and the Social Sciences* (London: Routledge, 2002).

62. Thomas Osborne *et al.*, *Governing Cities*, p. 15.

63. Patrick Geddes, *Cities in Evolution: An Introduction to the Town Planning Movement and to the Study of Civics* (London, 1915), and *City Development: A Study of Parks, Gardens and Culture Institutions* (Edinburgh, 1904); Helen Meller, 'Cities and Evolution: Patrick Geddes as an International Prophet of Town Planning before 1914', in Anthony Sutcliffe (ed.), *The Rise of Modern Urban Planning 1800–1914* (Oxford: Basil Blackwell, 1980), pp. 102–3, 199–218; and on Geddes see also her *Patrick Geddes: Social Evolutionist and City Planner* (London: Routledge, 1990).

64. Iain Border, 'The Politics of the Plan', in Iain Border and David Dunster (eds), *Architecture and the Sites of History: The Interpretation of Buildings and Cities* (Oxford: Butterworth Architecture, 1995).

65. Helen Meller, 'Cities and Evolution', p. 23.

66. On the Sociological Movement see R.J. Halliday, 'The Sociology Movement, the Sociology Society and the Genesis of Academic Sociology in Britain', *Sociological Review*, 16:3, 1968.

67. Anthony Sutcliffe, *Towards the Planned City: Germany, Britain, the United States and France 1780–1914* (Oxford: Basil Blackwell, 1981), chapter 6 on the international movement.

68. Thomas Osborne *et al.*, *Governing Cities*, pp. 11–15.

69. See above, pp. 88–9.

70. Anthony Sutcliffe, *Towards the Planned City*, pp. 28, 51–2.

71. Leif Jerram, 'Buildings, Spaces, Politics: Munich City Council and the Management of Modernity, 1900–1930' (University of Manchester PhD, 2001).

72. José Harris, *Private Lives, Public Spirit: Britain 1870–1914* (London: Penguin, 1993).

73. Jonathan Harwood, 'Heredity, Environment and the Legitimation of Social Policy',

in Barry Barnes and Stephen Shapin (eds), *Natural Order: Historical Studies of Scientific Culture* (London: Sage, 1979), also Donald A. McKenzie, *Statistics in Britain 1865–1930: The Social Construction of Scientific Knowledge* (Edinburgh: Edinburgh University Press, 1981).

74. Patrick Joyce, *The Social in Question*, pp. 10–12.

75. Paul Rabinow, *French Modern: Norms and Forms of the Social Environment* (London: MIT Press, 1989).

76. For international, comparative aspects see Anthony Sutcliffe, *Towards the Planned City*, also his (ed.), *The Rise of Modern Urban Planning*; and, on the German example, strongly influenced by the strength of the German state traditions, Brian Ladd, *Urban Planning and Civic Order in Germany, 1860–1914* (London: Harvard University Press, 1990).

77. Raymond Williams, *The Country and the City* (London: Chatto and Windus, 1973).

78. E.F. Biagini (ed.), *Citizenship and Community: Liberalism, Radicals and Collective Identities in the British Isles 1865–1931* (Cambridge: Cambridge University Press, 1996), also his *Liberty, Retrenchment and Reform: Popular Liberalism in the Age of Gladstone 1860–1880* (Cambridge: Cambridge University Press, 1992), chapters 1 and 6.

79. See above, pp. 121.

80. Patrick Joyce, *Visions of the People*, p. 44.

81. For the details of the political achievement of town planning and for accounts of Unwin and Parker, see the contributions in Anthony Sutcliffe (ed), *British Town Planning: the Formative Years* (Leicester: Leicester University Press, 1981).

5

The Republic of the Streets

Knowing and Moving in the City

Resisting freedom

This book is called *The Rule of Freedom*, and its chief emphasis is on the business of governing. To some it may seem that the cities I describe are somewhat free of impediments to this business, though I think that the question of 'resistance' to governance is in fact raised throughout the book in different contexts. I shall consider these contexts again here, in attending somewhat more systematically than previously to this question of the negotiation of, or the resistance to, what I have called the rule of freedom. Of course, aspects of governance often only concern the governed indirectly, if at all, and at several places in this book, for instance in chapter 3 on the emergence of a new ethics of governmental administration, I have emphasised the fact that those who wish to govern must work upon themselves first before they govern others (though the cultivation of governance in the governors must always make its way against *their* resistances). It is also the case, as in the example of the British mapping of India in chapter 1, that the illusion of governmental legibility may be as important as the actual, in practice illusory, achievement of real perfection in governing. There may be a considerable disjunction between appearance and reality, but in order for the business of governing to go forward, it is sometimes the appearance that matters.

Which is to say that the responses of the governed may not always be as important as some accounts imagine. Throughout the book so far I have strongly emphasised material dimensions of governing, indicating how 'technical' and 'non-political' solutions to problems, for example the achievement of an 'objective' cartography, or the new sanitary systems of the nineteenth century, particularly in their engineering solutions, meant that forms of competency, and of agency, were present in material things and processes, but not always present to the consciousness of contemporaries. Indeed, the achievement of a techno-administrative state in a liberal mode seems to have been one of the most profound developments in the period I have considered. The actual creation of consent, and forms of political reason impinging directly on the outlook of the governed, were not always necessary for this state to function, but of course the creation of technical solutions so as to appear *inevitable* did indeed involve persuasion and consent. However, once up and running, technical solutions to some extent had a life of their own, which was grist to the mill of governing liberally. As has been suggested at many places, the material embedding of power was itself made up of a myriad of practices which themselves composed overarching interventions in the world, interventions in the form of what I have called political reason, even when the rationale of these practices was not articulated discursively, or not articulated directly, and sometimes even when it was not present to the awareness of historical actors at all.

To some extent, I have emphasised culture as practice rather than representation. I have also dwelt on the dimensions of agency and performativity; as I put it in the Introduction, on how things work somewhat more than what they mean. While the two cannot be separated, an emphasis on agency leads to a different set of questions from one on representation and meaning alone. Human agency comes less to the fore, or rather attention is shifted to the complex interaction of human and non-human agency. In fact, 'resistance' is very much part of my interest in these interactions, the resistance of matter itself, as in chapter 2 on the thankless task of maintaining city infrastructure, but also the resistance of humans as they struggled to impart agency to matter, 'black boxing' it with varying degrees of success, to employ a term taken from science studies. That particular discipline emphasises how scientists and engineers struggle with the material world in order to 'capture' agency,[1] and if we conceive of agency as an *achievement* in the human as well as the material world, then we can think of 'resistance' as being inseparable from human attempts to capture their own agency as well as the agency of matter. It is in this light that one may conceive of several of the studies in this book, for example the achievement of a governmental ethics in part in the form of honourable secrecy, considered in chapter 3 (where habit struggles against 'habit'), or the performance of objectivity in institutional and daily social life seen in cartography and statistics, considered in chapter 1. Both are instances of a struggle to achieve the agencies of governing, human but also material, a struggle that was always provisional and elusive, like the scientists' struggle.

In the material, non-human realm, the provisional and contingent capturing of agency that parallels that of the human world is evident, among many other places, in the instance of Ordnance Survey mapping, in what I considered to be the complex and volatile 'layering' of knowledge and agency in the map itself. This aspect of the material map involved a temporary stabilisation of representational conventions, though the accompanying volatility of meaning evident in the map seemed to be related to the nature of liberalism itself, actively inviting the practice of freedom while at the same time facing the danger of being engulfed by it. Liberalism, as has been argued, could thrive on these contradictions, but was also vulnerable to them, in terms of the freedom beyond freedom. We are here in the area of the several 'others' of liberal freedom, an area that takes us further into the question of 'resistance', though the latter would seem to be not the 'other' of power so much as its complement.

From the point of view of an interest in agency and performativity, 'doing' in the social world only makes sense in terms of what doing is pitted against, namely what at the same time impedes, facilitates and necessitates action, so that 'resistance' is part and parcel of the means and the implementation of action. In many respects it seems to me that Foucault's own conception of 'resistance' has a good deal in common with this. For him, resistance is the condition of power relations, and, as he says: 'If there was no resistance, there would be no power relations . . . So resistance comes first, and resistance remains superior to the forces of the process; power relations are obligated to change with resistance. So I think *resistance* is the main word, the keyword, in this dynamic'.[2] However, contrary to orthodox notions of power, and this includes power as conceived in many social historical accounts, a subject-centred understanding of power is not involved here. Resistance is not necessarily linked to conscious choices and acts, but is understandable at a more basic conceptual level, in the sense that a movement that does not encounter resistance cannot be called a force. 'Resistance', in this sense, is intrinsic to how force and power operate. Power feeds on resistance, and vice versa. Resistance is not the opposite of power but its corollary. In this account power cannot be seen as originating in the subject, especially when conceived of as an 'individual'; rather, the individual is an effect of power, but also at the same time, it should be emphasised, the vehicle, or the element, of power's articulation. From this perspective, one in which pre-defined subjects do not enact power but, on the contrary, subjects are produced out of the engagement in power relations and therefore out of engagements involving resistance, the similarities with more performative accounts seem quite close. In both points of view, there is a strong sense in which subjects are realised in *doing*, in active engagement with the world.

Therefore, there is always a mutuality of power and resistance, which does not, however, mean that these are always equal or commensurate. I have so far attempted to allow for this mutuality in certain ways. For instance, the very nature and means of governmental power may become the very means by which those who experience power resist it. Indeed, governmental liberalism itself can be considered as the defining and overarching instance of this, by virtue of its being a form of political reason in great measure divided against itself, given its oxymoronic status as a mode of *rule* through *freedom* (the dangerous openness and plenitude of the Ordnance Survey map just referred to is one small material instance of this). However, particularly as emphasised in chapter 3, the contradictory nature of governmental liberalism, evident in its agonistic dimensions, could be a considerable source of strength. In more particular instances of power being the means of its own resistance, for example in chapter 1, I emphasised how statistics might combat statistics, and how more generally 'objectivity' might be marshalled so as to resist objectivity. In this way, the 'rules of the game' of power might be transformed so as to offer the ruled a means of negotiating, questioning and even resisting power, using resistance here in its more usual sense.

But at the same time these *were* the rules of the game, and as such a means of instituting power. Something of the subtle reciprocities of power involved is evident in the mapping of 'state space' considered in chapter 1, particularly in the case of Ireland. There the incorporation of 'local knowledge' in maps created what I called 'a reconfiguration of the field in which power and its reception operate', so that the new rules of the game, in terms of the epistemological framework of state space, both instituted and resisted power. This was a temporal, historical, matter as well as a spatial one, for old forms of knowledge and experience came into relation with new ones, in which they might be embedded. Other instances of this have also been apparent, for example the relationship between old and new ethics of public service and administration considered in chapter 3. In these temporal relationships spaces for instability, contradiction and resistance were opened up.

In the example of the mapping of Ireland, older forms of knowledge were also translated into new ones, for instance in the figure of John O'Donovan. The importance of translation, and translators, is therefore seen to be crucial, and indeed, whether conceived in this sense, or as 'hybrids', 'mediators' or as 'liminal' persons, places and things, this book as a whole has been greatly absorbed with these 'in between' things, for it is they that seem to offer a particularly productive way of understanding the reciprocities and mutualities of power/resistance. These things, and people, seem indeed to have been locations where the very nature of rule and the social order itself came into question, for instance markets and cemeteries. In this chapter the street itself, the 'republic' of the street, is seen in a similar light, as a place where the mutualities of power/resistance can be understood. In looking at things like markets, I wish to align anthropological notions of freedom, in the sense of the liminal, with governmental notions of freedom, as a strategy for exploring the latter and the resistances that ran through them. These resistances can be thought about in terms of that which exceeded freedom, exciting it into action but constantly eluding it. This I have called the freedom beyond freedom, which we might also think about as freedom's 'other'.

How best to think about these 'others' of disciplinary, governmental freedom, of the rule of freedom? One might think about freedom as release, not constraint, the letting go of control. And one might think about the other of rule as a lack of rule, as misrule, and unruliness. The other of the free is also the enslaved, the bound, for example the Indian immured in custom, or the working class immured in what to those who sought to govern it was its irrational culture of release and self-indulgence. This recalcitrant working class has been a considerable presence in this work so far. In the conclusion, the recalcitrant colonial subject will be considered further. In chapter 2 I opened up aspects of 'popular' culture in terms of the liminal sites in which 'resistance' could be located, in markets and fairs particularly. In the present chapter I take this further, exploring liminal sites and conditions in which contemporaries articulated what they literally took, in their own terms, to be 'freedom', locations of human release and unruliness which can be understood as the 'others' of liberal freedom. In particular, in the next section, I consider the pub 'free and easy' in this light, while more generally the street itself can be viewed in a similar way. As the major urban location for a significant dimension of the phenomenological, embodied city, namely moving in the city, especially in the form of walking, the street in the final section of this chapter serves as the focus for consideration of further aspects of power and resistance. In particular, an understanding of the tacit, habitual and practical aspects of negotiating the city that is to be found in walking enables further consideration of the freedom of the city.

In the next section I consider ways of knowing the city, in maps and guidebooks for example, but also in literary and other aesthetic representations, for instance the songs of the free and easy, though it is quite apparent that knowing and being in the city are in practice inseparable, song in performance comprising a mode of being, and walking in the city being a mode of tacit, habitual knowledge. None the less, it seems useful to distinguish between knowing and being in this approximate way. In thinking about walking in the city, I employ the work of de Certeau. From his post-structuralist perspective, the rational order of discourse is seen as constituting its own 'other' in terms of its non-representable part, that which is excluded, repressed or forgotten.[3] That this is so will be apparent in the treatment so far, for instance in the darkness and the illegibility presented to the light of publicity that were apparent in chapter 3, though it might be nearer the mark to say that governance seems to have generated its own 'others', constantly creating 'problems' for itself, which at the same time permitted it to function but constantly defeated it (I wrote earlier of the Sisyphean task of liberalism in this respect). Though the work of Foucault has, I think rightly, often been characterised as paying relatively little attention to 'resistance', this criticism is less apposite than is sometimes allowed, and not only at a theoretical level. In the example of the concept of heterotopia, of 'other places', there is explicit attention by Foucault to the nature of the other, and in the final section of this chapter I attend to this concept in terms of the nineteenth-century public park. Again, other dimensions of 'resistance' come into view with this.

The question of resistance, is of course, complicated by the very fact that the understanding of power in this book makes resistance sometimes difficult to identify. If power is dispersed in material things and processes, and all sorts of agency, as I said earlier, 'haunt' the material world, and if from a Foucauldian perspective power is not a zero-sum affair but is socially dispersed and multivalent, then, as was apparent in the Introduction, actually identifying what a 'political rationality' precisely was and is presents difficulties, and therefore so also does identifying resistance. None the less, the great advantage of the approaches I have used is the very recognition that power and also rule itself are dispersed far beyond the areas and channels in which they are usually acknowledged. In thinking about how we might conceive of liberal governmentality, power and rule were dispersed not only into an autonomous 'society' but also into a self-regulating economy. So far, although I have touched on economic aspects, they have not been as central as they could have been.

In the next section, 'Knowing the city', I want to consider how knowledge of the city was intimately tied up with understanding the city as a 'spectacle', a spectacle that was in turn intimately connected to the economic sphere of consumption, not just the consumption of the means by which the city was known, but also the consumption of the experiences of the city which these means opened up. In order to be consumed in this way, the city had to be presented in aesthetic forms, for example in city guides and the voluminous imaginative literature of the time on city life. As was seen in chapter 4, the aesthetic was part of governance, but the aesthetic productions evident in knowing the city, for example the literature of city 'types', seem at first glance to be outside governmentality. And indeed in many respects they were certainly outside the increasingly state-directed and political embrace of freedom as a principle of governance that I have so far considered. The instruments of knowing the city I consider in the next section certainly involved governing conduct, but this everyday governance of conduct is not the same as governmentality, which involves the coordination of these many, everyday practices of governing conduct in such a way as to make governing whole populations possible. None the less, the everyday conduct of conduct cannot simply be separated from liberal governmentality. In what follows I try to establish some lines of connection, but I also recognise that there are multiple points of disconnection too, in which 'resistance' was located. The chapter therefore comprises at once some account of resistance and some account of this grey area between what I call the everyday conduct of conduct and the operations of governmentality itself.

Knowing the city

Thinking about governmentality in terms of consumption and the aesthetic takes the idea into places where it seems somewhat attenuated and indistinct. None the less, the delegation of freedom and choice to the consumer in liberal society does seem to have been of great importance in how power and political reason have operated in that kind of society. This is especially the case in the twentieth century, where, for instance in the work of Zygmunt Bauman, social discipline in the contemporary world is now seen as in great measure displaced from formal government to the area of the consumption of goods and lifestyles.[4] In writing on governmentality itself, discipline through consumption has also been considered, for example in the work of Nikolas Rose.[5] However, these contemporary developments had their roots at least as early as the eighteenth century. The spectacle of the city became in fact itself a site of freedom, and this freedom to consume the city had inescapably disciplinary aspects. On the one hand, these aspects can be understood as serving to complement the operations of liberal governmentality, at least in so far as governmentality can be understood as circulating in the freedom of choice evident in these economic and aesthetic spheres. One might call this indirect- or quasi-governmentality. Historically, these dimensions of governmentality seem to have preceded that more direct political governance I have so far documented, so that one might also talk of a sort of pre-governmentality. However, on the other hand, the means of knowing the city could also serve as points of disconnection from or 'resistance' to governmentality. In this section, when maps are again considered, the aesthetic dimensions of fantasy can be understood as countering or disrupting the 'objectivity' and rationality that were important parts of governmental power, though fantasies of consumption might complement this power also. Here the emphasis tends to fall more on these complementary aspects. In the next section, on moving in the city, the emphasis tends to switch more to impediments to power. In both sections I am conscious that I merely open up questions for further consideration, and that I do limited justice to the problems involved.

In terms of representations of the city I want first to return to cartographic knowledge. The city was, of course, represented in many cartographic forms other than the Ordnance Survey, though the account of abstraction and objectification given for the OS maps does describe much of the development of maps in general. Indeed, after the 1850s there was widespread pirating of the Survey's information and its mapping conventions. Access to maps was accelerated by the removal of the paper tax and stamp duty in the 1850s, and the mechanisation of map production after 1870. There was a great proliferation of the number and types of maps, and increased access to them.[6] This was contemporaneous with the urbanisation of the population. The British became an urban nation partly through the means of the city map: the city and the map grew up side-by-side, the one influencing the other. Of all the maps available, that which perhaps did most to shape conceptions of the city was the map that purported to be a street guide.

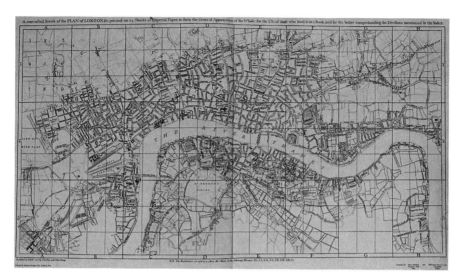

Figure 5.1 John Roques' map of London, 1746

Such 'guides' were to be found in city guidebooks (so-called), and in city and town directories. Sometimes they were sold separately as street atlases, culminating in the modern *A–Z*. If London is treated first, and the extra-cartographic aspects of guidebooks and directories later, John Roques' map of 1746 can be considered one of the first and most widely available forms of street finder (Figure 5.1).[7] The cultural geographer Miles Ogborn describes it as being a revelation to contemporaries, who, in however unwieldly a manner, for the first time saw the city as a whole yet in a detailed form.[8] He recognises this map's crucial role in producing what he calls the 'spaces of modernity' in the capital, spaces that had a close relation to governance. The London it delineated as a street finder was in the process of becoming one dedicated to free movement, the free movement of people and traffic. London was reproduced as a network of roads and traffic. In fact, the map itself was framed by representations of liberty and commerce. The modernity of the map is evident in other senses too, for instance the transition from personal patronage to map production for the market.

However, the street atlas in a compact and easily referred to form seems only to have come into its own around the mid-nineteenth century. *Collin's Illustrated Atlas of London with 7,000 References*, of 1854, is regarded as the earliest forerunner of a modern-day *A–Z* (Figure 5.2). 'Pocket

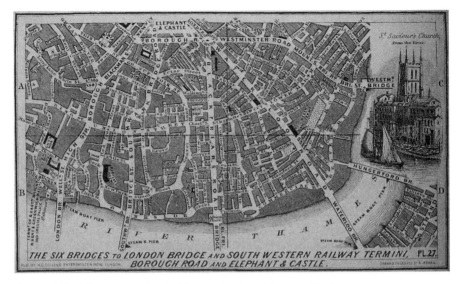

Figure 5.2   Map from *Collin's Illustrated Atlas of London*, 1854

plans' of the city, available from at least the late eighteenth century, if not greatly detailed, made city navigation of an approximate sort reasonably easy.[9] With the spectacular nineteenth-century growth of London, such navigation became increasingly difficult, the city constantly outgrowing attempts to know it cartographically. The city that nineteenth-century atlases and maps everywhere charted was even more a city of streets than in the eighteenth century, and even more abstract and geometric than Roques' map. In *Collin's Atlas* the city was made up of streets. The index listed streets and usually nothing else. Habitations were simply what occurred between streets. The city was mapped at ground level, without a vertical axis.[10] It was a composite of routes and passages, a space to be traversed and manipulated in order to find a destination in the quickest possible way.

The Introduction to *Collin's* asks if the reader has ever seen a stranger examining, 'almost hopelessly', the square yard of paper of which the older plans and maps were made up. Unless the 'whole map of London' is very large (and therefore impractical), it is 'a mass of confusion' or only gives the main thoroughfares. The *Atlas* is for 'street use', including the use of Londoners, of whom it says very few know the districts beyond their localities, and even fewer have an intimate knowledge of

London's whole extent. The maps can be consulted in the street 'without notice' and without inconvenience. The city is for moving through with ease and a certain anonymity. This is all the more necessary as London has entered a new sort of unknowability: London is now so big that to take it all in at one go is 'productive of little but useless annoyance and bewilderment'. The introduction to *London at a Glance* (1860) sets the words 'finding your way' in quotation marks, indicating a sharpened awareness of the city as a maze of tracks, and the atlas as a 'street finder'. In fact the Introduction speaks of the 'labyrinth of the Metropolis', and of itself as 'the guide', but also 'the friend', for all those who seek their way through it.

The unknowability of the city is in this friendly guide to be mastered 'at a glance'. In inverse proportion to the city's growth beyond comprehension it is rendered knowable by a technology of the glance. It is thus a place that one can know on the move, retaining one's autonomy as a private self negotiating the city. However, it can also enable the prudence of planning in advance. The Introduction claims that '[g]reat economy of time and money is to be had for the visitor by pre-arranging their visit by this guide.' The priority of the city as a place for the traffic of goods and people is apparent. This evident 'modernity' of the city cannot of course simply be equated with liberal governmentality, but the construction of ways of knowing and moving in the city which these maps facilitated had a relation to liberal modes of rule in terms of reinforcing modes of subjectivity and visual readings of the city that liberalism was itself concerned to reinforce. In particular these concerned the constitution of an autonomous, rather calculating and alert, private self, one realised in purposeful and easeful movement through a city itself conceived of as a place of traffic and unfettered communication.

Change tended in the same direction in the other British cities as in London.[11] What seems to be nearly a full range of maps and plans for the city of Manchester helps consideration of this change,[12] as do extensive runs of maps for other cities, for instance Liverpool.[13] The plans appearing in the city directories are as revealing as those in city guides. The directories of Pigot, and later Slater, used for all manner of purposes by city inhabitants,[14] were amongst the most important sources of cartographic knowledge of Manchester, but very similar city directory maps were available for all British cities.

In 1824 Pigot's directory map seems to have first featured concentric circles and radial lines dividing up the city into segments, so that geometrical space even more decidedly located the user in the city (Figure 5.3).[15]

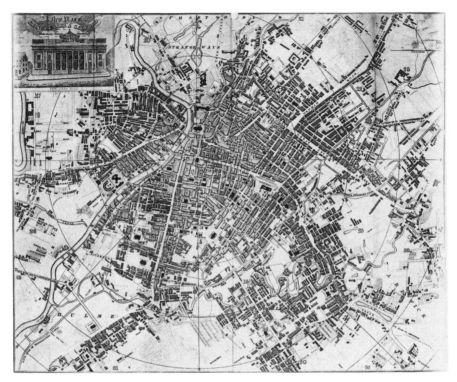

Figure 5.3   Pigot's 1824 directory map of Manchester

And it was the centre of the circles, the cartographical heart of the city, which is revealing. This was the Exchange building in Manchester, the core of the Manchester cotton textile business, and hence the economic hub of this cotton city. Map users were thus oriented around the foremost centre of economic exchange in the city, and indeed one of the foremost centres in the world at that time. The cartographic logic of the city map was about facilitating free movement and exchange. It was fitting therefore that this map should be centred on the Exchange itself. The city that was based on free economic exchange, for Manchester was the home of free trade, was mapped in terms of free exchange. One knew where one was in the city always in relation to the heart of capital. The street atlases that emerged in London around the middle of the century were themselves situated around another heart of exchange, namely the General Post Office near St Paul's.[16] Again the symbolic meaning is a powerful one: publications designed to effect rapid and unimpeded communication were centred upon another heart of communications, this time not goods but information.

However, as indicated in chapter 1, this emphasis on abstraction and objectivity fails to comprehend the effect of maps if these qualities are seen as the polar opposites of fantasy, the fantasy of governors and the governed. As for the former, it could be said that the very 'objectivity' of the map often represented a fantasy of total legibility, a fantasy, as for example in the minds of the governors of the British Raj, which represented a governmental utopia. As for the governed, the rationality of the map was not a negation of fantasies of the city, but often a provocation to them, and in such fantasies one can situate 'resistance' *and* the embedding of liberalism in the imagination. Analysts of visuality in the nineteenth century have suggested how the abstraction of vision, in allowing for its quantification and homogenisation, also created the conditions for its re-enchantment.[17] The reification of the world that abstraction created made possible new conditions for imaginative reworkings upon this world. In a parallel way, the very idea that the modern self was something that could be made went with the recognition that it could be unmade too, that it was plastic, and that it could be re-enchanted.[18]

This remaking of vision can be seen in terms of what has been called 'spectacular consumption', in which, through the agency precisely of things like guidebooks and city maps, but also literary representations of the city, the increasingly commodified and abstract 'everyday' world of its inhabitants was made into 'spectacle', and city inhabitants themselves into spectators. Among others, Vanessa Schwarz has considered this new framing of everyday life so as to form a 'spectacular reality' in her work on nineteenth-century Paris.[19] Alongside a new invention of the everyday, and the mass spectacle of the city, was the 'massified' gaze of the city spectator, in the sense of the growing need and tendency to classify the great urban masses then coming together. While the relationship between these developments – often considered under the rubric of 'modernity' – and liberal governmentality is obviously complex, the figure of the omniopticon, considered in chapter 4, the many viewing the many only now in disciplinary forms of freedom, needs to be considered in the light of this 'massified' gaze upon the everyday. Peter Fritzsche has described a similar process to that of Paris in Berlin, only a little later, around 1900.[20] Moving in the city, in the 'republic' of its streets, will in the next section take us further into this question of the omniopticon.

Beyond the forms of representation considered here, the 'rational' and 'objective' material infrastructure of the city, not least in the forms of lighting and sewerage systems themselves, became objects of fantasy. As Lynda Nead has shown for London, not only were these objects of fascinated attention themselves part of the spectacle of the city but, as in the case of what she calls a 'poetics' and 'semantics' of gas lighting, new developments in urban infrastructure elicited their own 'others', new forms of lighting, for instance, feeding on and generating new fears and understandings of darkness.[21] The city atlas and guide map illustrate something of this in terms of transport infrastructure. If these objectified the world, their visual realisations enabled projections of this world to take place that were far removed from the 'objective'. The London *A–Z*, for example, like its predecessors, is one instance of commodified vision which opened doors to many other commodified sights of London, making of the city a rational construction of parallel lines and geometric forms, but in this very process facilitating a mental movement through the city, leading one on from place to place, and opening out from one passage to another, often with unexpected results. The city map may be an oppressive grid of lines, but it may also be the key to the mystery which it itself produces.

Another example would be Harry Beck's famous tube map of London of 1933, the forerunner of the present Underground map. Inspired by electrical circuit diagrams, this represents an extreme development of the movement towards abstraction described in chapter 1. This map was the prototype of the present one. It bore little relation to real distances and real direction, and none at all to the streets above: it made of London a coherent and manageable entity in fact, amongst other things shrinking the distance between the suburbs and the centre, so that one did not need to leave London even when one lived in the suburbs (which were at this time being rapidly developed). Travelling to the centre was easy, the straight lines of the map emphasising this.[22] Out of an extreme form of abstraction came the fantastic megalopolis of a new London, a London intimately related to commercial developments, particularly in real estate. Travellers on the London Underground have been a slave to Beck's rational fantasy ever since.

Spectacular consumption and the 'massified' gaze that marked new forms of urban subjectivity were facilitated by more lowly forms of representation than the usual emphasis in the existing literature on the press and literary representations of the city. These mundane forms were closely related to the growth of the consumer as a free subject, which we can indeed relate to the dispersion of governance beyond the state alone.

However, in certain respects the emphasis on subjectivity is misplaced, for the inhabitants of the city became objects as well as subjects, particularly in the form of 'markets', which were the the objects of new forms of commercial activity, including the consumption of the city as spectacle. The importance of city directories in the creation of knowledge about cities' inhabitants is perhaps not generally recognised, nor is their function as databases for a commercial society. Beyond official information, some of which was anyway proscribed, the directories offered the fullest and certainly the most accessible information about city inhabitants. As has been seen, the use of the post and the directories developed in tandem: at least in part, the directories could be called the 'database' of the post.

The post hastened the naming of streets, the fixing of letter-boxes and, above all, the fixing of numbers to doors. (It was Baudelaire's view that this numbering was the death-knell of the urban anonymity upon which the *flâneur* depended.) The 1804 Manchester directory referred proudly in its title to being a list of inhabitants with numbers affixed to their doors, and it was in fact only in the preceding few decades, starting first in London, that home and person came to be joined together to any great extent in this way. The *Post Office Directory of London* (1800) indicates the closeness of the link, and this directory was in fact compiled by means of the employment of 'Inspectors of Inland Letter Carriers'. Directories do not appear to have borne this title before this time. With the institution of the Penny Post in the 1840s, the increasing number of city directories is apparent, and there was a marked increase also in the 1870s and 1880s, with the development of mass retailing.[23] Commercial directories, so called, started in the 1670s, to be followed by trade and professional directories in the 1760s. General trade directories commenced in the 1810s, and specialised trade directories in the 1870s. What is striking is the inclusion of vast numbers of city inhabitants in these general trade directories, way beyond what had earlier been included, and far exceeding those advertising skills and services in what was still a very skill- and labour-intensive economy. It was outside the capital that coverage was really striking. By the 1880s it is estimated that some provincial directories, including Liverpool and Manchester, recorded as many as 70 per cent of households. Occupations were frequently but by no means always listed, further identifying the commercial possibilities of the name itself.[24]

The directories were far more than mere listings of names and occupations. *Kelly's Post Office London Directory* gradually centred in itself the functions of a wide range of other, and older, publications. These included almanacs, parliamentary companions, financial yearbooks, professional yearbooks, peerage lists, street lists, and so on.[25] The Dublin directories especially, and to some extent the London ones, served as digests of information about the nation as a whole. *Thom's 8th Annual Irish Almanac and Official Directory with the Post Office Dublin City and County Guide* (1851) had 110 pages of the 'Statistics of Ireland'. In 1879 10 per cent of the same journal's 1,900 pages were similarly devoted. These included statistics described as 'population', 'geographical', 'crime', 'education', 'poor law', and so on. Other city directories included this kind of statistical information about their cities as a matter of course. In the Dublin case, as with all others, there was a vast amount of information about the city's political, administrative, legal, educational and other affairs as well. These directories were therefore one of the most significant means for the circulation of statistical as well as cartographic knowledge of the city. And these kinds of knowledge partook of new understandings of the 'social' emerging at this time, understandings crucially linked to categories like 'population' and 'crime', themselves critical for liberal governance through the social. To some degree the directories can be understood as the silent agents of what I call quasi-governmentality, just as they were of what has been referred to as the 'massified' gaze.

Parallel to the directories was the increasing number of city 'guides', which offered a much more discursive representation of the city. These, none the less, like the directories, were to a considerable degree still in thrall to the map, for even without specifying routes or walks, there were implied itineraries present in the directory maps because the 'principal buildings' of the city were very clearly marked out graphically, as well as written about. Manchester was perfectly typical of wider developments. The first city guide, of 1804, delineated a sort of hierarchy of these, in which 'public buildings' came first, the likes, in Manchester and everywhere else, of the town hall, the principal trade exchange, the post office, the workhouses, gaols and barracks, and even the gasworks. This account was followed by accounts of charitable, religious and educational institutions, places of amusement and commercial buildings. In Manchester, the Royal Exchange, the cathedral and the town hall throughout the century made up a trinity of the major 'sights' of the city. This trinity of commerce, religion and city government thus defined the city in these representations. These different elements were invariably placed in terms of an historical narrative of the town or city which itself emphasised progress and improvement. The 'spectacle' that mattered here was different from London, one of industry and commerce. (The great warehouses, the new street lighting, the 'class' composition of the city, and the details of a vast industrial output and of the wonders of the factory system marked the industrial spectacle).[26] It will be apparent that the gaze of the spectator constructed through the agency of these guides in large measure complemented governmentally liberal versions of the city, which is not surprising as the guides were in measure the outcome of this liberalism themselves.

However, 'urban spectatorship' had a longer pedigree than is often allowed, as did the massified gaze, elements that the work of Dana Brand allows us to trace in the case of London. Both can be discerned at least as early as the sixteenth century, when the development of a sophisticated consumer culture brought about the early emergence of the city and its inhabitants as themselves forms of spectacle.[27] The very size of London, a very early 'mass' city, encouraged the need to classify this mass. In Brand's account of the *longue durée* of the *flâneur* and of urban spectatorship, John Stow's *Survey of London* (1598) saw the city emerging as a feature of society subordinate to nothing else, independent of the values of Church and Crown. London was a microcosm of the world. It was also the source of that civilised behaviour known as *urbanitas*. This work gave rise to the genre of urban panorama books in the early seventeenth century, which had the effect of dividing the city into separate spaces so as to give the reader a sense of looking at it as a coherent entity. This anticipated later representations of the city as divisible into legible character types and representative places. Brand goes on to describe a persistent tension in the literature of urban spectatorship, namely that between recognising the contingency of city life and providing urban legibility: new genres continually negotiated this tension which lasted into the nineteenth and twentieth centuries as strongly as before.

In seventeenth-century negotiations of this tension, particularly in the Theophrastian 'character books', there emerged the idea of the spectator as knowing, as one who could determine the character and history of the stranger on the basis of a typically silent and brief urban encounter.[28] Knowing 'at a glance' obviously had a long history. This history seems to provide a very important context for what came later, in the liberal era, for it would appear that liberal governmentality can be understood as not only located in these 'extra-political' areas of representation (the aesthetic, the world of consumption), but also related to their long history, so that we might comprehend forms of political reason as embedded in this history. In this context, so much is evident in terms of the aesthetic dimensions in which forms of subjectivity were pioneered that would later have a direct relationship with governmentality. In these literary forms of urban spectatorship, therefore, one can perceive the elements of a quasi- or pseudo-science emerging around the spectator's division of the city and of its inhabitants into legible spaces and types. This science would later mesh more closely with the sciences of liberal governmentality, to which it anyway always had a fairly close relation, often surprisingly so. Science is too strong a word perhaps, though character books in fact drew heavily on physiological treatises, and we might usefully think here more generally of forms of popular knowledge taking science-like character-istics.[29] In these new kinds of subjectivity, forms of disciplinary power are obviously evident. Within the types and categories of this literature this is amply apparent, the one that is observed ceding power to the invisible, categorising, spectator.

There would seem to have been a hardening of impressions of the city into something analogous to, if not the same as, the self-evident, or naturalised, character of truth in much of scientific knowledge. This kind of urban typologising can be understood as achieving its own kind of 'naturalisation' in that, as Brand argues, the ease with which the inhabi-tants and spaces of the city could be distributed within different categories contributed to a sense of the fixed and absolute nature of these categories and of the social order they appeared to represent. Works like the seventeenth-century character books and the eighteenth-century works they gave rise to seem to have contributed to the growing belief that the organisation of society was natural and visible, and therefore did not need to be maintained by the exercise of coercive power.[30] Because this ordering of the social was constituted by the interplay of different acts of observation, each participating, observing individual could identify with this order as itself natural because dependent upon the truth of his or her senses, especially the sense of sight. This order could simply be seen, and randomly encountered in the 'normal' course of events, and there-fore everyone could be read and put in his or her proper place or slot in a typology. This social order did not, therefore, derive from an identifiable source, for instance the Church or the Crown, but was diffused through-out the entire social mass. What is evident here is not only a pre-history of urban spectatorship, but also a pre-history of a category of 'the social': while taking recognisably modern and 'scientific' form only in the later eighteenth century, and being systematically integrated into governance only in the early nineteenth, it is evident that the modern 'social' can to some extent be understood as pioneered in extra-governmental forms, particularly aesthetic ones, especially the communities of readers associated with these forms.[31]

The late eighteenth-century periodical press has been seen as representing a particular fusion of these earlier literary forms, and as a temporary stabilisation of their representational tensions. The consumption of the city as spectacle was evident, therefore, some time before its massive elaboration in the nineteenth century, particularly in eighteenth-century London.[32] The basis for the nineteenth-century *flâneur*, especially as discerned by Baudelaire, is apparent in the construction of a form of subjectivity which was restless, and constantly in search of distraction. Urban commercial life itself provided this distraction, in that the life of urban consumption was all-absorbing. Late eighteenth-century London guidebooks themselves presented the city in a manner which drew upon these representational traditions: the various 'sights' of the city were located in a framework that offered the reader the freedom of the city as a public space, open to the wanderings and the gaze of the walker, as we have seen for nineteenth-century guidebooks. This freedom was realised in terms of the public street as the locus of certain valued and civilised identities, identities which in fact revolved around the necessity of self-government, and which were modelled upon what, in the case of the London guidebooks, has been called a 'middling-sort masculinity'.[33] Public space taught private virtues, virtues which in turn could only be realised in such public spaces, in the sphere of urban interaction. Therefore, in these guidebooks, self-government was an essential means to enjoying the freedom of the city.

Urban spectatorship oscillated not only between recognising contingency and achieving legibility, but also between the aesthetic appreciation and the moralisation of the city which accompanied this tension. The period after the early nineteenth century can be recognised as one in which the emphasis on the contingent and the aesthetic gave way to the Victorian moralisation of the city, something closely related to the emergence of what I called the 'moral city' in chapter 4. The carnivalesque city of excess in representations of Georgian London was above all apparent in the writing of Pearce Egan, especially *Life in London* (1821), with its use of slang, and its subversive and extravagant picture of London life in the stories of Tom and Jerry. These very quickly came to be stigmatised as 'libertine'. In this period, above all in Dickens' *Sketches by Boz* (1836–7), the eighteenth-century periodical tradition of the detached yet appreciative *flâneur* can be said to have reached its pinnacle, only then to decline, because unable, like the urban panoramas so popular at the time, to capture the rapidly accelerating contingency of London life.[34] What succeeded these was a much more marked emphasis on social reform, which from the 1840s and 1850s was related to the currents of reform considered in the earlier parts of this book. At the same time, the emphasis on the city as illegible, mysterious and dangerous in these new departures was also important, reflecting as it did the carnivalesque city of earlier genres. There was a distinct movement from the illegibility of the carnivalesque city to a new city of mystery but also to a city of misery and indeed of disgust, a city which was now the object of social reform. The mysterious city and the city of social reform coalesced, with the works of G.W.M. Reynolds more representing the first genre, and those of Mayhew the second.[35]

In Mayhew's accounts of London the understanding of 'character' evident in the literary and other aesthetic conventions and traditions so far considered coalesced with the proto-science of sociology, but also that of anthropology. Both were related to the contemporary 'sciences' of phrenology and physiognomy. In fact, classification by class, race, gender and other categories was intimately linked at the time: not only was there seen to be a 'scientific' basis for such classification, but there was also understood to be an underlying physical basis for all such expressions of difference. In what amounted to an unprecedented desire to establish the foundations of human difference, amply reflected in all the instruments of liberal governmentality, notions of biological determinism were increasingly evident. As was the case with Mayhew, such ideas were often closely linked to 'popular' modes of representation, so that, for example, the great *Punch* tradition of graphical illustration of social mores and character reflected a strong belief that differences, especially differences of social class and race, were actually rooted in physical reality and had a physical explanation. Such literary and graphical representations served to legitimise the new sciences of human difference. Visual representation beyond *Punch* drew on this belief in the physical basis of social characteristics: for example, the very popular work of Albert Smith on London 'characters' defined itself as 'natural history' and 'physiology', and his studies of character as 'zoologies'. Amongst the most popular of all visual representations of London, the two great works of W.P. Frith, *Derby Day* (1858) and *The Railway Station* (1862), constructed panoramas of London in which the entirety of the city scene could be understood at sight, in terms of the physical characteristics which displayed social character.[36]

The panorama alerts us to changes in the technology of visual representation, above all in the case of photography. Photographic realism, like previous developments in the construction of the gaze of the *flâneur*, served here to further accelerate the naturalisation of the city as something self-evidently true. From the 1870s and 1880s technological developments enabled the use of hand-held cameras, and the capacity to take high-speed or 'snapshot' photographs. In the 1880s what were called 'detective cameras' were developed. The untrained or amateur photographer emerged, together with the amateur photographic society.[37] Street photography was the beneficiary, and the publication of books of street photographs the result. My book employs several instances of this photography. Like the person in the institutional photographs of the time, photographic realism can be said to have objectified what it represented by presenting it in the form of a 'document'. Photography was deployed in a whole range of institutions: by the police, in prisons, but also in asylums, in hospitals, reformatories, and so on. It involved the separation and individuation of the subject; the body was made docile, subject as it was to the unreturnable gaze of the camera as a machine.[38] The photographs created by this realistic gaze constructed in turn the 'dossier' by means of which power, especially state power, was increasingly wielded.

In time the accumulation of this sort of documentary photography formed an archive in which entirely new representations of society occurred, ones involving new norms of behaviour and new typologies to describe those whose behaviour was under scrutiny. This went for the city too. New ideas of verisimilitude based on realism lent the force of objectivity to these norms and typologies, particularly in terms of representations of the city and its streets. The city could now be made 'precise', its spaces being fixed in the photographic image. It had a new solidity based on this photographic 'accuracy'. Like a documentised person, the reality of the city is broken down, and its interior or its essence is made known, especially in the great collections of city photographs which began to emerge at this time, including photographs of city places and streets, especially ones facing demolition, collections in large part the result of the activity of the new amateur photography societies.[39] Rather as with the city map, the city was now opened to view in a new sort of way. City governments, always concerned with opening the city to view, themselves increasingly used photography in their various activities, for example in sanitary and housing regulation and reform.

Photography, with important exceptions, was still, however, somewhat removed from the dominant contemporary literary expression of fascination with the city, namely the literature of the street, or 'streetology' as one contemporary instance of this literature put it. This genre took many forms,[40] its chief interest here being less the variety of these forms than its place in the classification of the city seen so far. The end result of the acquisition of such classification was the possession of a certain knowingness about the city, nineteenth-century 'streetology' being a forerunner of twentieth-century street wisdom in this regard. This quality of knowingness is especially significant for it helps us understand some of the complex relations between 'liberal' forms of knowing the city and 'popular' forms, or at least forms existing beyond direct governance itself.

What can be termed 'townology', knowingness about the town or city as a *whole*, was in fact in the second half of the century more significant than 'streetology' in terms of popular forms of knowingness. At this time London was neither the only nor the main location of this townology, for parallel to the growth of towns and cities themselves there developed a much more coherent codification of knowingness than is evident in the literary forms so far considered. This is evident in the city periodical press of the later nineteenth century, which embraced political comment, social observation, information on city life, but above all satire on city affairs and people. This literature was evident in all the big provincial cities, and if it to some extent imitated London's *Punch*, it was in fact often wittier, more partisan, and certainly more concerned with and observant about city life. (Although featured in the illustrations of *Punch*, London did not figure so centrally in its writing.) Titles like *Town Crier*, *City Lantern*, *City Jackdaw* and *Free Lance* were evident in Manchester and Birmingham from the 1860s into the 1890s, when this literature was replaced by more directly commercial guides to city life, and to some extent by the treatment of urban life in the new, cheap, city evening newspaper press.[41] Newspaper publishing itself exploded in the 1850s, with the proliferation of newspapers in cities.[42]

As has been seen in chapter 3, newspapers were involved in the constitution of urban imaginaries in very significant ways, but the urban was not in general in this newspaper press the object of conscious attention, at least until later. A much more concentrated and fascinated attention is evident in the urban satirical press, and this can be briefly considered here, before the more decidedly 'popular' forms of knowingness in the 'free and easy' are explored, for this press was a rather refined version of the popular. I will take Manchester as an example. The Manchester satirical press especially concerned the city as an arena of pleasure.[43] Above all, this literature was an attempt to bring to the city what was earlier called 'the light of publicity'. However, the city that was now addressed was the marginal city, as it were, the new, unfamiliar, potentially dangerous city of pleasure and consumption, in Manchester the city of the music halls, the theatres, the bars and the brothels of the new entertainment district that had grown up to the east of the city centre. The light of publicity, had already been directed upon this city centre to enormous effect in the mid- to late-nineteenth-century transformation that created the city as a liberal monument which instituted a newly 'neutral' zone of public space. The Manchester satirical press and its cousins elsewhere indicate a further appropriation of the city in terms of a particular brand of knowingness. This knowingness had a decided disciplinary function, which complemented the operations of liberal governmentality.

Bringing light to those parts of the city that were still dark was part of a much wider *rapprochement* of polite and popular culture at the time, something, for example, evident in the new sorts of more sensational, 'popular' press which emerged from the 1880s: journals like the *Pall Mall Gazette*, which, though decidedly polite, represented an opening out of an older, provincial, often Nonconformist culture to the new world around it.[44] This also involved complicity with the 'respectable' poor or working class against the 'rough'. In fact, what was involved was the *constitution* of this divide, a projection of a desired working class.[45] While the singing saloon might be lost, and this press was stern in its condemnation of 'vice and immorality', the more informal, so-called 'free and easy', where the lower classes made their own entertainment, promised redemption.[46] For here might be found a form of entertainment which was alive and spontaneous (if a little coarse), yet at the same time innocently decent and respectable.[47] Here also might be found the respectable poor who would not be awed by broadcloth, and if treated like men would always act like men.[48]

However, being free in what this press called the Kingdom of Bohemia had strikingly different meanings for others in the city, and this is particularly evident in the case of the barroom entertainments of the poor, above all precisely in the form of the 'free and easy' of which I speak. This was the decided 'other' of liberal freedom, and its exploration helps us understand something of both power and resistance. It also helps open a bridge to the next section of this chapter, which concerns the experiential side of encounters in the city, as opposed to the paper encounters considered so far. Despite campaigns against so-called 'disorderly' and 'immoral' establishments, and despite the rise of organised leisure in the form of the music hall (and with it a growing if always qualified 'respectability' in these halls), the free and easy was perhaps the predominant form of popular entertainment at the time. Indeed, it can be said to have held its own strongly against commercial forms of entertainment long into the twentieth century. In Manchester in 1892 the vast majority of the 512 pubs and beer houses in the city (not counting the enormous number in contiguous Salford) held free and easies every week, often in adjacent 'singing rooms'.[49] At this time there were no more than eight or nine 'legitimate' music halls in the city, not counting the 'low' halls, which anyway had more in common with free and easies than the respectable halls. The expectations and conventions of the latter can be said to have in fact been shaped by this 'popular' form.[50]

This form was different from the village pub that can be said to have preceded it, and from the music hall itself. The constitution of both the audience and the event itself was more fluid and open than either. Professionals, semi-professionals, but especially amateurs followed one after another, with a sort of 'open-house' arrangement to the event. Accounts of performance suggest a sort of unfocused listening in which everyday life was not bracketed out.[51] The audience faced each other and not the stage or the performer. Drink and sociability were uppermost, drink being shared from jugs very often, and sociability being underlined by participation and the welcome given to strangers. There was none of the decorum, or the fixed attention, of the commercial musical hall, where the performer was separated from the audience. The context of performance was one of noise, smoke, eating, drinking, talking and constant movement. There was a sort of sensual overload, a sense of the tumultuous, something akin to being in the streets of the city, or to the fair (for instance, the ancient and now superseded fairs of Saint Bartholomew or Donnybrook). Most important of all was the element of 'release', the physical sense, indeed, of being 'free and easy', released from the cares of the everyday, but not divorced from it. Audiences included women, of diverse ages, including mothers feeding children, and families were frequently present, as were prostitutes, and even though the largest group were young men, in contrast to the male pub the free and easy was much less exclusively gendered.[52] The line between the rough and respectable was itself blurred and observers from the Manchester satirical press had surprisingly little confidence in making social identifications, being confounded to see the mix of what they thought distinct social types. The music was as mixed as the audience, embracing the sacred and the profane. A sense of the liminal was everywhere apparent and with it the active symbolic exploration of social order itself.

The song culture that was such a central part of the free and easy was therefore embedded in the experience of the urban. The songs them-selves frequently addressed urban experience, providing a sort of com-mentary on city life, but also a kind of 'conduct book' for the poor in terms of managing the everyday problems of city living. The experience of which the songs spoke might include the goings-on in the halls in which they were sung, but also in the streets in which they were per-formed, for, as well as at the free and easy, popular ballads were sold and performed on the street. A song might in fact be about the street in which it was performed. But it was at a perhaps deeper level that the songs echoed the experience of the urban, for performance was embedded in the sensory flow of urban experience, whether in the free and easy or the street. The mode of listening, unfocused or 'distracted', was related to the tumult of both the hall and the street, the endless flow of impressions, and the contingency and unpredictability of city life. Songs had to compete with a myriad other impressions, and the form of popular song bears testimony to this: the words, metre and tunes of songs battered powerfully at the senses and at memory, with their repetitions, their attempts at catchiness, and at securing imitation. Rather like urban slang, they were a means of being part of what was going on, being up-to-date, being in the know, and like slang, and indeed fashion itself, their attempts at memorability and instant recognition were a consequence of their embeddedness in the flow of urban sensation, which both created and in the end destroyed them.[53]

The songs therefore were not simply about city life, but their actual contexts of performance and reception involved modes of being in the city. This can be illustrated by the situation of the street singer, one aspect of urban song culture among many brilliantly analysed by Philomen Eva.[54] The street singer was both insider and outsider. The unsavoury reputation of the singing fraternity, their existence as a street 'tribe' indeed, made them outsiders. However, the singer was also an integral part of the city and the street, and for the poor he (the singer was usually a man) was at once a figure of sympathy as well as someone to be distanced, the former especially because he sang of the condition of the poor (not only to a poor audience of course, but that audience was undoubtedly the greatest one for his sort of music). The street singer was liminal in another sense too, for in the myriad of 'songs about the times', songs about politics and current events, he brought the 'outside' world within, realising it by relating it to the experience of those who listened, or who read the texts of the songs, and indeed sometimes performed them themselves. He carried both the positive and the negative associations of the street, and his music reflected this, in being both a celebration of the city and a recognition of its dangers.

As a classically 'liminal' figure, the street singer vastly multiplied the interpretive possibilities of those who received his music. He was in a sense therefore someone who was 'licensed', and therefore 'free', his very freedom implying that of his listeners. Meaning in street music, but just as much in the music and song of the free and easy where the performer had an analogous function, was inherently open and ambiguous, leaving listeners themselves to be outsiders or insiders, innocent or knowing about the city, fearful of it or celebrating it, and so on. In the music that was the staple of the free and easy, the 'sign of the voice' present in the bare printed text of the song was amplified in performance, the singer mediating the 'voice' of the simple verbal text in many different ways, ways that were always informed by the constant tendency of the music, for all its sentimentality, to undercut itself by burlesque, and by a frequent movement into the absurd. There was no 'authentic' meaning in this song culture, only a range of mobile and fluid possibilities for identity formation.[55] It was these that negotiated the social order, and the forms of governmentality that gave it expression, so that 'resistance' was here not a matter of direct, articulated opposition (even though it sometimes could be this). Rather, the governmentalised city was lived out, implemented *and* 'resisted' in the form of the fluid and mobile possibilities for identity formation of which I speak. It is at the interface of different versions of freedom that we may locate both power and resistance, therefore, so that outcomes were heterogeneous and ambiguous, as I put it in the Introduction.

The liminal moment represented by the street singer was apparent in the experience of the free and easy itself, the experience of a release from the everyday that was yet embedded in the everyday. Release was experienced above all in the actual mode of being involved by being there at all, a mode of being intimately related to different stages of inebriation of course. Just as in street music, the performer, the performance and the subject of the song not only embraced the experience of the city, and were a mode of being in the city, but also embraced the possibility of a kind of 'freedom'. The way in which freedom was experienced was closely related to the experiential possibilities offered by the city as a focus of the multiple interpretive possibilities available to participants. There were others of course (domestic life, romantic love, nostalgia for home, and so on), each in practice framing the others. Attending to the explicitly urban, in terms of the sort of mental mapping of the city evident in these broadside songs,[56] and considering this mapping as an expression of the 'freedom' possible through the songs and through participation in the free and easy, it is useful to invoke the concept of carnival. Carnival represented one of the poles evident in the operation of literary representations of the city, in particular the sense of a city escaping attempts to bring legibility to it, and the same is evident in these lower-class forms.

Bakhtin's account of the 'folk laughter' evident in carnival certainly fits this song culture.[57] There is the same upending of respectable norms in the vivacity and indeed 'vulgarity' of the songs, a freedom from restraint that issued in a sort of manic pleasure, in laughter, and in distinct elements of the absurd and the grotesque. The dimension of subversion is certainly present, though what is more evident is perhaps a kind of competence, or rather a set of competencies, about dealing with the city. A popular or lower-class 'knowingness' is again evident, something that ran in parallel with but obviously diverged from the kinds of knowingness to be encountered higher up the social scale which have so far been considered. In talking of the knowingness of the music hall, Peter Bailey can be understood as speaking also for the free and easy and its song culture, which drew upon the broadside ballads, but outlasted them to accompany the growth of music hall into the twentieth century.[58]

Like the free and easy, music hall offered audiences 'texts' with which to develop their own competence in negotiating everyday life in the city. They offered what a clearly unsympathetic contemporary characterised as 'the quick, clever tact by which one vulgar mind placed itself *en rapport* with a number of other vulgar minds'. Knowingness projected a sense of identity and belonging as 'the earned return on experience': contrary to some interpretations of the music hall as a culture of consolation,[59] it is perhaps better described as an arena of competence, certainly in the experiential dimension considered here. Just as there was no 'authentic' meaning in the songs of the free and easy, neither did they give authentic expression to carnivalesque revolt or consolatory acceptance of the social order. Rather, the free and easy offered simply a resource for negotiating the city; as I say, a set of competencies. Carnivalesque revolt and consolation both tend to romanticise power and 'resistance', not that the romantic overtones of the word 'resistance' help matters here. A better term might in fact be the 'negotiation' of power, rather than resistance to it, so that the free and easy was ultimately a key site of such negotiation because it was at the interface of different experiences and notions of 'freedom', and so at the interface of liberal governmentality and its reception.

As will become clear in the next section, where the 'daydreaming' and automatic behaviour evident in moving in the city can be seen to have an analogy with the distracted and automatic kinds of behaviour witnessed in this song culture, while one can see this culture as evidence of 'resistance' in the mainstream sense, its relationship to dominant modes of power was always complex. In the example of the free and easy itself, the knowingness which audiences projected was in turn co-opted by cultural entrepreneurs in the entertainment industries and in the popular press, and projected back to audiences in a subtle cycle of a 'popular' *and* entrepreneurially shaped knowingness.[60] The latter sanctioned an ethic of the music halls which was concerned with the people's right to a good time. This in its populism was closely linked to commercial, capitalist projections of liberality and open-handedness, and therefore to a sort of 'liberal' freedom to be realised in pleasure.

Moving in the city

In a celebrated account Michel de Certeau speaks of how

> [t]he long poem of walking manipulates spatial organisations, no matter how panoptic they may be: it is neither foreign to them (it can take place only within them) nor in conformity with them (it does not receive its identity from them). It creates shadows and ambiguities within them. . . . Within them it is itself the effect of successive encounters and occasions that constantly alter it and make it the other's blazon: in other words it is like a pedlar, carrying something surprising, transverse or attractive compared with the usual choice.

He also speaks of

> [t]he ordinary practitioners of the city 'down below', below the threshold at which visibility begins. They walk – an elementary form of the experience of the city: they are walkers, *Wandersmänner*, whose bodies follow the thicks and thins of an urban 'text' they write without being able to read it. These practitioners make use of spaces that cannot be seen; their knowledge of them is as blind as that of lovers in each other's arms.[61]

If de Certeau's account is rather at odds with the notion of 'resistance' developed here in its somewhat romantic dualism of high power and low resistance, then the sense of people following a text that they write without being able to read is suggestive for thinking about other 'negotiations' of the city, and about power and its living out. It helps us think beyond the confines of 'texts', understood in the traditional sense, the sense considered in the first section of this chapter on the paper street and the paper city, even if the free and easy takes us beyond these confines into embodied forms of knowingness that were analogous to those of movement considered here.

In thinking about moving in the city, anthropological work on movement is similarly suggestive. This considers place instead of space, and thinks of places as constituted by narratives so that in fact time and space are indistinguishable. Places are brought into being by the encounters of life and hence are constituted in terms of life histories. In this kind of reading of space, places are not points but poles, loci of movements towards and away from. Space is here a thing of embodiment, practice, constant adjustments, in fact the 'seeing' of a destination before it is visible, as if this destination 'pulled' the traveller onwards, as in the example of South Sea Island navigation.[62] To think about space in this way is to think about movement. Subjects are always emplaced and cannot in fact be subjects unless they are such: persons are not bounded entities but 'grow along the lines of their paths'. We have, here, the invitation to consider ways of moving in the past and the use of narratives to which these ways of moving were related.

De Certeau, of course, worked along the lines of narrative with the idea of what he called 'spatial stories'. Such stories can be related to the distinction between the map, concerned with seeing and with establishing boundaries, and the 'tour', evident in bodily practices of movement beyond seeing alone, and involved with crossing boundaries. The 'everyday stories' of moving in the city thereby involve 'bridges', so that if the map 'cuts up', the story 'cuts across' and links what it crosses. The tour makes the frontier a point of contact as well as difference. To walk, therefore, can be considered in a similar sense as to tour, for 'to walk is to lack a space', and in the the act of walking itself to make this lack of space into a place.[63] The act of walking is therefore an essential condition of the bridge or frontier, so that walking gives definition to urban space. From this perspective too, the act of walking can be understood as an elementary, phenomenological condition of freedom, an essential bodily mode of experiencing freedom.[64]

The demarcations of space which are places are therefore instituted by movement, and movement is governed by narrative. We have seen something of these narratives, the narratives of liberal governmentality in terms of the built forms and design of the city, also, more literally, the narratives present in guidebooks, imaginative literature, the periodical press, street ballads. However, these stories have a certain legibility: while they relate to 'everyday stories', they do not quite bring us to a sense of embodied movement in the city, the practice of the city, in fact the often unconscious urban 'text' that walkers in the city write without being able to read. Getting at this is very difficult, but we can begin an account at a crucial point in the history of movement in the city, namely the so-called 'transport revolution' of the late eighteenth and early nineteenth centuries.[65] This involved the institution of the roadway as a place of free communication, yet one that remained for some time also unfree. The tremendous changes in road construction, which put Britain far ahead of any other state, including France, were not in fact fully influential until the second decade of the nineteenth century. They were accompanied by a massive increase in the number of turnpike roads and trusts. The latter concerned traffic between towns, yet passage within towns was also subject to commercial restrictions, a liberal economy here being in flat contradiction to free movement. In 1838 there were still 1,116 trusts and almost 1,000 tollgates and side-bars in England and Wales. Turnpike trusts thereafter declined, but in London these were not all abolished until 1871 (restrictions applied over bridges in London, and into the enclaves of the wealthy, but were liberally scattered over the whole city as well). However, the outcome of the transport revolution was that with journey times between cities dramatically cut, and movement within towns and cities increasingly free, the number of road travellers increased greatly.

So too did the number of rail travellers, though it was not until the second half of the nineteenth century that a combination of direct governmental intervention and cheap fares meant that rail travel became the experience of those who were not relatively well-off. In 1854, 88,000 Londoners used the horse-drawn bus daily, 54,000 the train, 30,000 the river, 52,000 their own or hired carriages, but 400,000 walked. If the proportion who travelled by train and omnibus (especially) increased considerably thereafter in London, walking, or travel by cart over longer destinations, were the options for many people, in the 1830s the latter at a quarter the price of coach travel, but at barely more than walking pace. In terms of moving about the city, there was a clear class distinction. It was not until the development of the tram system (often municipally run), between 1880 and 1914, that the ranks of the walking poor were seriously depleted: Robert Roberts' account of life in pre-1914 Salford speaks of the electric tram as the means by which slum dwellers saw Manchester for the first time.[66]

It was precisely at the time of the transport revolution, when walking was no longer a necessity, that it became the object of self-conscious interest. What might be termed ideologies of walking began to emerge.[67] Once the necessity of walking was lost, the old association of walking with labour, in the sense of travail, began also to be lost, as did its association with danger – bad roads were still facts of early nineteenth-century life, and only in 1835 was a nationally maintained highway system inaugurated.[68] To understand the associated ideologies it is instructive to compare the new road system with the old road system in the open field parishes, a system displaced by the eighteenth-century enclosure of common land, and by the new principle of the roadway as the site of direct, free and unrestricted passage.[69] The parish road was designed to circulate animals, people and goods around the local field system. It was a self-enclosed, circular system, lying side-by-side with other similar parish road systems. Walking in these was indeed deeply related to labour, labour as work itself, for walking was tied to the practices of agriculture. In this system walking kept one in one's place; in the new system it involved changing places. The parish road system was seen as mysterious and hostile by outsiders, especially city dwellers. The new road system was one that connected places, a 'through' road that went from one place to another in as near to a straight line as was possible. Walking set boundaries in the old system, and broke them in the new.

With the decay of the old system, and the closing of the old paths, ways of passing through the world were quite literally lost for ever. Walking, and travel in general, was displaced from the purpose of reaching a destination to the process of travel itself. Existing travel literature, up to the late eighteenth century, whether in terms of pilgrimage or the Grand Tour, was concerned with destination.[70] New travel literature, involved with the creation of the 'tourist gaze', concerned itself with the process of travel itself. As John Barrell has argued, with the desuetude of old paths and old ways of passing through the world, the sense of place came to be profoundly altered.[71] Walking became the object of different sorts of representation, and thereby divorced from its earlier, implicit bodily knowledge and competencies, and hence from its historical, material and contextual conditions. The mode of seeing in this new view of place, where place was understood as a series of points of connection, was a detached one, based as it was upon continuous, linear movement. This detached mode of perception was not a sense of 'place-in-itself', as in the example of the poet John Clare that Barrell cites. Local knowledge was not a part of it; rather, the subject brought to the landscape abstract knowledge which was then applied. Wordsworth, for example, located place platonically in the idea of nature, and the spirit of place was to be found by looking through it, rather than being in it, as in the example of Clare.

The 'spatial stories' of the Wordsworthian peripatetic in particular came to have a profound influence on nineteenth-century ideologies of walking, and the new practices of walking these gave rise to. These involved different narratives of walking, linking places together in a way that contrasted with the corporeal practices of earlier times. These new ways, for instance in the ideology of the Wordsworthian peripatetic, in applying a more abstract, if aesthetic, knowledge to movement, forged new connections between past and present, the individual and the community, and the physical and the natural, as Anne Wallace's fine account of Wordsworth-inspired walking indicates.[72] This particular element in the new consciousness of walking, combined, of course, with other influences, received institutional and political expression very early on in the Association for the Protection of Ancient Footpaths of 1824, and the similar Manchester association founded in 1826, but perhaps most effectively in the Commons, Open Spaces and Footpaths Preservation Society of 1865.

These expressions embraced all shades of political opinion, but their radical potential was especially marked. As Rebecca Solnit has recently remarked, Britain is perhaps unique in embracing walking in and for itself, unmixed with other activities. She observes how '[w]alking has a resonance, a cultural weight, that it does nowhere else', and that '[t]he British swore allegiance to footpaths, not boulevards'.[73] Much of this almost religious intensity to walking in Britain was no doubt owed in part to the early and extensive urbanisation of the country, together with the long-continuing power of aristocratic land-holding, so that asserting rights to walking the countryside became closely involved with British ideas about freedom itself. This is especially so in relation to property rights. As Solnit observes, 'Walking focuses not on boundary lines of ownership that break the land into pieces but on the paths that function as a kind of circulating system connecting the whole organism. Walking is, in this way, the antitithesis of owning.' American land, by contrast, though more often in public ownership and with easier access, lacks this circulating system, this capacity to *pass through* private property, and so in some way challenge its absolute rights, so preserving an alternative vision of the land as the property of all, and in this sense the locus of a rather British version of freedom.[74]

This, historically, has been a powerful, if perhaps a minority, element in British culture. The predominant experience was one of towns and cities, and of walking and moving in them. And the people of the nineteenth-century city who increasingly walked these rural paths did so not in the ways their rural predecessors had done, but in ways shaped by urban walking. How did people learn to walk in these new urban ways? What they had to walk upon in fact encouraged them to pass through the street in the new linear fashion, just like the new roads that cut through the parish system. The transport revolution and its aftermath represented a transition in the material history of the street, from the old sense of a stratum, a series of artificial layers, to the sense of the street as a place of passage. The wheel was increasingly adapted to the road, and the road to the wheel. The pedestrian was literally marginalised, as the carriageway grew in size and importance: the Macadamised roadway in fact took up more of the road space than previously. Traffic was increasingly triumphant. In the eighteenth-century street the carriageway and the footpath were at the same level, separated off by posts and chains sometimes, and with a cobbled 'pavement' perhaps.[75] The pedestrian was more dominant, and the wheel less dominant. In the nineteenth century, restricted to the new pavements, the pedestrian had to fight his or her way in a more crowded area. As can be seen in street photographs of the late nineteenth century, however, there was a considerable tension between the city as a place of order, and the invitation to a sort of freedom. The street photograph in Figure 5.4 in fact presents us with the possibility of recreating some sense of the practice of the nineteenth-century street.

There is solidity, stone and order everywhere, but there is also, frozen in this past present, a very high degree of movement. Within this movement there is order. The horse-drawn trams run along particular lines, and traffic keeps to its designated side of the street, also cabs line the side of the road. But the kerb itself is extremely low, and if we compare this scene to the city of the present, what is striking is the degree of latitude allowed to movement. There are no rails to separate street and pavement, just as the division between street and pavement is attenuated by the low kerb. There are no street crossings. The streets are wide, especially given the volume of traffic (which at busy times could, of course, be immense; this seems to be a relatively quiet time). The pavement is also very considerable in breadth. Throughout the city a systematic process of road widening and new road construction had from the 1840s resulted in just these sorts of more fluid open space. There is a considerable degree of informality in the use of public space. This fluidity was evident in the photograph of Deansgate in Manchester discussed in the Introduction

Figure 5.4   Piccadilly Square, Manchester, 1890s, view from northeast corner

(Figure 1). People were in fact quite exposed to the view of others: the trams have large windows, and the double-deckers are open. Cabs have a certain privacy but are still relatively open.

While Manchester is the example here, as street photography from other British cities very clearly shows, it was entirely representative of the country as a whole.[76] This city can be understood as one where the exercise of freedom was in fact invited in ways much more marked than in the city of today. Compared to the eighteenth-century chained and posted street, therefore, and although the momentum towards the street as a place of passage and traffic was relentless, a space was established that had a certain potential as one of self-rule that we might consider to be 'liberal', for only within this fluidity and indeed tension between order and movement could there exist the spatial potentials for enacting freedom. At the same time, given this tension, there was always the capacity to exceed the rule of freedom. Like the free and easy, the street can be understood as another existential arena of freedom.

One can consider this tension in terms of the history of street traffic, particularly in London.[77] The development of the legal apparatus for control of London's traffic by the police was a slow process. The 1817 Traffic Act was concerned with the idea of the city as a stratum, and it attended to the condition of the streets and not to the traffic. This was the case until the Police Acts of 1839 and 1835, which involved police intervention in non-criminal street activities for the first time. The 1867 Traffic Acts increased police powers over the regulation of traffic and street activity to a degree that disturbed many Londoners. Subject to approval by different bodies, streets could be closed off and traffic laned, police could direct traffic, and they could order drivers to attach lamps at night and display their licence plates. However, these laws were discretionary as well as stated in very general terms. By the last quarter of the century the police had some success in getting drivers to pay attention to hand signals, but not a lot in getting them to stay in line and to control their speed. The impression of the late nineteenth century is one still of considerable anarchy and *laissez-faire*, with cabs, omnibuses and wagons fighting each other to control the centre of the road, or the margins for picking up and setting down. It is very striking how omnibuses before the 1867 Acts could stop anywhere and on any side of the road. Even then, after the Act, there were still no fixed stopping points.

It is somewhat surprising, therefore, given their relatively limited nature, how these powers excited the anxiety of Londoners. This anxiety reveals the tensions, and sometimes the confrontations, within liberalism (in both its political and governmentalised forms), between interventions to secure free movement, and fear that these interventions would endanger freedom. The attitude of the first head of the Metropolitan Police, Richard Mayne, is very revealing. Mayne was on the side of those who feared centralisation, including Benthamite centralisation, preferring policing to operate through the medium of the citizen as policeman (which of course included self-policing). Mayne was in favour of licensing of all sorts, but only so that the public might be involved in the control process themselves. The discretionary Acts of 1867 were to his liking. As was said at the time, Mayne had 'no call to the social mission'.[78] In terms of the law of the road, it would not be inappropriate to speak of the figure of the Free-Born English Pedestrian at this time. In a legal case in the mid-1860s, brought by a young widow who sued for the loss of her husband, a pedestrian struck down by an omnibus, the decision went for the widow and in favour of the freedom of the pedestrian, which reflected the still widespread sense that the highway was free to all users, not least the foot traveller. As one contemporary in this context reported, 'Your only true republic is a crowded street.'

This belief in the unconditional freedom of the pedestrian was in contradiction to the ancient usage of keeping to the left, which the police attempted to enforce with only limited success, and which the courts only very conditionally determined.[79] At the same time, however, and as reflected in the jury's response in the 1865 trial (they ordered very limited financial recompense to the widow), the feeling grew that responsibility was with the pedestrian, even though in the early twentieth century London pedestrians still disliked studded crossings as an incursion on their freedom. However, the pedestrian was increasingly restricted to the pavement, and if in some senses there was a high degree of fluidity between road and pavement, the distinction between the two was none the less increasingly marked – the very conjunction 'kerb'/curb indicates this propensity to delineate one from the other. However, reflecting the tension between the fluidity and the distinctiveness of the division between the roadway and pavement, the margin between the two took on new meanings as a liminal space. The Macadamised roads were cambered, and therefore detritus drained into the margins at their sides. These roads, in the nature of their construction, were muddy, extremely noisy and very dusty, depending on the time of year. Crossing from pavement to street might be perilous. The streets themselves were slippery and dangerous to animals and humans,[80] though matters were improved slowly after the 1870s with the development of asphalt and the use of wood. The liminality of the roadside inhered in large measure in how it put circulation in question, as a place of peril, dirt and congestion. The often difficult negotiation of the passage from pavement to road had to be made there, with cabmen and omnibus drivers fighting for position and for customers. It was a place where passengers were translated into pedestrians and vice versa.

Cambered roads had to have gutters, and the latter term, as well as 'kerb', evokes the symbolic power of these margins, in particular their unsavoury aspects. Commerce gravitated to these margins, but commerce which itself was of a marginal sort. These margins were places occupied by street traders, costermongers who in fact were marginal within the law, very often having a semi-legal status. In the music hall of the time, the costermonger was a classic marginal or liminal figure in his relation to the law, but especially in his relation to ideas about work, where he symbolised a condition of independence aspired to by many in the audience.[81] Rather like the street singer treated in the preceding section, he was both part of and outside the communities to which his figure spoke. If free, the costermonger was still harassed, and if independent, he was also dependent. He was envied for his freedom yet despised for his anarchy and dependence. The street trader therefore also inhabited spaces in which many cultural transactions occurred as well as commercial ones. As was seen in chapter 2, street markets, like the great municipal markets, were places where blood and rotting matter, both vegetable and animal, ran in gutters. These street margins were therefore places where boundaries of all sorts were negotiated and explored, in particular those between nature and culture, and life and death. Around these road margins accrued both 'literary' and 'everyday' 'spatial stories', the narratives of literature and music hall, and the 'bridges' or 'poles' by means of which, through the corporeal 'tour' that was constituted by spatial practices in the city, the city became known by being moved through and hence experienced bodily.

Learning to walk in the teeming streets of London presented challenges which, we have seen, were taken up in a variety of literary forms, in guidebooks, imaginative depictions of cities and their streets, the periodical press and broadside ballads. Learning to see the city through the late eighteenth-century guidebook for instance involved learning to walk in it in particular ways. These ways were inseparable from the creation of the material technology of paving, evident in Westminster in the 1780s, and then spreading throughout and beyond London.[82] This walking was not that of the narcissistic *flâneur*, or the aristocratic or indeed the 'bourgeois' promenade. Unlike these, what seems to have been a forerunner of nineteenth-century 'liberal' walking was encouraged, which emphasised a controllable private self that could not be completely of the city yet was very much in it. Walking was conducted in such a way as to resolve the problem of being a private person in public. One walked so as to retain privacy, while responding all the time to the public context in which walking occurred, a context which, through the activity of walking, was civilising.[83] While the paved city made this kind of walking more likely, the actual nature of the republic of the streets made it difficult. Given the tumult of the street, effort was displaced to other locations, particularly the new public parks which emerged from the 1840s in Britain.

These parks need to be distinguished from eighteenth-century and nineteenth-century pleasure grounds. These were built with high enclosing walls, unlike the much more open, if often railed and tree-lined, public park. Money was paid for admission to the pleasure ground, but the park was 'free' (carrying with it much of the meaning and purpose of other 'free' institutions, like the public library). Compared to many of its continental versions, the English public park was porous as well as free, for physical entry was easier, and 'liberty of usage' more marked (for instance, the grass could be used).[84] The Manchester Parks Committee in the 1840s was extremely concerned to make the park accessible to all, unlike the pleasure ground.[85] The pleasures of the park, unlike the

pleasure ground, were active, not passive, in the sense that the purpose
was enjoyment to a purpose, namely the recreation of the self through
the recreation of the body. Walking was a very significant part of this
purpose. It was an integral part of the design of parks.

The writings, and parks, of Frederick Law Olmsted give us perhaps the
clearest insight into the park as an instrument governing conduct. Olmsted was one of the first, and in many ways the greatest, of all the
'professionals' of park design and management which the intense international interest in public parks of the mid-nineteenth century gave rise
to. Perhaps the greatest of his many achievements in the United States
was New York's Central Park, begun in 1858. The inspiration of this, and
all his work, was the English country park: in particular, one of the first
public parks in Britain, Joseph Paxton's Birkenhead Park, built in 1847,
across the river from Liverpool, set him on the path of public park design
as what he called a 'landscape architect'. Paxton's park applied the model
of the English country park to the needs of the city dweller in what
Olmsted took to be 'the democratic condition of society' that then
obtained.[86] Greatly influenced by British social reformers of all sorts, he
sought the governance of conduct not in formal government itself but in
the 'social improvement' the park could engineer. He thought of himself
as an administrator as well as an artist, and, as the Executive Director of
the US Sanitary Commission, he was indeed a major figure in the
administration of the Northern war effort in the US Civil War, appropriately enough for such a pioneer of the union of art, engineering and
administration.

Olmsted was in fact a self-conscious designer of freedom (he almost
became head of the organisation governing enfranchised black slaves, the
Freedmans Bureau), his purpose always being to inculcate ennobling taste
in a democracy made up of free persons. This is evident in his writings on
park design. In his 'Public Parks and the Enlargement of Towns' (1870),
in countering the deleterious effect of city life, his concern was to make
the park an 'edifying spectacle' in which 'the people' themselves would
be the source of that spectacle.[87] For the vision of the park evident here
is one involving what he called the 'gregarious' and 'neighbourly', a vision
of Brooklyn Park as what was earlier referred to as an omniopticon, in
which the multitude watched and experienced the multitude, in this case
at the great 'neighbourly festivals' held in the Park at weekends, when
thousands of families congregated for picnics and neighbourly interaction. The object of walking in the park was to see what Olmsted called
'congregated human life'. This pioneer's attempt to work with the socia-

bility of the city's inhabitants can be seen as a precursor of that governance of the social considered in chapter 4.

It is in fact in the physical business of walking, of movement itself, that we most clearly see the governance of conduct, and the solicitation of freedom in the movement of the human body. In his 'The Psychological Effects of Park Scenery' (1868)[88] Olmsted argues that the park should be a place that through the governance of movement invites users to discover *for themselves* beauty as well as a democratic version of 'gentility', by means of what he calls 'grace' and 'ease' of movement. Walking as an essential bodily, phenomenal mode of freedom became a carefully calculated process of discovery by the active walker, in which 'a sagacious consideration and application of the known laws of cause and effect' would mean that nothing in the park 'will be without design and purpose'. For example, wandering should be made easy, by means of graceful contours, yet there should also be a degree of obscurity in the landscape to provide a motive for wandering in the first place. There should be variety in the landscape so as to make movement a pleasure, yet variety should be of a simple character so as to make walking capable of engaging what Olmsted called 'the common and elementary impulses of all classes of mankind'. 'Natural', and aesthetic, pleasure is to be stimulated by easeful movement so achieved, for instance the uplifting sense of both the illimitable and the limitable, secured by the planting of trees so as to suggest infinitude in the suddenly opened panorama, and finitude in its closing. At the same time there was the most careful policing of the park, involving extremely elaborate orders for park keepers which balanced the detail of regulation with the notion that policing should be best achieved indirectly, with a light touch through the manner and mien of the park keeper himself.[89]

In British parks everything that could interfere with rational and uplifting walking was banned: gambling, dogs, drink, swearing, dirty clothes and games in the wrong parts of the park. In some cases, for instance Crossley Park in Halifax, donated as so many northern parks were by big local industrialists and run by the municipality, the park was positioned on a prominence, so as to picture the town or city as itself an edifying 'spectacle', and indeed, in reverse, to frame the park when seen from the town. The new urban cemeteries were also locations for uplifting walking of a quasi-municipal kind, with accompanying spectacles of the urban. The construction of the park, inculcating desired behaviour of a sort conducive to liberal selfhood, was complemented in this purpose by the siting of the walker in respect to the observation of others.[90] This rationale of the park, developed by Olmsted in the 1860s and 1870s, had, however, already been expressed in Britain, particularly in the 1833 Report of the Parliamentary Committee on Public Walks, which voiced a less democratic and republican version of liberal walking than did the American, also a more class-ridden one. Walking was seen as the way in which the walker displayed himself and his family properly, the idea being that the upper-class person would produce emulation in the lower-class person, and teach by example.[91] One taught and one was taught through what J.P. Kay called the 'social observation' of walking.[92] The poor man walking out with his family in the company of his betters will desire to comport himself in a respectable and rational manner. The classes were to meet on terms of equality, without shame or affectation. British parks also frequently housed other means of inculcating the spirit of mental and physical improvement, such as libraries, art galleries and museums.

It would be wrong, however, to consider the park as simply an elaborate disciplinary machine, however omni- as opposed to panoptic it may have been. Here Foucault's notion of heterotopias, of 'other' or 'different' spaces, is useful.[93] Heterotopias may be contrasted with the 'ordinary' emplacements of the world, which are marked by a considerable degree of compatibility with other places, and are relatively unregulated as well as spatially porous. They are characterised by loose boundaries, and connected to other temporalities outside themselves. Conversely, heterotopias are sites where the ordinary emplacements of society are simultaneously represented, contested and reversed. They are localised, but also outside all other places. As 'actually existing utopias', Foucault instances a somewhat bewildering array of them, from brothels and ships to gardens (all 'heterotopias of deviation'), to 'crisis heterotopias', places where things need to take place 'elsewhere', things like the care of the old, and the regulation of menstruating women. They juxtapose incompatible emplacements, for example the garden as both a spiritualised and 'earthy' place. They are associated with temporal discontinuities, representing absolute breaks with ordinary time, and Foucault mentions the cemetery alongside this example of the garden. These discontinuities open out into multiple chronologies, for example the seasons of plants and metropolitan time schedules, or the maintenance of green space across generations. Heterotopias also presuppose a system of opening and closing which isolates them, while making them penetrable only at certain times. In relation to the rest of space they are either spaces of illusion, denouncing the rest of space as even more illusory (for example, brothels), or they create a different 'real space' which is perfect, as well organised as everyday space is imperfect, for example, the garden.

Now, it should at once be said that we are here concerned with complex 'ordering' processes, not with a simple matter of the imposition of *order* in the singular.[94] And heterotopias are involved in this ordering, an ordering that is associated with disciplinary power *and* ways of countering such power, so that heterotopias, as Foucault suggests, have multiple and often opposed effects *within* the same heterotopic spaces. Of course, gardens are not parks, though parks may be considered as gardens on a grand scale, and there may be gardens in parks, but none the less the two are not the same, and certainly not institutionally. Parks, as it were, set gardens to work for the ends of governance, the public parks movement in the nineteenth century being a case in point. However, if the park–garden relationship can be understood as situated near the disciplinary end of power, as it were, then it seems to me that the park, so conceived, is also a site of deeply ambiguous processes of *ordering* going on in heterotopias. As such the park can be understood as complementing and subverting, and enchanting and challenging, the city in the midst of which it was placed. It did this because it was the ultimate 'other' space in the city, the green, earthy, rural and natural heart of the built, crowded and man-made city.

In the present context, concerned with walking and not parks as such, there is insufficient space to explore this in the detail needed, but it is useful none the less to point to the work of Robert Rosenberg, *Landscape and Power in Vienna*, a history of power and the garden in that city, including the public park, which develops some of these aspects of heterotopias, with the added virtue of situating them in an historical typology of the garden, each form of which has its own, differing, heterotopic qualities.[95] However, this account tends to be a little reductive, equating gardens with socio-political formations in an over-direct way, while at the same time almost entirely highlighting disciplinary aspects alone. By contrast, other uses of the idea of heterotopia, while recognising its ordering qualities, emphasise it as almost exclusively involved with sites of alternative as opposed to dominant forms of power.[96] None the less, Rosenberg's typology is useful: there was the seventeenth- and eighteenth-century baroque garden, or garden of order, based on absolutist models of power, which was followed by the eighteenth-century garden of liberty, based on English aristocratic models, and perhaps the most dominant of all forms in Europe and in the United States, as in the case of Olmsted.

In nineteenth-century Vienna, the garden of liberty was transmuted into the municipal park, which, like its British counterpart, functioned as what was in effect a garden of reform, for example the Vienna *Stadtpark* of 1861. The relation to the city is absolutely central here, as is apparent in a somewhat different way in the Rathauspark of 1873. As understood in the previous chapter's account of the visual economy of the city, this park was a vital element in Vienna in particular but by extension in other cities as well, for the Rathauspark connected the disparate and disconnected planes of the vertical and the horizontal by siting the town hall as the park's architectural focus and *raison d'être*. At the same time the park was everywhere opened to the city, framing it and being framed by it in different ways. By contrast, despite its name, when one entered the Stadtpark one left the town behind, entering another world. (In many ways this was the experience of British public parks, though the business of framing still went on.)

As to the sorts of walking that people brought with them when they walked in the new public parks of the nineteenth century, the 'pre-industrial' modes of walking considered in the context of the parish road system again come to mind. In the study of new kinds of city policing in chapter 3, it was remarked how the new and incessant police injunction to those who 'loitered' on the street to 'move on' was greeted with extraordinary hostility. This was especially evident in the early industrial villages of the West Riding of Yorkshire and other northern industrial settings which spanned the distinction between the cultural world of the parish and that of the city. This defence of not moving on was related to the maintenance of local 'feasts' and 'wakes' in these northern industrial areas, so that walking was here a spatial story enunciating the force of local community bonds. Without being overly teleological, one might identify later popular and 'non-official' modes of walking in terms of the tacit, local forms of movement evident in the nineteenth-century urban neighbourhoods and slums which followed 'early indus-trial' kinds of walking. The street in such later settings, to some extent protected by its very poverty and reputation from too much regulation, was a place for recreation, for children playing, for parents sitting out in the evening, particularly in the summer, for lovers meeting, for gamblers gambling, and indeed for a host of activities which meant that the public/private distinction was in practice very porous. These activities involved life under the 'gaze' of disciplinary practices somewhat removed from liberal panopticism, in the form of the imperceptibly lifted curtain announcing the ever-present scrutiny of the street matriarch at her window, as in the 'classic slum' of Salford so memorably described by Robert Roberts.[97]

None the less, these areas were increasingly hemmed in and as it were policed by the more open and public parts of the city. To appreciate the extent to which cities were transformed, it is only necessary to keep in mind the example of the non-western street, as in India.[98] There linear movement, of the sort institutionalised by liberalism, was next to impossible. Instead, the street was made up of a host of different time and space paths. It intersected with the bazaar, for example, and can indeed be conceived as a place of intersection, rather than as one of connection and passage. It was an 'unenclosed space', made up of many functions (working, living, socialising), and one which drew forth the horror of the colonial power, which did its limited best to create separate paths and directions so as to counteract the labyrinth. Just like the character of the space itself, communal regulation of the street was contingent, local and contextual, as is evident in the political, gendered and religious forms this regulation took.

In contrast, nineteenth-century urban space in Britain was being possessed in new sorts of ways. However, these ways, if linked to liberal walking, should be seen as extending beyond it. There was, first, a sort of 'automatic' walking to which the city gave rise. This 'automatism' was in some respects produced by liberal governmentality, yet at the same time it can be understood as exceeding governance, and in fact as a form of 'resistance'. Jonathan Crary, among others, has drawn attention to how governmental procedures and the training of attention in capitalist forms of the mass media not only depend upon but also actively train and produce automatic routines.[99] Reverie, as it were, can be trained, yet there is a sense in which trance, inattention and the daydream also have a certain potential to ignore, undermine and 'resist' dominant forms of power. And they do this in the same way as that which de Certeau describes, one in which the body follows an urban text people write without being able to read, a text inscribed in the individual, implicit action and behaviour making up everyday 'spatial stories'. In the Conclusion, I shall address this further in terms of modes of movement in the contemporary world, using the example of California freeways to say something about comparative aspects of freedom.

In terms of nineteenth-century Britain, this is how W.E.A. Adams, a Tyneside radical working man, described the compartment of a section of the 400,000 people who regularly walked into and out of London in the 1850s:

> The order observed in the streets, the unwritten law of the people, was even then remarkable. I may give an example, the *Morning Star* was at that time the leading radical daily in London. . . . It was my custom every morning to buy a copy at a news stall near the Horns Tavern at Kennington. My business was in Fleet Street.

He then describes the route taken by himself and the throng of people who accompanied him.

> So orderly was the traffic throughout that route that I could, by keeping to the right, read my paper the whole time. And I had nothing left to read in it – at least nothing I wanted to read – when I reached Fleet Street, nearly an hour's walk from Kennington. The feat – if it was a feat – was only possible when people kept in line. All I found it necessary to do, where the traffic was thickest, was to walk immediately behind somebody else. Pedestrians at that period who did not observe the rule of the pavement had as bad a time of it as a dog in a fair. Indeed, they were so buffeted about . . . that they very soon discovered that it was really compulsory to 'keep to the right'.[100]

Adams suggests that this mass sense of order was relatively new, though keeping to the right was certainly evident in London in the 1820s. This understanding of absorbed urban walking did indeed form a trope in literary accounts of urban life which was evident before the 1850s, but what does seem new is the sheer massification of scale, and the attendant deepening of the effect for those who participated, and for those who represented the activity.[101] This sort of abstracted, interiorised, walking is decidedly related to but not quite the same as that designed to cultivate a public of private persons in which walkers would encounter their fellow walkers and the city itself as a civilising spectacle. Somewhat later than Adams, Mayhew described the 'revolution' in a person's life and feelings when coming to live in London. Anticipating Simmel's description of the anonymous, objectivised city, Mayhew described a loss of individuality consequent upon the intense pace and competitiveness of this new sort of city. 'In London a man rubs out, elsewhere he rusts out.' In London one is a 'party', subject to the customs of the city. These customs are given bodily form in what he calls the 'living stream' in the streets. In other cities you may saunter, but in London you go direct. This was the living stream that tended 'greatly to the habit of abstraction and the bump of concentratedness'. One needs to cultivate interior space, but also to be sharp and alert. One is, as it were, closed up in and by the city, closed in on oneself, so that one is absorbed, and, for example, does not give to the beggar and the poor. One is closed in by all the rituals which this automatic London life involves, the ritual of going to work, but also those of leisure (for example, the tyranny of visiting). Therefore, the living stream of the city is but one part of the city's unrelenting, abstracting grip. No matter how one yearns for release, this grip is tight.[102]

There is, therefore, a way of walking which is at once abstracted and alert. There are also the routes which this way of walking marks out. In Mayhew's account, as in Adams', the living stream of London is above all that which flows in and out of the city every day, increasingly the commercial City itself, and which is in fact to be encountered most clearly at the place where this tide ebbs and flows most, fittingly enough called the Strand. There people from the south came into and left London, over the river by foot, and by means of the railway into Charing Cross. (Adams' route from Kennington in the south was near to this manifestation of the living stream.) What are some of the other routes taken into and through the city, ones that seem to have been 'habitual', perhaps in this abstracting way imposed by the city? And how can this habituation be understood? I invoke the idea of the *via sacra* loosely, in order to convey the sense that while patterns of use were ever-changing, at the same time they often existed in terms of urban pathways that endured, and endure, over long periods of time: what is so often striking about cities is how the street pattern continues over many decades, and indeed many centuries. These spatial pathways therefore carry with them different layers of time, and this is particularly evident in relation to particular localities, *loci sacri* as they may be called.

Such pathways and places may be of greater or lesser antiquity, for instance the patterns of use relatively quickly built up in the neighbour-hoods of the industrial city to which I have referred. 'Classic slums' have to age a little before they become classic. The 'slum' district of Ancoats in Manchester is an example of this, as an industrial 'neighbourhood' from the very earliest days of cotton factory industrialisation in the late eighteenth century a particularly interesting one. Going through many trans-formations in the nineteenth century, it retained an identity as a coherent entity, for those who lived within it, and those who lived outside, including those who through the designation 'slum' wished to subject it to the regime of the social. The pathways which demarcated the area, and in this sense actually constituted it, in fact appear to have subsisted over many decades. They were known to insiders and outsiders alike, and their walking was the token of this knowledge, a knowledge to varying degrees conscious and habitual.[103]

This neighbourhood contained within it other smaller sites, for example

Shudehill Market. This was a corporation market of the new reformed kind, but on Saturday nights it spilled over into the surrounding streets, the walking of which became a major element in the ritualised framing of time that made up the 'working-class week'. Time and space were further fused, in that the experience of the market crossed generations, as market night was often a family affair.[104] This occupation was of spaces that were of relatively recent origin, but in considering the *via sacra* of the city the antiquity of particular market sites as *loci sacri* is very striking. This has been seen in the case of Smithfield in London, and was equally so for the other great produce markets of the metropolis, particularly Leadenhall and Billingsgate, where antiquity was measurable not in decades or centuries but millennia. Street markets themselves often continued over surprisingly long periods of time on the same sites, and carried with them many of the powerful associations that we have seen to characterise markets as liminal spaces, especially those of their more antique cousins.

One of the two great street markets of mid-nineteenth-century London, the Cut in Lambeth, was in fact the New Cut, built upon a 'cut' which had been a track through the city that had existed for centuries before. The market therefore reinforced a traditional, habitual pathway through the city. As early as 1700 this particular 'cut' had connected the river and a local pleasure garden, and in the early eighteenth century a new cut had been made across the fields to Old Bargehouse Stairs, from where watermen would take people across the river to Temple Steps.[105] Both new and old 'cuts' were rich in temporal and spatial associations. The Lambeth Sunday market was one of the sights of London, in particular the notable sight of men in their Sunday best enacting a kind of 'working-class' promenade. Traditional routes were therefore sites in which space was *claimed* by different groups, so that, as elements in the spatial stories of everyday knowledge, they delineated a kind of popular social geography of the city. London, in fact, can be considered in its very antiquity as being made up of a whole series of routes, or 'cuts', sometimes with and sometimes against the grain of the existing street pattern.

The 'Fields' of London, the old 'fields below' the new streets,[106] can also be considered in this light, as part of an urban palimpsest on which the new was written on the old, but the old none the less manifested itself. For instance, there was Bonners Field in the East End, the occupation of which as a site for radical political movements in the early nineteenth century continued traditions of plebeian collective assembly that went back centuries. Bonners Field was built over around the mid-

nineteenth century, but part of this building involved the construction,
very near the original site, of Victoria Park, which accrued to itself
precisely this tradition of public assembly, public speakers moving directly
from one to the other location. In the late nineteenth and twentieth
centuries Victoria Park became a major venue for political meetings and
for the enjoyment of the poor in the East End of London.[107] A somewhat
different instance of this was the translation of the 'Royal Park', such as
Hyde Park, into the 'People's Park', with its Speakers' Corner, old
possibilities for movement within bounded space being overlaid by new
ones.

   It is, however, London as a totality that also needs addressing, particularly in relation to the routes that negotiated its primary division into the
City, the East End and the West End. One of these was certainly the route
through Fleet Street to the City, a route impeded by Temple Bar until its
demolition in 1878, itself a notable victory for circulation over tradition
(though as we have seen, and contrary to many accounts, the City was not
a bastion of reaction).[108] More important than this, however, was the
primal route mirroring the primary division between the East End and
West End, namely the old route of Tyburn.[109] The route of the condemned prisoner led from Newgate Prison via the Tyburn Road, which
was later to be Oxford Street, to the place of public execution at Tyburn,
close to what was later to be Marble Arch. This was a *via dolorosa* which
was an expression of disciplinary power of a pre-liberal sort (one in fact
harking back to the power of sovereignty), in which the body itself was
punished, and in which this punishment became a spectacle through
which the multitude who watched were disciplined. However, at the same
time, it was in practice also a means by which this multitude measured
and bargained with the powers that sought to discipline it. This route can
be seen as the the central east–west axis in the primal geography of
London, which in the nineteenth century connected the 'popular' locations of the east with their terminus in the west, in Hyde Park. (The
public scaffold was taken back to the exterior of Newgate in 1783.) In
Hyde Park, near to the carnival of Tyburn, was later re-enacted in a
decidedly different context a carnival of democracy at Speakers' Corner,
a carnival of the age of a new mode of governance, namely that of
liberalism, not sovereignty.

   Before this time, popular defences of London's sacred ways are in
evidence in the Queen Caroline Affair of 1820–1. When the authorities
diverted the funeral *cortège* of the Queen into a circuitous route aimed at
avoiding passage along the Oxford Street axis, there were widespread

public disturbances, marked by the blockading of all roads that were alternatives to passage along this axis, so that in the event rights to popular possession of public routes could be asserted.[110] In the nineteenth century, at the time when Speakers' Corner was coming into existence, the east–west route was claimed in public procession by radical political movements, particularly the Reform League in the 1860s.[111] One typical procession route was from Clerkenwell, then a great radical artisan centre, via Holborn and Oxford Street, thence to Marble Arch. At this time, and subsequently, there was a sort of triangulation of political space in London, the points of the triangle being Hyde Park, the East End and Trafalgar Square. Processions between the first two points were often followed by movements of people to the latter, and then back to the East End. The way to and from Hyde Park, especially down Park Lane, went by the homes of the rich and powerful, so that the possession of public space also involved a clear message to those on the route. Trafalgar Square itself became a notable destination for processional routes in London, in 1887 extensive public disturbances taking place, especially in Pall Mall, a similar location of privilege to Park Lane. However, the spectre of liberal governmentality is ever-present: this was a very different world from the eighteenth-century one, for the reform processions were part of a 'liberal' dispensation very unlike that inhabited by the eighteenth-century way of execution, just as the carnival of democracy that was later to be Speakers' Corner was different in kind from old Tyburn. Speakers' Corner was a part of this new dispensation, but it was also an outcome of the radical tradition of the reformers of the 1860s. *Their* mode of public walking was above all 'orderly', and being orderly in this way was at once a victory for liberalism and an appropriation of it which acted as 'resistance', for it involved using the the language and practice of liberal order to criticise its dominant forms.[112] As in the Tyburn execution, the social order was played out, in very different forms from previously.

In terms of ways of moving in the city beyond walking alone, learning to ride in the teeming streets of London, whether by omnibus, tram or cab, presented as many difficulties as walking. Because the tram did not enter the centre of London, and because the railway termini were so spread out, the omnibus took on a particular importance. However, until late in the nineteenth century the omnibus was the preserve of the better-off. (Services started too late for working men and were too expensive.)[113] It is only with the development of the tram system from the 1880s that public transport began to offer truly mass transit. While there was regulation of the operations of the bus companies, none the less the ordinary daily business of travel was a surprisingly anarchic experience.[114] Buses picked up and set down on request. What regulations there were were limited, and anyone could start a company, and any fare could be charged, though big companies moved in quite early, among them a French entrepreneur, M. Foucauld, who was in fact encouraged by another great engineer of Victorian communication systems, in the form of the sanitary system, Edwin Chadwick.

Buses fought each other for custom, careering through the streets. Conductors, or cads (cadgers) as they were called, took fares as and when they could, and paid their employers what they thought fit. There were no formal tickets until a system was instituted in 1891. Driver and conductor shared the takings. The cad was therefore a sort of subcontracted employee, a condition of labour in fact widely evident in industry throughout most of the nineteenth century. The cad touted for custom, and had his own favourite passengers, who might command a seat close by him, and who in turn would not neglect to 'remember' the conductor. Uniforms were not usually worn. Special relationships grew up between cads and passengers, the former waiting for the latter at set times. Altogether, the cad became an exemplary instance of the urban 'type'. The driver also was a 'type': he might wear a top hat and flower, and from the height of the bus hailed passengers, ogled girls and chaffed other drivers. Drivers were commonly thought to be part of the fraternity of the turf. The cad had the prerogative of keeping down ladies' crinolines when they squeezed onto the bus, the source of much caddish ribaldry.[115]

Unlike the railway compartment, the interior of the horse-drawn omnibus was narrow and cramped, and one had to squeeze in and out, idealisations of the order of the interior of the omnibus in Victorian paintings notwithstanding.[116] Lighting within the omnibus was poor, and the floor, covered with straw, was dank and smelly. Photographs of omnibuses in the street, in the 1890s, convey the marked conviviality, also the contingency and fluidity, of social interactions in the city, with those on the open top of the bus leaning over to talk to those below. As with low street kerbs, and the absence of street barriers, the whole emphasis was in fact on openness, with a high premium on seeing and being seen. (Omnibus windows, at least after the mid-nineteenth century, were quite large, and could be opened at will, which was a frequent source of argument.)[117] Argument does not seem to have been foreign to the Free-Born English Passenger: regulations had it that each passenger had 16 inches of sitting room, and it was not unknown for people to bring measuring tapes with them in order to secure their rights. When a ticket system did emerge, it does not seem to have been to the satisfaction of the passenger.

The ticket system was in fact one of the everyday victories of the rational management of circulation, something in this instance quite closely related to the implementation of liberal governance through municipal regulation. It is with this little victory, one of many charted here and cumulatively of great effect, that I shall conclude this account. The conductor stopped being a kind of middleman, with a direct relationship with the passenger, whose custom he solicited. Instead, the balance of power swung to the companies, and instead of this direct relationship, the impersonal, institutionalised relations of a more modern system of capitalism developed. Although subject to the vagaries of the relationship with the cad, which could include cheating and various other tricks,[118] the passenger, under the old system, partook of a city which was anything but anonymous. After the ticket system the ordered queue began to be manifest, and the whip hand passed from the cad/passenger duo to the company. Before then the bus cadged the passenger, as it were, and afterwards the passenger the bus.[119] The ticket system, when it at last came, was accompanied by an increased level of licensing, and police regulation and inspection. Relations between bus crews and passengers were widely felt to be not as cordial as previously. As for the drivers and the cads, although from early on they had been the subject of surveillance, their power was substantially intact until 1891, after which, despite a bitter strike, they were at last controlled. One report of 1902 said that conductors were now morose and suspicious, unlike former times. (Passengers were said to be rather similar.)[120] Glummer times seem to have arrived.

In terms particularly of the free and easy and of walking in the city, I have in this chapter tried to get at some of the subtle operations of liberal freedom at just the points which reveal the intricate relationship of power and resistance, namely what seems to have been a significant *location* of the connection of different notions of freedom, as well as in terms of a significant existential *condition* of being free in the city. If the general direction of change towards more 'liberal' forms of ordering seems apparent, then the appropriation of this change for diverse ends and to diverse effect is apparent too. If we see in the appropriation of old routes and old spaces, as in the example of popular politics, certain possibilities for exciting resistance, then this capacity was framed in terms of new rules of the game of power which those who appropriated often had little control over. None the less, the subtle trade-offs in this game are everywhere apparent in the republic of the streets, for example the new regime of modern traffic and its renegotiations in practice, including the ambiguous form of the Free-Born English Pedestrian. There is also the action of what I earlier called the techno-administrative state, and the slow and silent power of different material agencies in bringing about the rule of freedom, but also in effecting material resistances to this rule, as well as in provoking its active human negotiation. It is to instances of the liberal form of this state other than Britain alone that I shall now turn by way of conclusion.

Notes

1. For an exemplary study, see Andrew Pickering, *The Mangle of Practice: Time, Agency, and Science* (London: University of Chicago Press, 1995).
2. Michel Foucault, 'An Interview: Sex, Power and the Politics of Identity', interview with B. Gallagher and A. Wilson, *The Advocate*, 400, 1984, p. 29. For a valuable discussion of power, resistance and contradiction see 'Special issue: conflict, contradiction and governance', *Economy and Society*, 25:3, August 1996, esp. Pat O'Malley, 'Indigenous governance', where the subtle operations of governance and its reception are viewed in terms of the 'translation' of the two, and the 'incorporation' of resistance into governance and vice-versa.
3. Michel de Certeau, 'Practices of Space', in Marshall Blonsky (ed.), *On Signs* (Baltimore: Johns Hopkins University Press, 1984). One obvious 'other' of the city of light and publicity was the city at night. See Joachim Schlor, *Nights in the Big City: Paris, Berlin, London 1840–1930* (London: Reaktion Books, 1998). That the city of darkness and the city of light were explicitly gendered is apparent in numerous works, in particular Judith Walkowitz, *City of Dreadful Delight: Narratives of Danger in Late-Victorian London* (Chicago: University of Chicago Press, 1992).
4. Zygmunt Bauman, *Work, Consumerism and the New Poor* (Buckingham: Open University Press, 1998).
5. Nikolas Rose, *Powers of Freedom: Reframing Political Thought* (Cambridge: Cambridge University Press, 1999), pp. 85–9, 164–5, 159–60, 245–6.
6. David Smith, *Victorian Maps of the British Isles* (London: Batsford, 1985), chapter 4; James Elliot, *The City in Maps: Urban Mapping to 1900* (London: British Library, 1987).
7. On London maps, see Andrew Davies, *The Map of London: From 1746 to the Present Day* (London: Batsford, 1987); Ralph Hyde, *Printed Maps of Victorian London* (Folkestone: Dawson, 1975), which has much information on the range of maps available in the nineteenth century; James Howgego, *Printed Maps of London 1553–1850* (Folkestone: Dawson, 1978).
8. Miles Ogborn, *The Spaces of Modernity: London's Geographies 1680–1780* (London: Guilford Press, 1998), pp. 28–38.

9. For example, *Cary's New Pocket Plan of London, Westminster & Southwark* (London, 1793), 'with penny post receiving houses, and hackney coach fares', which has a considerable index, including references to 'public buildings', but in which much is left off, particularly in the highly congested city centre, given the ½ inch to 1 mile scale. See also *A New Pocket Plan* (London, 1797); *Smith's New Plan of London* (London, 1801), ½ inch scale; *Wallis' Guide for Strangers* (London, 1826).

10. Jeremy Black, *Maps and Politics* (London: Reaktion Books, 1997), p. 51.

11. The British Library's Map Library has extensive runs of street maps and 'street atlases' for British towns and cities. All such items for nineteenth-century, late eighteenth-century and early twentieth-century London have been consulted. See, for example, *W.H. Smith's Bartholemew Plan of Liverpool* (Liverpool, 1895), 6 inches to 1 mile.

12. Manchester Central Reference Library has extensive holdings of city maps and plans over several centuries, and there are handlists of maps and plans which are even more extensive. Together these give what must be a reasonably full account of the mapping of the city over time. See J. Lee, *Maps and Plans of Manchester and Salford 1650–1845: A Handlist* (Altrincham: Sherrat, 1957); Charles Roeder, 'Maps and Views of Manchester', *Transactions of the Lancashire and Cheshire Antiquarian Society*, 1904. See too John Harland, *Collecteana* (Manchester: Chetham Society, 1866), and John Leigh, Appendix to Procter's *Bygone Manchester* (Manchester, 1880).

13. Nineteenth-century holdings of Liverpool maps in the British Library have been consulted.

14. For a map in one of the early guides see *Bancks and Thornton's Pocket Plan of Manchester* (Manchester, 1800).

15. *Pigot's 1824 Directory of Manchester and Salford* (Manchester, 1824).

16. *Collin's Illustrated Atlas of London* (London, 1854); *Reynolds Pocket Atlas of London* (London, 1859).

17. Jonathan Crary, *Techniques of the Observer: On Visuality and Modernity* (London: Harvard University Press, 1990), pp. 19, 24, 149.

18. Miles Ogborn, *The Spaces of Modernity*, pp. 39–45.

19. Vanessa Schwartz, *Spectacular Realities: Early Mass Culture in Fin-de-Siècle Paris* (London: University of California Press, 1998), chapter 1.

20. Peter Fritzsche, *Reading Berlin 1900* (London: Harvard University Press, 1996).

21. Lynda Nead, *Modern Babylon: People, Streets and Images in Nineteenth-century London* (London: Yale University Press, 2000).

22. Jeremy Black, *Maps and Politics*, pp. 15–17, 49; Sarah Hartley, *Mrs P's Journey: The Remarkable Story of the Woman Who Created the A-Z Map* (London: Simon & Schuster, 2001).

23. Gareth Shaw and Allison Typer, *British Directories: A Bibliographical Guide* (Leicester: Leicester University Press, 1989), part 1, chapter 2.

24. Ibid., table 8, p. 45.

25. P.F. Atkins, *The Directories of London 1677–1977* (London: Mansell, 1990), p. 8, figure 2.

26. Henry Duffield, *The Pocket Companion, or The Strangers Guide to Manchester and Salford* (Manchester, 1852), pp. 12, 23ff.; and see also the first Manchester city

guide, James Aston, *The Manchester Guide* (Manchester, 1804), the interesting *Visitors Guide to Manchester 1857* (Manchester, 1857) and *John Heywood's Illustrated Guide to Manchester* (Manchester, 1891).

27. Dana Brand, *The Spectator and the City in Nineteenth-Century American Literature* (Cambridge: Cambridge University Press, 1991), chapter 2 on the development of the *flâneur* in England.

28. Ibid., pp. 20–6.

29. Ibid., p. 21.

30. Ibid., p. 25.

31. Patrick Joyce, 'Introduction', in Joyce (ed.), *The Social in Question: New Bearings in History and the Social Sciences* (London: Routledge, 2002).

32. Peter Stallybrass and Allon White, *The Politics and Poetics of Transgression* (London: Cornell University Press, 1986), chapter 3.

33. Miles Ogborn, *The Spaces of Modernity*, pp. 110–11.

34. Dana Brand, *The Spectator and the City*, chapter 3, especially pp. 45–63.

35. Trefor Thomas, 'Introduction', to his (ed.) *The Mysteries of London* (Keele: Keele University Press, 1996); Anne Humphreys, *Travels into a Poor Man's Country: The Work of William Henry Mayhew* (Georgia, US: Albens, 1977); Bertrand Taithe, *The Essential Mayhew: Representing and Communicating the Poor* (London: Rivers Oram Press, 1996).

36. Henry Mayhew, *London Labour and the London Poor, Volume Three, The Prisons of London* (London, 1862); Mary Cowley, *The Artist as Anthropologist: The Representation of Type and Character in Victorian Art* (Cambridge: Cambridge University Press, 1989); see also Kerry Meadows, *Heads of the People, Or Portraits of the English*, 2 volumes (London, 1878).

37. John Tagg, *The Burden of Representation: Essays on Photographies and Histories* (Basingstoke: Macmillan, 1988), chapters 1–2.

38. Ibid., chapter 3, especially pp. 99–101, 154–5, 157, 174–83, 191–2, 203 on 'realism', and Thomas Annan, *Photographs of the Old Closes and Streets of Glasgow 1868–1877* (New York: Dover Press, 1977); John Thompson and Adolph Smith, *Street Life in London* (1877–8, republished Wakefield: E.P. Publishing, 1973).

39. See, for example, the urban photography of the Manchester Amateur Photography Society Survey, 1890–1901, in the Documentary Photography Archive, Manchester.

40. Charles Hindley, *History of the Cries of London, Ancient and Modern* (London, 1884); *Streetology of London, or the Metropolitan Papers of the Itinerant Club*, No. 1, July 1837; *Vagabondia: Anecdotes of Mendicant Wanderers in the the Streets of London* (London, 1817); and for some later variants, *Phil May's Guttersnipes* (London, 1896), and W. Pitt Ridge, *London Types, Taken from Nature* (London, 1926). For the case of Dublin streetology, differing from the London example, see Sidney Davis, *Dublin Types* (Dublin, 1918), especially 'Introduction'.

41. Lucy Brown, *Victorian News and Newspapers* (Oxford: Oxford University Press, 1985).

42. Aled Jones, *Powers of Press: Newspapers, Power and the Public in Nineteenth-Century England* (Aldershot: Scolar Press, 1996).

43. On this press in the provinces see Simon Gunn, *The Public Culture of the Victorian Middle Class: Ritual and Authority in the English Industrial City 1840–1914* (Manchester: Manchester University Press, 2000), chapter 3; and on the city as an arena of pleasure see, for example, *Free Lance* articles for 20, 27 July, 31 August, 7, 12 December, and 12 February 1867; on a contemporary journalist who wrote for the *Free Lance* see the obituary of J.N. Allen, *Free Lance*, 30 November 1867; see also Charles Tomlinson, 'Gutter Merchants', in *Byways of Manchester Life* (Manchester, 1887).

44. Patrick Joyce, *Democratic Subjects: The Self and the Social in Nineteenth-century England* (Cambridge: Cambridge University Press, 1994), pp. 180–1, 207–8.

45. See the discussion below, pp. 246, also Gareth Stedman Jones, 'The "Cockney" and the Nation, 1780–1988', in Gareth Stedman Jones and David Feldman (eds), *Metropolis: London, History and Representation since 1800* (London: Routledge, 1989).

46. *Free Lance*, 7 December 1867.

47. *City Lantern*, 14 May 1875.

48. On 'Mr Smith' and 'Mr Swell' see *Free Lance*, 28 January 1876.

49. Philomen Eva, 'Popular Song and Social Identity in Victorian Manchester' (University of Manchester PhD, 1996), 'Introduction'; and see also Patrick Joyce, *Visions of the People: Industrial England and the Question of Class 1840–1914* (Cambridge: Cambridge University Press, 1991), chapters 10, 13.

50. Philomen Eva, 'Popular Song', p. 143.

51. Ibid., chapter 4.

52. See the accounts of the halls and the free and easy in Fred Leary, 'Manchester Ballads', Manuscript Section, Manchester Central Reference Library, Local Studies Unit.

53. Philomen Eva, 'Popular Song', especially chapter 5.

54. Ibid., chapter 3 on the street singer.

55. Ibid., part II for the analysis of the songs.

56. A range of broadside ballads about the city circulating in Manchester between the 1830s and 1860s represent a sort of imaginative cartographic mapping of the city as a place of plebeian pleasure and sociability. They represent a variant of carnivalesque knowingness. This is city of freedom and release. Another strain represents the massive 'improvement' of the city centre, which both celebrates and criticises aspects of the rapid change of the time. But what is most evident is this division into two cities, the city of power and restraint being conceived of as distinct from the city of pleasure and release. The encounter of these two cities in the songs is where one may track something of power and resistance. Lack of space prevents an analysis of the songs.

57. Mikhail Bakhtin, *The Dialogic Imagination: Four Essays by Mikhail Bakhtin* (Austin: University of Texas Press, 1981), and *Rabelais and His World* (Bloomington: Indiana University Press, 1984).

58. Peter Bailey, *Popular Culture and Performance in the Victorian City* (Cambridge: Cambridge University Press, 1998).

59. Ibid., p. 149.

60. Ibid., pp. 77–9, 149–50.

61. Michel de Certeau, *The Practice of Everyday Life* (London: University of California Press, 1984), p. 93.

62. Thomas Gladwin, *East is a Big Bird: Navigation and Logic on Pulawat Atoll* (London: Harvard University Press, 1970); Lucy A. Suchman, *Plans and Situated Actions* (Cambridge: Cambridge University Press, 1987).

63. Michel de Certeau, *The Practice of Everyday Life*, chapter IX.

64. Rebecca Solnit, *Wanderlust: A History of Walking* (London: Verso, 2001), chapter 2, 'The Mind at Three Miles an Hour'.

65. This account is taken from Philip S. Bagwell, *The Transport Revolution from 1770* (London: Batsford, 1974); see also Sidney and Beatrice Webb, *The Story of the King's Highway* (London, 1913).

66. Robert Roberts, *The Classic Slum* (Manchester: Manchester University Press, 1971), pp. 115–16.

67. Rebecca Solnit, *Wanderlust*, chapters 6–9.

68. Anne Wallace, *Walking, Literature and English Culture: The Origins and Use of Peripatetic in the Nineteenth Century* (Oxford: Oxford University Press, 1993).

69. John Barrell, *The Idea of Landscape and the Sense of Place 1730–1840* (Cambridge: Cambridge University Press, 1972).

70. Anne Wallace, *Walking, Literature*, chapter 1.

71. John Barrell, *The Idea of Landscape*, chapter 1.

72. Anne Lawrence, *Walking, Literature*, pp. 106, 108, chapter 3, *passim.*

73. Rebecca Solnit, *Wanderlust*, pp. 160, 161.

74. Ibid., p. 162.

75. James Winter, *London's Teeming Streets 1830–1914* (London: Routledge, 1993), chapters 3 and 6.

76. Chris Makepeace (ed.), *Manchester As It Was* (Nelson: Hendon Publishing, 1972), and subsequent volumes 2 and 3. See, for example, on Birmingham, Keith Turner (ed.), *Central Birmingham 1870–1920: The Old Photography Series* (Birmingham, 1974); John Marks (ed.), *Birmingham on Old Postcards*, volumes 1 and 2 (Birmingham, 1983).

77. James Winter, *London's Teeming Streets*, pp. 40–4.

78. Ibid., pp. 51–64.

79. Ibid., pp. 44–5.

80. Ibid., chapters 7–8, 10.

81. Peter Bailey (ed.), *Music Hall: The Business of Pleasure* (Milton Keynes: Open University Press, 1986); Jackie Bratton (ed.), *Music Hall: Performance and Style* (Milton Keynes: Open University Press, 1986), and Dagmar Kift, *The Victorian Music Hall: Culture, Class, Conflict* (Cambridge: Cambridge University Press, 1996).

82. Miles Ogborn, *The Spaces of Modernity*, pp. 91–104.

83. Ibid., pp. 104–14.

84. Hazel Thurston, 'Introduction' to her *Royal Parks for the People* (Newton Abbot: David and Charles, 1974). On Hyde Park, the exemplar for many subsequent public parks, see the especially useful John Ashton, *Hyde Park from Domesday Book to Date* (London, 1896); Mrs Alec Tweedie, *Hyde Park: Its History and Romance*

(London, 1908); Edward Owen, *Hyde Park: Selected Narrative, Annual Events . . . During Twenty-one Years of Police Service* (London, 1906).

85. Teresa Wyborn, *Parks for the People: The Development of Public Parks in Manchester 1830–1860* (University of Manchester Working Papers in Economic and Social History, No. 29, 1994).

86. Charles E. Beveridge (ed.), *Frederick Law Olmsted: Designing the American Landscape* (New York: Rizzoli, 1995).

87. Charles E. Beveridge and Carolyn Hoffman (eds), *The Papers of Frederick Law Olmsted: Supplementary Series Volume 1: Writings on Public Parks, Parkways and Park Systems* (Baltimore: Johns Hopkins University Press, 1997), pp. 171–206.

88. Ibid., pp. 147–71.

89. Ibid., 'General Orders . . .', pp. 281–308.

90. Mark Girouard, *The English Town: A History of Urban Life* (London: Yale University Press, 1990), chapter 16.

91. Teresa Wyborn, *Parks for the People*, pp. 2–3.

92. Letters, *Manchester Guardian*, 14 September 1833.

93. Michel Foucault, 'Different Spaces', in James D. Faubion (ed.), *Michel Foucault: Aesthetics, Method and Epistemology* (London: Allen Lane Penguin Press, 2000).

94. Kevin Hetherington, *The Badlands of Modernity: Heterotopia and Social Ordering* (London: Routledge, 1997).

95. Robert Rosenberg, *Landscape and Power in Vienna* (Baltimore: Johns Hopkins University Press, 1995).

96. Kevin Hetherington, *The Badlands of Modernity*, p. 8.

97. Robert Roberts, *The Classic Slum*, pp. 25–8.

98. Tim Edensor, 'The Indian Street', in Nick Fyfe (ed.), *Images of the Street: Representation, Experience and Control in Public Space* (London: Routledge, 1998).

99. Jonathan Crary, *Suspensions of Perception: Attention, Spectacle and Modern Culture* (Cambridge, Mass.: MIT Press, 1999), pp. 77–9.

100. W.E.A. Adams, *Memoirs of a Social Atom* (1903, reprinted New York: Augustus M. Kelley, 1968), pp. 312–13.

101. Jane Rendell, 'Displaying Sexuality: the Early Nineteenth-Century Street', in Nick Fyfe (ed.), *Images of the Street*.

102. Henry Mayhew, *London Characters* (London, 1881), pp. 277ff.

103. On Ancoats, see Malcolm Lynch, *The Streets of Ancoats* (London: Constable, 1985); and the special number of *Manchester Region History Review*, VII, 1993. For a very revealing survey of Manchester city centre streets, covering many of the main ones, see the run of articles at roughly monthly intervals in *Momus*, between 4 November 1880 and 21 July 1881.

104. Andrew Davies, *Leisure, Gender and Poverty: Working-Class Culture in Salford and Manchester 1900–1939* (Buckingham: Open University Press, 1992). And for markets, see W.J. Passingham, *London Markets: Their Origins and History* (London, 1935); W. Addison, *English Fairs and Markets* (London: Batsford, 1953); Mary Benedetta, *The Street Markets of London* (London, 1936); James Greenwood, *Journeys Through London; Or Byways of Modern Babylon* (London, 1873), chapters ii, xxvi–vii.

105. Fred Willis, *Peace and Dripping Toast* (London: Phoenix House, 1950), chap. xx.

There is an enormous literature on the streets of London in the British Library, and the following are especially useful: Thomas Burke, *The Streets of London Through the Centuries* (London, 1940); and Alfred Rosling Bennett, *London and Londoners in the 1850s and '60s* (London, 1924), the latter a mine of information.

106. Peter Ackroyd, *London: The Biography* (London: Chatto and Windus, 2000).

107. Charles Poulson, *Victoria Park: A Study in the History of East London* (London: Stepney Books, 1976).

108. Lynda Nead, *Modern Babylon*, pp. 203–11, and see Henry Johnson, *Temple Bar and State Pageants* (London, 1897).

109. V.A.C. Gatrell, *The Hanging Tree: Execution and the English People 1770–1868* (Oxford: Oxford University Press, 1994).

110. John Ashton, *Hyde Park from Domesday Book*, p. 173.

111. Anon., *Government of the People! The Great Reform League Demonstration in Hyde Park* (London, 1866[?]).

112. Donald C. Richter, *Riotous Victorians* (London: Ohio University Press, 1981).

113. *London General: The Story of the London Bus 1856–1956* (London: London Transport, 1956); John Hibbs, *The History of British Bus Services* (Newton Abbot: David and Charles, 1968).

114. Trevor May, *Gondolas and Growlers: The History of the London Horse Cab* (Stroud: Alan Sutton, 1995); T.C. Barker, *A History of London Transport* (London: Allen and Unwin, 2 volumes, 1973, 1974), volume 1; I. Yearsley, *The Manchester Tram* (Huddersfield: Advertiser Press, 1962); Manchester Corporation Transport Department, *A Hundred Years of Public Passenger Transport in Manchester* (Manchester, n.d.).

115. Henry Charles Moore, *Omnibuses and Cabs: Their Origin and History* (London, 1902), is by far the most revealing account.

116. Charles E. Lee, *The Horse-Drawn Bus As a Vehicle* (Newton Abbot: David and Charles, 1974): Vernon Summerfield, *London Buses* (London, 1933) and *London Transport: A Record and Survey* (London, 1935).

117. See the discussion of street photographs above, pp. 202–3.

118. Henry Charles Moore, *Omnibuses and Cabs*, especially chapter 8, also chapters 6–7, 9, 12.

119. Ibid., chapter 5, esp. pp. 53–5, 71, and Alfred Rosling Bennett, *London and Londoners*, p. 82.

120. Mrs E.T. Cook, *Highways and Byways in London* (London, 1902), chapter xviii, and Frederick Willis, *101 Jubilee Road: A Book of London Yesterdays* (London, 1948), chapter 3.

6

Modern Freedom

Comparisons and Conclusion

If in the history of walking the British had their footpaths and the French their boulevards, this only shows how much national differences in the history of liberal governmentality mattered. At the same time there was an international history parallel to this national one, the west, loosely considered, seeing the operations of similar governmental initiatives and technologies across national boundaries, part of the long history of 'globalisation'. There was indeed a general and progressive process of *internationalisation* of governmentality in the nineteenth century – the internationalisation of social statistics and of the statistics movement in the mid-nineteenth century was mentioned in chapter 1.[1] Another example would be the international town planning movement of the late nineteenth and early twentieth centuries, considered in chapter 4. I will consider the 'English park' a little more closely as an instance of these parallel histories, migrating as it did into many different national locations.

As was seen in the previous chapter, Frederick Law Olmsted was a key figure in the international dissemination of the English park: in fact figures such as he were themselves elements in the internationalisation of governance. The model of the eighteenth-century Whig aristocratic park clearly spoke to similar governmental needs in rather different state regimes and national circumstances. Olmsted's appropriation of the park is evidence of this for the United States, as is the 'park of liberty' in

Austria-Hungary. The English model of landscape more generally was crucial for Olmsted, as for the many others involved in aesthetic governance, but he adapted the model to US circumstances, in terms of grafting upon English models his own idealisation of the American frontier homestead and the Connecticut Valley community of his youth.[2] In the making of the US public park he brought to bear in park design his own version of contemporary American notions of nature and democracy, and indeed of the nature of space. And of course he built parks in the particular material conditions of US cities. In other respects Olmsted's influence upon the governance of American space has been profound, and profoundly inflected by American contexts. It was he 'who advocated the continuity of the suburban front lawn as a means of expressing amplitude and democratic solidarity', so that the 'American obsession with front lawns' represented at once the subjugation of nature to civilisation and a recognition of nature's value.[3] Alongside the creation of the collective went that of the individual, the lawn being utterly similar irrespective of geographical location (similar precisely in its democratic 'ordinariness' and openness) while at the same time utterly distinct in its individuated form as private property.

In thinking about common processes of urban governance, what is striking in, for example, Britain and the USA in the nineteenth century is how similar urban governance was: in the eighteenth century, far from seeing the absence of governance, American towns and cities saw the active governance of the economic sphere in a highly regulated way,[4] one akin to European models of 'police' governmentality. In the nineteenth century, somewhat later than in Britain, but very similar to it, there was a systematic attention to the regulation of *social* life. However, in terms of national inflections of common processes it would be necessary here to take into account the particular sorts of problems governance presented in different locations, particularly notable in the US context, given its urban and demographic history, being the management of 'the stranger', something not nearly so evident in the British and other cases.[5] In thinking about common processes across national or state form boundaries, it is necessary to evaluate the city *itself* as an instrument of liberal governance. How did states use cities as the means or instruments of governance? I have highlighted the British case, where this use seems to have been much in evidence, and in the discussion of India that follows I situate this use in a colonial context, where the city had less central a role.

Continuing with the US example, the theme of movement in the city considered in the last chapter can be developed further in a

consideration of the US freeway. This can also serve to show the utility of
the governmentality optic in looking at the present as well as the past.
Again, common governmental forms and needs are evident in the international example of the express roadway, but I concentrate here particularly on American expressions of these forms and needs. At the same
time, even in these American expressions, a certain 'western' expression
of contemporary freedom seems evident. In using this example I also
want to suggest again the utility of considering the often neglected
dimension of mundane life and material technologies. On the contemporary Los Angeles urban freeway, 'we' in the west can be said to have
reached the apotheosis of the city of free circulation. As the culmination
of ways of moving in the city evident in one capital of the late nineteenth
century, London, can this capital of the early twenty-first century be said
to exemplify something of how modern freedom is governed and lived?
David Brodsky's eulogy to the Los Angeles freeway system considers how
it creates a mental map which makes the city into a place of passage
between points, freeing people from locality and what is 'in between'.[6] Of
course, new communities are made possible by the freeway, for the
political, economic and physical structures of the city were shaped by it,
but what seems apparent is that the city is reduced to a network of lines
of passage, rendering what abuts on these lines invisible. This is paralleled
by the freeway itself becoming invisible to what surrounds it: Brodsky
reports on how the freeway is often physically set apart from its surround-
ings, and is perceived to be so dissociated by city dwellers themselves that
mental maps of localities miss out freeways, just as mental maps of the city
leave out some localities.

These ways of knowing and being in cities are not accidents. They are,
in this case quite literally, engineered into urban landscapes, and so are
the forms of conduct they help shape but of course do not determine. In
this sense, then, we can think of the freeway as a technosocial solution to
city life which is also technopolitical in the governmental sense developed
in this book. This is the sense of 'liberalism': the freeway seems similar to
the instances of nineteenth-century urban infrastructure already
described, instances that appear to perform the constitutional dislike of
liberal regimes for more direct political intervention upon subjects.
Freeways are set apart (sunken or elevated), often landscaped, they may
have sound walls, and so on. They are monofunctional, and unidirectional
(so that the effect of breakdown is traumatic). For a European driver,
certainly this one, the feeling that the road and not the driver drives the
car is overwhelming: wide laning, smooth banking, copious signing,

contribute to this, as does the construction of the motor car itself, with its size, power and automatic functions. Engineering interventions are inseparable from a vast battery of legal regulations concerning roads, motoring and vehicles which govern this abiding experience of a lonely freedom, one in which the driver controls but is also controlled by distant and seemingly benign forces (on good days; malign forces on bad days).[7]

A certain autonomous subjectivity seems to be made possible by a technology which actively seeks liberation from both place and circumstance. This subjectivity is marked by the isolation, individuation and separation of the person. However, while these systems in their very materiality have a degree of autonomy which it is important to emphasise, they are not only always related to political systems but also embedded in all manner of cultural representations, so that the experience of the freeway is associated with forms of identity and conduct which are inextricable from American understandings of freedom and space. The American lawn, the American park, the American freeways, seem to draw on similar feelings about space. (It is interesting that Frederick Law Olmsted's son was a major influence behind the first serious plan in 1924 of what would be the future Los Angeles freeway system, a plan that represented a landmark in the history of the idea of traffic *flow* as all-important.) The practice of freedom on the freeway is, for example, to be seen alongside the dream of a complete mobility it often seems to realise, a dream associated with the importance of freedom to move in US, especially Californian, society, and the experience of actual and frequent movement in American society. Also, having a car, and thus being free, relates to notions of freedom in US society that reverberate at many levels, some political in an orthodox sense. If the British have their footpaths, the French their boulevards, then the Americans have their freeways and their cars – even though we in Britain now seem to be heading down the motorway to hell. Technopolitical systems therefore mediate national differences, as well as being mediated by them, emphasising, as in this case, the increasingly common experience of roadways and movement across national boundaries. Common too is the increasing merger of human and machinic agency evident in the revolution in information technology. The motor car itself, the means of transacting the experience of the road/freeway, is one site of this merging.

However, like the case of the 'automatic' aspects of walking evident in the British example, 'resistance' seems to be inseparable from governance here too. The capacity of the reverie, the daydream, to resist what Jonathan Crary has considered as the systematic training of attention apparent since the late nineteenth century is a valuable avenue to explore.[8] Here it is again useful to invoke a theme frequently present in this book, namely that of the liminal, in this case the liminality of travel, of being 'in between', especially in these contemporary conditions of attempted separation from place and circumstance. In such situations, as I have suggested, the social order may itself be put in question. 'Resistance' may be found on the bad days, when the dysfunction of the entire system seems evident. On the good days, when movement is free, the road system presents itself as a utopia of socio-technological order; on the bad days, a dystopia. The vision of the city itself that is gained from the vantage of the freeway, as a symbol of order and disorder, is in turn shaped by these experiences of the freeway system as utopia and dystopia. 'Resistance' may in part therefore lie in the *collective* experience of the freeway, in the sense of it as what Brodsky, citing Joan Didion, calls 'the only secular communion' Los Angeles has.[9]

Here the daydream, as part of the governance of conduct *and* of resistance to this, becomes evident in the 'detached involvement' of driving, when forms of public order and social cooperation are realised at the level of practice. The social cooperation of the daydreamers may both cement and undermine dominant versions of this public order, undermining them by presenting other possibilities of order. This vision and experience of traffic, if collective, and thus part of our new 'social', seem, however, in this case also to be lonely, but who knows what awaits us all in the daydreams and rages that breed on the US freeway? We await our fate. That fate is to some degree a 'western', also a European one. However, it is also distinctively a British one, for the particular form governmentality has taken in Britain has obviously been greatly shaped by the distinctiveness of Britain. In conclusion I want to turn to something more of that distinctiveness, but before I do so I shall explore in detail how the metropolitan experience of governmentality was shaped by, and in turn shaped, the experience of colonial governmentality. That experience too, especially in India, was part of the distinctiveness of the British case.

Dislocated liberalism: ruling the Raj

It is a commonplace that the practice of metropolitan governance often originated in colonial situations, not that the empires in question needed necessarily to be 'western' ones. The famed panopticon of Bentham was in fact first used in his brother's factory in the Ottoman Empire between 1768 and 1774.[10] Sitting uneasily between east and west, the Russian Empire of the late nineteenth and early twentieth centuries (and this includes its Soviet manifestations) developed very similar categories and practices for operating on 'populations' to those of its western counterparts, including many of the accoutrements of the contemporary 'social' we have seen operating in Britain, but in the Russian case developed by the military and leaning heavily towards ethnographic knowledge,[11] as in British India.[12] In the latter, as was seen in the case of mapping, the activity originated in the eighteenth century, though finding origins here is rather pointless, the process between metropole and colony being rather a circular one, as indeed was the case with Ordnance Survey mapping itself. None the less, the fertility of the colony as a seedbed of metropolitan governmentality cannot be denied. As has been seen, the same group of intellectuals and politicians who were responsible for the reform of the British civil service were earlier on involved in developing the Indian civil service. It was in India that the mandarin elite of this service (at its peak some thousand people governing 300 million Indians) deployed all the governmental nostrums of the nineteenth-century metropole.[13]

The fertility of the colony in exciting governmental creativity, whether in the colony or the metropole, is especially evident in situations where the very fundamentals of western culture were themselves excited into creative life by the apprehension of difference that the colony represented. Drawing upon the work of Foucault, Timothy Mitchell has considered the creation of the idea of 'external reality' itself as a mechanism of power. The naturalisation of the distinction between representation and reality is constituted by, and reflected in, western notions of the separation of built form and culture, so that the framing of space evident in the colonists' 'model villages' of colonial Egypt, for example, was based on codes and symbols separable from the physical world. These codes and symbols literally framed space and thereby instituted abstract space, by means of networks of cellular housing adapted to age, sex, social condition, and so on.[14] Non-western divisions of space inside the house and between the house and outside were contextual and relational, based on resemblances and differences drawn from the physical world. There was no framing of space in these houses.

In accounts of colonial governmentality the emphasis on the significance of *difference* has, rightly, been immense. None the less, as I shall argue later, an emphasis on similarity, emerging from the claims to universality inherent in liberalism, however we view that term, is not to be neglected. An adequate comparison of metropolitan and colonial govern-mentality would need to bring out differences *between* the different colonial powers and their colonies, something I am not placed to do. Instead, I shall consider the British case alone, emphasising India and liberal governmentality. In recent years there have been a number of outstanding accounts of colonial governmentality, especially Gyan Prak-ash's *Another Reason* and Nicholas Dirks' *Castes of Mind.*[15] The former shows clearly how science and technology were deployed in Indian colonial governmentality, where they were not, as in the metropole, predicated upon the notion of a free civil society and a free self, or the attendant notion of the city as a site of liberal freedom. At the same time, it is quite apparent that very many of the techniques of metropolitan governmentality (the census, statistics, public works, and so on) were just as evident in the colony, so that *both* experiences of government were central to the shaping of the modern nation-state. None the less, the colonial state was based on difference: Nicholas Dirks in fact shows that, instead of civil society, it was the category of 'community' in the form of caste that, especially after the traumatic breakdown of government in 1857, formed the central principle of colonial governmentality; Prakash echoes this affirmation.[16] It was the very concept of difference itself that legitimated colonial rule.[17]

India became an 'ethnographic state', anthropology supplanting his-tory as the principal colonial modality of knowledge. It identified as a subject a 'native' population that was to be ruled. Colonial history conceded to anthropology the study of an historical subject that had not yet become modern. Anthropology became the history of those without history. It was caste that articulated this legacy of tradition, standing in place of the historical mindedness that was seen to be absent from Indian sensibilities. By contrast the public which the metropolitan archive addressed was already within history, for this history in the form of the nation was its legacy, unlike the Indian. This was so even though this public, and the form of the 'working class' especially, were in the utmost need of 'improvement'. As Cromer put it of Egypt, there was absent in the empire 'the traditional, communal bonds between rulers and those who were ruled', the bonds of 'race, religion, language, and habits of thought'. Bureaucracy was the sister of caste. As Dirks argues, in India sovereignty performed itself not only through caste but, before 1857 in particular, also through the administration of state security and private property, so that sovereignty became yoked to bureaucracy.[18] The Indian bureaucracy became organised around knowing its objects of rule, through caste, through the needs of security, and through the interests of property. It is striking how in these mid-nineteenth-century experimental years of Victorian governmentality, for all the advances in bureaucracy and the attempts to know its populations in Britain, at a time when in India knowledge became more important than the colonial state, as Dirks puts it, in Britain it is the reverse that was still the case, or rather, as was evident in chapter 1, a particular balance was achieved then so that the state might know enough not to need to know too much.

Were we to trace Indian governmentality at the micro-level, for example the governance of movement, the emphasis on difference would be the same. Linda Baer's study of the Indian railway system contrasts it with the British one, in which '[r]ailways were perceived as enabling a new degree of social as well as commercial intercourse in which the whole population was made mobile and could actively be brought into play in securing the wealth of the nation'.[19] In the daily management of the railways there was a strictly limited penetration of a 'colonial public sphere'. A concern with discipline and surveillance was overwhelming: as soon as travelling Indians entered the space of the railway station, they came under the disciplinary powers of the Railway Acts and of the railway staff who enforced these.[20] If in law the travelling Indian 'public' enjoyed certain rights as a public, for the Railways as a 'common carrier' were a 'public carrier' in the terms of the Indian Railway Acts, the series of public offices, offences and rights that were a consequence of these posited hierarchical relations of super- and subordination in India that did not apply in the metropole. (There was, for example, no such offence as trespass on a British railway platform.)

And further, in terms of the city itself as an instrument of colonial governmentality, a similar story of difference would emerge. This is strikingly evident in the case of Lucknow, singled out by the British after 1857 for a massive transformation not only because it was the epicentre of rebellion in that year, but also because as a pre-colonial city, the largest and most prosperous one, it signified so strongly the otherness of an India now felt to be greatly threatening.[21] If, along European lines, the social imaginary of the city was in a sense liberal, as now a place of free flows and free circulation, what is striking are the limitations on this vision and its practices: the limitations of the city, and all Indian cities, divided into the separate areas of a 'black town' and a 'white town', the limitations of the spatial and legal segregation of the military's cantonments and the civilians' 'civil lines', indeed the demarcations of the ordinary space of the habitation itself, particularly in the form of the bungalow.[22]

At the same time, if we were to look at Britain of the 1830s we would find, for example among the sanitary inspectors considered in chapter 2, a vision of the ruled as almost sub-human, a vision with striking similarities to the Indian situation. This warns us against separating colonial and metropolitan governmentality too sharply, and therefore creating teleological readings of both. Liberal governmentality in Britain was, one might say, feeling its way into explicitly political existence in these years, and if it always worked with a more developed notion of freedom than in India, this existence was being elaborated then and there, on the spot. As seen in chapter 1, there is an ever-present danger of imagining a prescient, all-seeing state, whereas the state often groped its way along as it went. And the way that it went, so often being instantiated in material objects and processes, might be similar in colony and metropole, as well as something that the state might have little control over. At the time of sanitary reform in Britain, at least in some cases, it was felt that the realisation of this particular social imaginary of the city might create conditions in which it would not be necessary to grant freedom in other spheres, for example the political. The *disciplinary* aspects of liberal governmentality should be remembered. Liberal governmentality, like all forms of governmentality but perhaps especially so, was tentative and uneven, developments in one area working at different rates to those in others. Therefore, one might see governmentality in Britain and India developing together, in mutual fertilisation, the 'liberal' variant emerging dramatically in Britain, but not being totally absent in India.

Consequently, if the place of difference in colonial governmentality was immense, that of similarity should not be minimised. As Prakash has remarked, colonial governmentality had to be western and Indian at the same time. None the less, the emphasis on difference may be somewhat overplayed. I have already spoken of a colonial public sphere and an Indian public, however limited and contradictory, and of a certain 'liberalism' in urban governance. In terms of orthodox understandings of liberalism, Thomas R. Metcalf has considered the duality always evident within it, that between difference and universality. While an emphasis on the former was especially evident after 1857, the universality of liberalism was always in play, giving rise to some of the most momentous clashes within the governing classes until the granting of Indian independence in 1947. This universality was particularly evident in the instances of private property, the rule of the law, the liberty of the individual, and education in western knowledge.[23] It could not help but shape the colonial subject at least partly in its own image. A degree of tension, indeed contradiction,[24] always characterised what I think can be called the liberal dimensions of colonial governmentality, and in this respect the latter therefore seems to have had something in common with the agonistic element that I have argued was so important within metropolitan governance through freedom.

Metcalf, and Stokes before him,[25] show how liberal ideas partook of decidedly different views in India. The 'liberalism' of Bentham and the early Utilitarians in India conceived of the aim of government not as liberty but as the greatest happiness. This turned on the idea that men pursued their own self-interest, so that ultimately the judicious use of force, wielded by a powerful legislator, was its own justification. In this view law was the instrument of sovereignty, and spoke the language of command. Rights were not natural but were created by law. As Stokes indicates, early 'liberalism' in its Indian settings was rooted in enlightened despotism, so that we might in fact consider it in terms of the 'police', not 'liberal', mode or phase of governmentality. In this sense, liberal governmentality was foreign to India This view of government did not end with the Utilitarians, but in spokesmen like James Fitzjames Stephens was reflected in opinion not only in India but at home too, especially that domestic opinion which was frightened by Gladstone's positive embrace of liberty as a mode of governance.[26] Indeed, this conservative liberalism, in essence more akin to what might be called a conservative than a liberal mode of governmentality, was perhaps the dominant form of British opinion in India.

None the less, just as in the metropole if in a more contradictory and limited way, colonial governmentality was inflected by a certain degree of agonism between authority and liberty. If the momentous step taken in Britain to govern in the name of liberty was not taken in India, then the active mobilisation of freedom as a rationale and technological principle of governance was not totally absent. The earlier account of the performance of liberalism dwelt on how the younger Mill embraced liberty and self-government at home. Somewhat before this, Macaulay did so in India. He sought in the reform of the Indian civil service an educated and improved 'native public opinion'; he looked forward to the day when, adopting 'European institutions', Indians might govern themselves. Before his time the training of a bureaucracy was already moving forward in parallel with the training of this native opinion in self-government: Haileybury College at home (1805) and Fort William College in Calcutta

(1800), both for the training of the British bureaucrat, were quickly followed in 1816 by the Hindu College in Calcutta, for the training of the Indian. In fact, this active governance through an 'improving' education aimed at some measure of colonial self-governance preceded many domestic developments in Britain.

I have called this contradictory and limited, and so it was. If we take municipal reform, except in Calcutta this was greatly circumscribed, and its principle of representation was not persons or localities but 'communities', and representation was more often by nomination than election, the aim being to secure a community's supposed natural leaders. The contradictions of equality and difference are evident, and they are equally evident in J.S. Mill, who, while embracing liberal universalism, was entirely characteristic of all of liberalism in its Indian governmental setting in situating this universalism in terms of a view of progress. As evident in chapter 3, Mill understood the exertion of the will against the force of habit as essential to the development of both the self and society. There was a clear threshold over which some cultures had crossed, but most had not, including India (a distinctly geographical as well as historical threshold, as the nearer one came to England the nearer one came to civilisation). India was still immured in habit, in the form of 'Custom'. The universalism of liberalism, being predicated on the idea of a notion of progress which consigned the Indian outside the pale of progress, was therefore at heart a fundamental contradiction. In fact, this very universalism depended for its existence on realising India as its own 'other'.[27]

If fundamentally contradictory, the liberal dimensions of colonial governmentality were important: Cromer recognised this importance in Egypt, seeing that in the absence of the 'traditional, communal bonds' of the metropole, the 'artificial bonds of a reasonable and disciplined sympathy' with the native populations were needed. Perhaps, in the light of Cromer's remark, one can talk of an 'artificial' governmental liberalism, or, given the fundamental contradictions at work, a 'bastard liberalism', though that term may not convey the sense that colonial governmentality was not merely a departure from the metropolitan norm, but in fact something *sui generis* and structurally different if also intimately related. Perhaps a better term might be 'dislocated liberalism', conveying the sense of something fundamentally out of place. It may be useful to consider the hybrid and contradictory nature of colonial governmentality in terms of the central place in British rule of intermediaries of all kinds, themselves hybrids of sorts: from the earliest days in Calcutta, for example, British rule depended upon these, and they existed at all levels of social life.[28] The intermediary was necessitated, and its reproductions accelerated, by the apprehension of colonial difference. This draws attention to the role of difference within metropolitan liberal governance also, which was always present, though the ties of blood and culture were sufficient to cast the figure of the intermediary more in the guise of a component in governmental liberalism, an instrument for bringing about that governing 'at a distance' through freedom characteristic of metropolitan Britain. I am thinking here of the various versions of a 'respectable' working class as acceptable proxies for the uncertainly 'othered' mass of the governed, proxies that figured prominently in nineteenth-century political reform.

Intermediaries might be informal, even illegal. They might be governmental in a sense that was not liberal, such as the dependence on a range of intermediary positions in the Army in India, in the forms of the Indian soldier, the *sepoy*, or in the form of the 'martial races', who were even more set apart from both the native Indian soldier and the colonisers. These became an important element in the second half of the nineteenth century, most famously in the case of the Gurkhas. The civilian aspects of a colonial society systematically governmentalised by engineering and technology at this time were in a number of their most important respects run by another group of intermediaries, namely the Anglo-Indians, who had a vital role in running the postal, telegraph and railway systems. And, within the purview of a colonial governmental liberalism, one could conceive of the western-educated Indian in a similar light.

In thinking about governmentality, it may be useful to approach the intermediary as, if not quite a 'technology' in the sense of the sewer or the market, then having a certain technical relation to governance. Considered as a governmental *technique* the intermediary can be understood as providing a *metric* for governance, one that in a liberal frame measured the advances of progress, but in a more general governmental sense the effectiveness of governance itself. A whole bureaucratic machinery is suggested, but also informal procedures, both replete with a myriad of distinctions and markers enacting the measurement of the efficiency of government's attempts to govern – the provision of ladders of educational attainment, for example, or the markers of a martial race as set out in Army recruitment manuals.[29] Now, from this perspective, in terms of 'liberalism', similarities with the situation in metropolitan Britain become evident, for there the creation of a 'civilised' working class/people was central to the progress of governance. Indeed, the passing of the 1867 Reform Act in Britain turned upon arguments that the people were now

sufficiently advanced on the road of progress and improvement to warrant
the vote. However, this road was measured against a yardstick of progress
which defined metropolitan advance against colonial retardation, the
political nation at home being comprehensively redefined in terms of
racialised notions of progress.[30]

Progress became a means of excluding the other in this case, and of
defining metropolitan governance in terms of difference, but the point
here is the similarity of governmental manoeuvres in the construction of
the intermediary. In Britain this was the respectable working class, existing
between the already respectable classes and the 'residuum' below, and in
India a native public opinion between the actual (real and powerful)
public opinion of the colonisers and the benighted multitude. If nothing
else, the parallel draws attention to the role of the state in the construction of the public sphere, which in many accounts seems to emerge
magically outside governance. This was not a virgin birth, and the state
was the progenitor of the public sphere in India as well as in Britain. Of
course, if from this perspective differences between the two were of
degree rather than of kind, these differences were enormous. The colonial
public sphere in India was not only more controlled but was also aimed
at defining a 'social' composed not of free individuals but of particularistic
communities. More than in Britain too, the state was the arbiter of what
public discourse was legitimate and what illegitimate, so delimiting public
from private in an authoritarian way. (Religion was, for instance, outside
the public sphere and therefore private, along with Indian domestic
life.)[31]

The reconstruction of colonial Lucknow, for example, was accompanied by the systematic constitution of intermediary groups aimed at
promoting loyalty. Local elites, the 'nawabi' notables of the city and the
surrounding province of Oudh, were the object of a battery of economic
and legal measures aimed at attaching them to the Raj. A 'liberal'
dimension, however, becomes very quickly apparent, in that by 1861 the
city had its own British India Association aimed at securing not only
loyalty but also the active penetration of European culture.[32] The model
of both this Association and the myriad of others like it seems to have
been the colonial capital of Calcutta, where the Bengali landowning
zamindar class were taken as an example of public service. In some
measure this and similar associations aimed to make the city itself a
principle, or metric, of cultural advance, integrating rural elites into
civilised European urban life and so facilitating intercourse with the
colonial rulers. In Calcutta itself the so-called *bhadralok*, a term denoting,

roughly, the Bengali western-educated middle class, is perhaps the best-known example of such an intermediate group in Indian society.

In fact, as numerous historians of India have shown, such groups, and the public opinion and public sphere they inhabited, represented a warrening from within of western modernity by indigenous needs and cultural resources, so that these groups established the foundations of nationalist resistance to British rule rather than the foundations of British rule itself. Partha Chatterjee, Gyan Prakash, Dipesh Chakrabarty and others have developed subtle readings of the appropriation of western modernity for indigenous ends.[33] From another perspective Christopher Bayly has developed sophisticated readings of how indigenous populations reinvented the western public sphere in order to discover 'India'. At a time when the colonial power was attempting to render India into a diversity of communities the better to rule it, Indians were inventing India as a unity so as themselves the better to bend western governmentality to their own needs.[34]

In so far as the city was a domain of colonial governmentality, and in a sense itself an intermediary and metric, there seem to be considerable differences between Britain, at the time the most urbanised country in the world, and a profoundly rural India, its great cities notwithstanding. The city did not have the same place in colonial as in metropolitan governmentality. None the less, with around a million people by 1900, Calcutta was a great city by any standards. It was also developed in a quite systematic way by the British as the colonial capital, self-consciously the 'second city of Empire'. Yet, just as the Indian street was in a different conceptual universe to that of the metropolitan city, so Indian conceptions of urban space were also at great variance with European notions. As Sumit Sarkar has suggested, although nineteenth-century Calcutta could be said to be the making of the *bhadralok*, they did not feel at home there. The ancestral village home was often the site of the most intimate notions of belonging.[35] Members of the *bhadralok* seldom wrote about the city, and indeed associated it with degeneracy. It was not until the early twentieth century that the city was associated with progress, and it eventually became part of nationalist political mythology (including the twentieth-century invention of a nineteenth-century Bengali urban renaissance in Calcutta). *Bhadralok* conceptions of urban space themselves seem to have been rooted in traditions that conceived of the urban as in fact centred on many highly localised spatial settings within the larger city, settings in large part organised around faction, religion and caste, such as the nineteenth-century *dals* (factional groupings), which both physically and emotionally had the village within the city as their heart. The physical structure of the city was therefore unlike that of European cities, Calcutta being a vast collection of poor tenanted settlements, the so-called *bustees*, complemented by bazaars whose economic, and spatial, logic was entirely different to urban Europe's.[36] This was the 'black town'. The 'white town' was different, and it is there that one can locate some of the contradictions of difference and universality in colonial governmentality.

I have previously considered particular 'problematisations' of the city in liberal governmentality, namely the sanitary, moral and social 'diagrams' of the city, tracing these out in terms of urban design and architecture. It seems to me that each of these imaginaries of the city had a colonial counterpart. They also might be said to have had counterparts in other, non-liberal forms of governmentality, for example Soviet and by extension communist governmentality, where they were aimed at equality, not freedom or hierarchy as in the liberal and colonial variants. In revisiting the moral city in the colony, we find the same institutions and influences as in Britain. For example, the *Bombay Builder*, founded in 1865, was a cousin to its English and Irish counterparts considered in chapter 4. Like these it venerated Ruskin and the gothic, expressing the general recognition at the time of the failings of the universalism of the neoclassical style to suitably represent the character of European civilisation. The gothic could do this better, especially as European civilisation was now seen in terms of the historical, the national and the Christian. The gothic, with its idea of craftsmanship and intuitive artistry of a native, that is to say, English, sort, was decidedly historical, national and Christian. However, as the capital, Calcutta was most consistently developed in a neoclassical vein, it being felt that the Roman associations of the neoclassical would best represent the power, majesty and supremacy of the west.[37] None the less, it seems to me that the real originality of the Raj as a distinctively *British*, and English, form of empire in fact lay in the gothic and the historical, in short in the form of what I have called the moral city. The late nineteenth-century neoclassical upsurge in Calcutta was in fact an historicised neoclassical, owing a great debt to indigenous British forms of classicism, especially the baroque classicism that developed after Victoria's Jubilee in 1887.

This imperial gothic, while decidedly part of the moralisation of the city, functioned in a rather different way from gothic in the metropolitan city. It helped create a 'traditional' past for the empire, for the colonisers but also those among the colonised whom this built version of an 'Indian public sphere' embraced. It can be seen, therefore, as negotiating the contradictions between asserting imperial supremacy and making limited concessions to forms of liberal self-rule. Bombay was above all the centre of Indian gothic, the University, the city Corporation Building (1893), the Post Office, the Railway Station (1878–87), the Office of Public Works, the places in short where Indians, especially educated Indians, were exposed to 'the west', were all part of a comprehensive gothicisation of the city in the second half of the nineteenth century.[38]

However, this 'traditional', historicised past was still very much a European one, and it was the historicist eclecticism of what followed the gothic that represented best the deepening sense of the need to recognise the importance of 'native' architectural traditions, a recognition that sometimes went in parallel with the development of more progressive forms of liberal thought about Indian self-rule. The Corporation Building (Figure 6.1) was in fact already a fusion of gothic and 'oriental' styles, and therefore a fitting emblem of the contradictions of governmentality in India, where city self-government, if preached, was relatively little practised. This eclecticism has gone under the name of the 'Indo-Saracenic', the general thrust of which was towards supposedly 'Indian' traditions. Yet this only served to reveal even more the contradictory nature of the liberal dimensions of colonial governmentality, for these buildings showed little regard for local townscapes, traditional building plans and the geographical and religious specificity of indigenous styles.[39] In essence, they were an appliqué of supposed tradition upon what were inside basically western buildings. The crown of power was hollow.

As one colonial variant of what I have called the social city, the rebuilding of New Delhi after 1913 involved a formal geometry of space, and zoned housing by class, status and race, so that social structures of an abstract sort were, as in Britain, rendered directly on the ground. The social machine here served the ends of empire; at home, the ends of what was increasingly becoming a social liberal administration. In Britain the social city was planned in order to accord with the presumed sociality of its inhabitants, so as to maximise their happiness, extending to city inhabitants what was to be an increasingly social democratic and 'communal' form of happiness. One exponent of this happiness, Patrick Geddes, in fact abhorred the monumentality of New Delhi, in which this particular colonial version of the laws of the social took precedence over working in compliance with local needs and traditions. He was instrumental in getting Henry Vaughan Lanchester appointed the first official town planner in India. None the less, in the 1930s it was if anything still the

Figure 6.1   Bombay Municipal Corporation Building, 1893

model of the sanitary city that dominated Indian urban development, especially in Calcutta, and the influence of Geddes was very limited.[40]

The planning of New Delhi not only emphasised the separateness of the British city from the Indian settlement (evident in Figure 6.2), it also emphasised class distinctions amongst the British themselves:

> The residential pattern of the city reflected the civil service hierarchy, with upper-level employees segregated from lower-level employees, and the British separated from the Indians. In some ways, the distribution of population was like the caste distribution of the traditional Indian town. The highest ranking officials, the gazetted officers, were placed near the government centre, with

Figure 6.2   The juncture of old and new Delhi, date of photograph unknown

Indian princes at the eastern end of the monumental axis. European clerks
were housed beyond the officers' district, and Indian clerks still further away.
At the greatest distance were the lowest ranking Indian employees. Land
elevation was also used to emphasise status, with European clerks on higher
land than the Indian clerks, and gazetted officers higher than the clerks. Within
the various housing districts, a pattern of fine distinctions was developed in
which rank was defined by size of plot, cost of house, and street location.[41]

This spatial subdivision of the city extended downward to peons, sweepers
and *dhobis*. Again, the cross-fertilisation of metropolitan and colonial
governmentality is evident, though the differences are none the less clear.
In understanding the specifically British, or English, nature of governmental liberalism – at least in distinction to other national expressions –
colonial encounters were of course hugely significant but other factors
came into play too, and in conclusion I will consider some of these.

Conclusion

It is amply apparent that the form in which liberal governance realised itself historically *was* the nation-state, as this intensive study of the British example indicates. The consideration of British, French and German variants of urban planning in chapter 4 made it clear that forms that were similar in their governmental liberalism might none the less reflect important national differences. The French aimed at rebuilding the city, the Germans at planning the extant city, and the British showed a considerable ambivalence about the city. These differences reflected complex cultural and social changes over time at a national level, which are themselves closely related to complex political changes, above all at the level of the state. The opening discussion in chapter 3 dwelt on how eighteenth- and nineteenth-century British state formation marked Britain out from continental developments. As the discussion of the 'police' and liberal variants of governmentality in the Introduction indicated, there does indeed seem to have been an important anglophone–continental European distinction in governmentality, for all the important similarities. As Foucault himself saw, British traditions of local and parliamentary government, also its religious traditions, differentiated it from Europe, marking out a certain precocity in the generation of liberal forms of governmentality. At the same time, as was evident in chapter 3, the local, 'parish state' of eighteenth-century Britain was really very similar to the supposedly more European police forms of governmentality.

It is this particular balance of central and local in state formation that was so important in the British case. Perhaps, here, one should say the English case, for two things are striking about the British example. One is the great longevity of what became the British state, its roots extending at least as far back as medieval times. The other is the central place of England in this process of state formation, so that the formation of the British state was essentially a case of English state building.[42] In this regard Ireland was part of this process of state building, rather than of colonialism,[43] even though in chapter 1 I marked out its decidedly anomalous status by the term 'semi-colonial'. Nor, in considering state formation, should we adopt a Whiggish history which envisages the state over time as progressively deepening its hold on the lives of its members, for early state forms extended far into the fabric of society.

None the less, the originality and precocity of nineteenth-century Britain in developing forms of liberal governance should not be underestimated. The active embrace of governance through freedom, as well as rule through everyday life and what I call the ordinary, was indeed something new: these were not merely ruled over but were now the media of rule in a manner that had not previously been the case. This originality owed a great deal to the balance of which I speak; the oxymoronic nature of liberal governance as *rule* through freedom can be seen to be rooted in this balance. Freedom was a mode of rule which depended on a *strong* state, and this realisation is an important contribution to the understanding of liberalism in general. As an exemplification of a strong state, the sovereignty of the English state in the form of the Crown in Parliament was a notable example, a sovereignty that was at the same time highly dispersed.

At the same time, we can talk of this dispersal in another sense too, that of material things and processes. The strength of liberal civil society, so central to liberal governance, was in no small measure owed to the humble material things considered in this book. Unheralded engineers and architects begin to rival the tribunes of the state as pioneers of liberalism. At the same time, the highly dispersed agency that marked material governance should caution us when speaking of a strong state, for as has been seen, it is useful to think of the state as often myopic, not far-seeing, feeling its way precisely in terms of the unforseen consequences of this dispersal. It might be a slave to its material forms and these might be a source of its weakness as well as its strength. The Foucauldian analytic has the advantage of calling the state to account.

None the less, the precocity of nineteenth-century governance is undeniable, an originality that has been the subject of this book. The sweep of the book has taken us from the sanitary city of the early nineteenth century to the social city of the early twentieth. It has also taken us from the systematisation of the rule of freedom first evident in the early nineteenth century to its more state-directed social forms a century later. This new dispensation obtained for a good deal of the twentieth century, until, in its last quarter, the market replaced 'society' and the social as the model for governance. Something of this needs to be considered here. From the 1970s onwards not only economic life was marketized, but equally all areas of social life. For example, in welfare and education a whole range of institutions were reconstituted as a series of internal markets, in line with what has been called 'the new public management'. This change involved the transition from the idea of public service to one of private management, and parallel to this culture of accountability was the emergence of an 'audit society' in which formal, and professionally sanctioned, monitoring systems replaced the trust that the earlier version of the relationship between state and society had invested in professional specialists of all sorts (including historians and social scientists).

The social state gave way to a state that was regarded as 'enabling', permitting the citizen, the firm, the locality, and so on, to freely choose. This politics of choice had various expressions, in which the state was seen as more or less benign, in its more benign form being seen as a means of articulating 'community' as a kind of third term, which was in fact part of a political 'third way' in Britain, between the individual and the state. Community therefore became a sort of de-socialised social. This new relation of state and society involved the devolution of rule upon the citizen himself or herself, with the idea that the capacity for self-realisation could only ultimately be a question of individual activity. The enormous proliferation of 'self-help' institutions and activities is testament to this. Governance now occurred through the realisation and practice of an 'inner' self (as Nikolas Rose puts it, a 'depth within'), and of freely chosen forms of identity in everyday life (a practice of lifestyle 'without'), in which the place of consumption and the market in this particular practice of freedom is of course central.[44]

The beginnings of all this now lie almost two centuries before our present, in the active creation of rule through freedom that I have considered by means of the example of the city. The city is only one means by which the history of 'liberalism' can be traced, but none the less, I think, a productive one. The literature on governmentality enables us to understand the history of our own liberal present in ways that, I think, are deepened by this history of the city in liberalism that I have attempted, deepened by the historical sense itself and by the richness brought by understanding not only liberalism but also the city in a new way. This has first involved considering the ways in which people and things were identified so that they might be brought within the view of government. Statistics but especially maps were seen to be crucial to this process, one intimately tied to the consolidation of what was called 'modern abstraction'. If we conceive of the latter in terms of the objectification and standardisation of the world that abstraction brought, then we might also think of what was going on as modernity itself. Liberal governmentality from this point of view could indeed be thought of as the political arm of modernity.

However, it is less grand narratives of modernity that concern me here than the ways in which an objectivised world helped compose social imaginaries of power, or urban imaginaries, which themselves became 'naturalised' as part of the common sense of their time, and of our time as well in considerable measure. This normalisation of governable worlds took form around imaginaries of the city as places of flow, movement and free circulation. In chapter 2, normalised in this way as the subject of discourses and practices of health, and indeed of life itself, the city could be acted upon in order to secure governance. The imaginary of the 'sanitary city' was translated into material forms and material power in terms of urban infrastructure, things like sewers, abattoirs and markets. These comprised early forms of the technoscientific state, and were in effect technopolitical solutions. Chapter 3 considered the parallel attempt to realise the urban as the basis of forms of free and open liberal community, including the community of knowledge users who employed public libraries. This attempt grew out of a sense of the shortcomings, the incomplete nature, of the diagram of the city as a sanitary one. Securing governance thus moved forward jointly in terms of action upon what I called the moral city, as well as the sanitary city, with actions above ground, in terms of the building and planning of the city, as well as below. This also involved the governance of time and of history running parallel with the governance of space, as was apparent in chapter 4. Towards the end of the nineteenth century I identify the 'social city' as a shape of things to come.

As the realisation of a new urban imaginary, the social city brought with it a new range of specialists in a field of governance, just as earlier versions of the city had. Chapter 3 considered the emergence of experts in what might be thought of as the foundational science of government, namely modern administration, in the shape of the early civil service. The modern civil service was at the centre of a new ethics of governance, one concerned with *performing* the ethics of power as evidence of the truth of power. This performance was directed to the civil servants themselves as much as to others, so that they should be worthy of the trust of governing. Chapter 3 also considered the new political world, another free domain like 'society' and the 'economy', in which these new servants of the state operated, and from which they differentiated themselves. None the less, in this differentiation were played out some of the ambiguities and complexities of liberal governance, apparent in what I termed the agonistic strain in liberalism, its definition of itself as a moral struggle, a struggle in and with the world of the political.

This agonism tells us something of the deeper truth of liberalism itself, namely how its longevity and success seem to be related to how, in attaching itself to our sense of being free, it connects itself to one of the most powerful sources of our being. The subtlety but also the failures and compromises of liberalism have interested me throughout the book, especially in chapter 5. There what I called the republic of the streets was the arena in which subtlety and ambiguity were most apparent. I have tried to get at some of this by a consideration of power and resistance as played out in terms of 'popular' imaginaries of the city, the paper city as I termed it, alongside the lived city, the city that was moved through, and especially walked through. In the republic of the streets the many viewed themselves in terms of governance and resistance to it, and in the increasingly demotic nature of governance, that governance of and through the ordinary of which I speak, our present governance is presaged. It was then that the rule of freedom came of age.

Notes

1. See also John Koren, *The History of Statistics* (London, 1918).
2. Charles E. Beveridge (ed.), *Frederick Law Olmsted: Designing the American Landscape* (New York: Rizzoli, 1995).
3. Richard S. Weinstein, 'The First American City', in Allan J. Scott and Edward J. Soja (eds), *The City: Los Angeles and Urban Theory at the End of the Twentieth Century* (London: University of California Press, 1996), p. 26.
4. J.C. Teaford, *The Municipal Revolution in America: Origins of Modern Urban Government, 1650–1825* (Chicago: University of Chicago Press, 1975).
5. Alan I. Marcus, *Plague of Strangers: Social Groups and the Origins of City Service in Cincinnati 1819–1870* (Columbus: Ohio University Press, 1991); and see also Carl Smith, *Urban Disorder and the Shape of Belief* (Chicago: University of Chicago Press, 1995).
6. David Brodsky, *Los Angeles Freeway: An Appreciative Essay* (London: University of California Press, 1981).
7. On Los Angeles freeways see also the entries on 'government' and 'freeway' in Leonard and D. Pitt (eds), *Los Angeles A–Z: An Encyclopaedia of the City and County* (London: University of California Press, 1999); and on California, space, freedom and the American dream, see the various works on California by Kevin Starr, for example *Material Dreams: Southern California through the 1920s* (New York: Oxford University Press, 1990).
8. See above, pp. 225–6.
9. David Brodsky, *Los Angeles Freeway*, pp. 1–5.
10. Timothy Mitchell, *Colonising Egypt* (Cambridge: Cambridge University Press, 1988), p. 35, note 6.
11. Nicholas Dirks, *Castes of Mind: Colonialism and the Making of Modern India* (Princeton: Princeton University Press, 2001).
12. Peter Holquist, 'Population Statistics and Population Politics in Late Imperial and Soviet Russia', in Ronald G. Suny and Terry Martin (eds), *A State of Nations: Empire*

and State Making in the Age of Lenin and Stalin (New York: Oxford University Press, 2001).

13. Clive Dewey, Anglo-Indian Attitudes: The Mind of the Indian Civil Service (London: Hambledon, 1993).

14. Timothy Mitchell, Colonising Egypt, chapter 2, 'Enframing'.

15. Gyan Prakash, Another Reason: Science and the Imagination of Modern India (Princeton: Princeton University Press, 1999); Nicholas Dirks, Castes of Mind.

16. Gyan Prakash, 'The Colonial Genealogy of Society: Community and Political Modernity in India', in Patrick Joyce (ed.), The Social in Question: New Bearings in History and the Social Sciences (London: Routledge, 2002).

17. See also Ann Stoler, Race and the Education of Desire: Foucault's 'History of Sexuality' and the Colonial Order of Things (London: Duke University Press, 1995).

18. Nicholas Dirks, Castes of Mind, p. 123.

19. Laura Baer, 'Travelling Modernity: Capitalism, Community and the Nation in the Colonial Government of the Indian Railways' (University of Michigan PhD, 1998), p. 50.

20. Ibid., pp. 25, 113–15, 116.

21. Veema T. Oldenberg, The Making of Colonial Lucknow 1856–1877 (Princeton: Princeton University Press, 1987).

22. Sumanta Bannerjee, The Parlour and the Street: Elite and Popular Culture in Nineteenth-Century Calcutta (Calcutta: Seagull Publishers, 1989); S.N. Mukherjee, Calcutta: Myths and History (Calcutta: Subarnarekha, 1977), and Calcutta, Essays in Urban History (Calcutta: Subarnarekha); Pradip Sinha, Calcutta in Urban History (Calcutta: Firma KLM Private Ltd, 1978), which is especially useful and interesting; Sukanta Chadhauri, Calcutta the Living City, 2 volumes (Delhi: Oxford University Press, 1990); Anthony D. King, Colonial Urban Development: Culture, Social Power and the Environment (London: Routledge and Kegan Paul, 1976).

23. Thomas R. Metcalf, Ideologies of the Raj, The New Cambridge History of India, II. 4, (Cambridge: Cambridge University Press, 1995), p. 31.

24. Ibid., 'The Claims of Equality', pp. 197–203.

25. Eric Stokes, The English Utilitarians in India (Delhi: Oxford University Press, 1959).

26. James Fitzjames Stephens, Liberty, Equality, Fraternity (London, 1875); Thomas R. Metcalf, Ideologies of the Raj, pp. 56–7.

27. Uday Singh Mehta, Liberalism and Empire: A Study in the Nineteenth-Century British Political Thought (Chicago: University of Chicago Press, 1999).

28. Sumanta Bannerjee, The Parlour and the Street, chapter 2.

29. David E. Omissi, The Sepoy and the Raj: The Indian Army 1860–1940 (Basingstoke: Macmillan, 1994).

30. Catherine Hall, Keith McClelland and Jane Rendell (eds), Defining the Victorian Nation: Class, Race, Gender and the Reform Act of 1867 (Cambridge: Cambridge University Press, 2000).

31. Thomas R. Metcalf, Ideologies of the Raj, p. 187.

32. Veema T. Oldenberg, The Making of Colonial Lucknow, esp. chapter 6.

33. Partha Chatterjee, The Nation and its Fragments: Colonial and Postcolonial Histories (Delhi: Oxford University Press, 1997), especially chapter 2, and p. 26; Dipesh

Chakrabarty, *Provincialising Europe: Postcolonial Thought and Colonial Difference* (London: Princeton University Press, 2001); see also David Scott, 'Colonial Governmentality', *Social Text*, 43, 1995.

34. C.A. Bayly, *Empire and Information: Intelligence Gathering and Social Communication in India, 1780–1870* (Cambridge: Cambridge University Press, 1996).

35. Sumit Sarkar, *Writing Social History* (Delhi: Oxford University Press, 1997), chapter 5 on Calcutta.

36. On Calcutta urban space see the works cited in note 22 above; also J.S. Grewal (ed.), *Calcutta: Foundation and Development of a Colonial Metropolis* (Chandigarh: Urban Historical Association of India, 1991).

37. Thomas R. Metcalf, *An Imperial Vision: Indian Architecture and the British Raj* (London: University of California Press, 1989), chapter 6.

38. Norma Evenson, *The Indian Metropolis: A View Towards the West* (New Haven: Yale University Press, 1989).

39. Ibid., pp. 90–4.

40. Jonathan Lang, *Architecture and Independence, the Search for Identity: India 1880–1980* (Delhi: Oxford University Press, 1997); Robert Grant Irving, *Indian Summer: Lutyens, Barker and Imperial Delhi* (New Haven: Yale University Press, 1981).

41. Norma Evenson, *The Indian Metropolis*, pp. 151–2.

42. See the symposium on the British state, 'What and When Was the State?', *Journal of Historical Sociology*, 15:1, 2002.

43. Stephen Howe, *Ireland and Empire: Colonial Legacies in Irish History and Culture* (Oxford: Oxford University Press, 2000).

44. For a fuller account, see Nikolas Rose, *Powers of Freedom: Reframing Political Thought* (Cambridge: Cambridge University Press, 1999).

Index